Mrs. Ziegfeld

Mrs. Ziegfeld

The Public and Private Lives of Billie Burke

GRANT HAYTER-MENZIES

Foreword by Eric Myers

McFarland & Company, Inc., Publishers
Jefferson, North Carolina, and London

Unless otherwise noted, photographs are from author's collection.

LIBRARY OF CONGRESS CATALOGUING-IN-PUBLICATION DATA

Hayter-Menzies, Grant, 1964–
Mrs. Ziegfeld : the public and private lives
of Billie Burke / Grant Hayter-Menzies ;
foreword by Eric Myers.
p.   cm.
Includes bibliographical references and index.

ISBN 978-0-7864-3800-6
illustrated case binding : 50# alkaline paper ∞

1. Burke, Billie, 1885–1970.
2. Actors — United States — Biography.
I. Title.
PN2287.B78H39   2009   792.02'8092 — dc22   [B]   2008052173

British Library cataloguing data are available

On the cover: Billie Burke in *Happy Husband* (1928);
Ornamental trim ©2009 Shutterstock

Manufactured in the United States of America

*McFarland & Company, Inc., Publishers
Box 611, Jefferson, North Carolina 28640
www.mcfarlandpub.com*

To the memory of
Patricia Ziegfeld Stephenson (1915–2008),
the greatest Ziegfeld Girl of them all,

and Les,
who has more heart, wisdom and courage
than any wizard could give,

and Jessie,
faithful companion on the Yellow Brick Road

Acknowledgments

The writing of a biography, like the staging of a play, requires more than the mere creative effort of the playwright. For one thing, the playwright makes use of suggestions, impressions, sudden flashes of inspiration, sudden realizations of potential failure, that are not entirely his own but often come from people around him. He who thinks he does it alone is not part of the stream of life that is blood to the veins of a play, symphony, comedy routine, or a book like the one you are holding in your hands.

Without the help of her daughter and son-in-law, Patricia and William Stephenson, both of whom I met in their last summer, I could not have hoped to learn about the warm, wise and very real woman behind the comic concept popularly known as Billie Burke. And without the generous memories of Billie's granddaughters Cecilia Duncan and Susan Plemons, I could never have understood what it was like to grow up with, be nurtured by, and nurture in their turn a grandmother who to children around the world was the pink tulle vision of gracious sorcery, Glinda the Good Witch from *The Wizard of Oz*. When I first met this family, they had just been to the Los Angeles production of *Wicked*—92-year-old Mrs. Stephenson was, in fact, happily wearing a t-shirt bearing the green profile of the star of the show. On arrival, my brother and I both stopped as we approached the Stephenson home as we heard from the swimming pool, where Mrs. Stephenson's great-grandchildren were playing, the Flo-look-alike great-grandson say to his sister, who had risen from the water with her long red hair flowing over her shoulders, "You've been Glinda-ized!" Had we had any doubts of the address, we would have known from that remark that we had found the right place. It was the right place in so many ways — the place to understand Billie Burke, and to be welcomed into the sort of happy family only a fairy great-grandmother could bequeath to posterity.

I have many others to thank for helping me along this particular yellow brick road. Ned Comstock, archivist par excellence at the USC Cinema-Television Archive, Doheny Library, and all-around great guy, guided me through the forests of clippings, letters and photographs in the Billie Burke papers and made it possible for me to document and assess, for the first time, Billie's early stage stardom, that almost-lost theatre history that explains so much of her movie persona.

I thank Richard Lamparski, who shared funny and moving memories of afternoon tea with Billie, and Barbara Rush, who shared with me fond recollections of making a film with a woman she regarded as a legend in her own time. (And thanks also to an autodidact after my own heart, Kendall Hailey, who kindly put me in touch with Ms. Rush.) And I thank Jim Crabtree, producing director of the Cumberland County Playhouse in Crossville, Tennessee, who described for me his childhood experience of playing opposite a woman who, despite the passage of time, never stopped being a star.

Without Peter Fitzgerald, whose documentary *The Making of 'The Great Ziegfeld'* and, especially, his generous sharing of his contacts with Billie's family, this book could not have been written. Without John Fricke, the real wizard of *Oz*, who shared his vast knowledge of the 1939 film and Billie's role (and singing) in it, the richness of her contribution could never have been so clear to me or so beneficial to the writing of this book.

My dear brother, Sean William Menzies, not only accompanied me on most of my forays into archives and libraries, but was there for our special afternoon with Patricia and Bill Stephenson. Luckily for me, he was taking notes when I lost myself in listening to stories about Billie the mother and grandmother. He allowed me to use him as a sounding board for the welter of symbols and theories around Billie's role in *Oz* and the ultimate role in our shared human cosmology of Glinda the Good and her Baumian cohorts. Most of all, he was there in our childhood in front of the flickering television screen, as we lay side by side in our pajamas watching the annual broadcast of *Oz* and crying (as we still do) when Dorothy has to return to Kansas, but glad (as we still are) that she makes it there at last.

My wonderful cousins, Bob and Roberta Blank, opened their Los Angeles home to me on my trips back into Billie's past — I thank them for their hospitality and, above all, for their belief in me. I thank Corrine Balcaen for her generosity of time and friendship, without which trips to far-flung places to burrow through archives in search of Billie Burke would not have been possible.

My dear friend, William Luce, the greatest biographer I know, remembered for me the time he met Billie in Twenty-Eighth Church of Christ, Scientist, in Westwood Village, California, and how he never forgot her brilliant smile. Bekah and Fern Galindo kindly shared their first edition of *The Wizard of Oz* with me.

Dr. Anne Fliotsos's paper on Billie was the first opening of the door to understanding the arc of this woman's and actor's life, on stage and off— without Dr. Fliotsos's showing the way, I would never have reached the writing of these acknowledgments.

Very special thanks for advice and encouragement to Muriel Donaldson, Nathalie Lewis, Patrick McGilligan, William Mann, Judith Mayne and Anthony Slide.

Last but not at all least, I am thankful for the generosity of the Lilly Library, Indiana University, Bloomington, Indiana, the Howard Gotlieb Archival Research Center at Boston University, and the Cinematic Arts Library at the University of Southern California, Los Angeles.

Any omissions, errors, faults or flubs are my own.

Contents

ix

Foreword
by Eric Myers

"Are you a good witch or a bad witch?"

Billie Burke's opening line in *The Wizard of Oz*, on the heels of her entrance via iridescent bubble, is one of that film's countless unforgettable moments. For most of us who grew up watching the movie on television, it was our first exposure to the lady.

But Glinda, the very personification of charm, grace, and serenity, was to be Burke's least typical role. Arriving near the midpoint of her talkie career, the role was preceded and followed by a long line of inimitable, flouncy flibbertigibbets. Burke played those types so well that she was rarely allowed to do anything else, and in her way, she became as typecast as Hattie McDaniel or Marjorie Main. We may never know what she might have accomplished had she been given the chance to expand her range.

In this long-overdue scholarly work, Grant Hayter-Menzies gives us a complete biography of the courageous lady who lurked beneath all that flightiness. She was a woman whose career mirrored the entire history of American entertainment during the first half of the twentieth century. From her early stage stardom as an adorable Victorian sprite to her years spent making silent films, through her bittersweet marriage to the greatest Broadway impresario of all time, and on to her 1930s rebirth as a Hollywood character actress who would become a fixture on screen, radio, and television for the next thirty years, Burke weathered the changing tastes and fancies of a fickle public.

Few were aware of the doubts and uncertainties that plagued her throughout her widowhood, as she watched her finances plummet along with the nation's depressed economy. Yet she persevered, and survived by doing what she did best: putting herself in front of audiences who rarely failed to delight in the sight of this famous stage beauty growing old with uncommon grace and good humor.

Few actresses today would be able to pull off her madcap brand of comic high style. It is quite telling that when *Dinner at Eight* was recently revived at Lincoln Center, Tony-winning actress Christine Ebersole, cast in Billie's role of the superficial society doyenne Millicent Jordan, made no attempt whatsoever to echo Billie's perfect screen performance. Instead, she took quite the opposite tack by making Millicent into a virtual Gorgon — a monster of monomaniacal comic intensity.

It was a totally effective performance on its own terms; one that expunged all of Billie's flightiness. And it was the right choice. No one will ever be able to duplicate Billie Burke.

Eric Myers is author of *Uncle Mame: The Life of Patrick Dennis* and co-author (with Howard Mandelbaum) of *Screen Deco* and *Forties Screen Style*. His writing has also appeared in the *New York Times, Variety, Opera News, Art and Auction* and *Time Out New York*.

Preface

She was probably wearing the fluffy evening gown in which she appears in her first scene in George Cukor's 1932 drama, *A Bill of Divorcement*.

All Billie Burke remembered of that evening when her whole life, already changed in pieces, finally altered itself completely, was that she was in full costume, and was speaking lines to the young Walter Pidgeon, in a test to determine his suitability to play her fiancé in the film, when the call came. Someone told Cukor that Billie was needed urgently on the telephone. Already on edge over her husband's illness and their fractured finances, Billie took the receiver and heard Sidney Boggis, valet of many years to her husband, Florenz Ziegfeld, Jr., speak not with his habitual British cool but with fright. "Come quickly, madam, come quickly," was all he could say. Billie hurried to Cedars of Lebanon Hospital, just down the street from RKO, where Flo had been placed less than a week earlier. She ran into his room, and found him there—dead. Ziegfeld had dropped in Sidney's arms only a few minutes before.

It was the supreme irony of many such ironies of Billie's life, that she should be playing on film the wife of a sick man whom she is about to leave, and be called away from the set to find that she had reached her real sick husband, whom she would never leave, too late to see him go.

It was close to 11 P.M. on July 22, 1932, and Flo's death was already being hammered out in newsprint—a nurse on a newspaper's payroll had called in the details before Billie had even made it to Flo's deathbed. He was 63 years old, and had died of, among other things, an enlarged heart. Some, as did his widow, chose to see it as death from a broken heart. But it was Billie Burke's heart that had to be strong. Collapsing into misery the first few terrible days of life without this man who had made her life worth living, Billie rose to the occasion and showed not only the strength that had helped her survive plenty of lesser shocks, but proved that out of death comes life. She remade herself, a forgotten leading lady of the stage, as one of the screen's most beloved comediennes.

Billie Burke's career and life often twined together in this manner—so many of her roles called on her to play parts that were fragments of her real life: the sought-after young stage beauty, the wronged wife, the spendthrift matriarch of bankrupt wealth, the woman too old to be acting so young. And behind it all was a woman who had not even intended to become an actress; who, had she possessed the undivided atten-

3

tion of the only man she had ever really loved, Flo Ziegfeld, might have left the stage and played in life the decorous society figure she portrayed on stage and screen. And yet how much poorer the history of entertainment would be had we not had Billie Burke, who regardless of her other significant performances will always be Glinda the Good Witch of the North in *The Wizard of Oz*, merrily adjuring new generations to "follow the yellow brick road" and to remember that "there's no place like home."

Her story is that of an actress remade before she could take a hand in the transformation. Billie professed to abhor the film industry when a famous stage actress and then had to approach it hat in hand, wearing a different mask from the one she had worn for so many years — from stage beauty to character actress. She went from the powerful Mrs. Ziegfeld, whose word in her husband's ear could get critics fired, to dithering clown in diamonds and lace, twittering her way through a few classics and a lot of mediocrity, but becoming in Glinda a symbol of the simple creed of always looking at the bright side, regardless of wicked witches and unpaid bills and dreams collapsed in disarray. This apparent wisp of a woman, with the disturbed-chandelier tinkle of a voice and sparrow-like flutter of hands, survived some of the worst storms that can sweep over anyone's life, and came out of the tempest stronger than anyone would have believed — perhaps herself most of all.

"In almost 80 movies," wrote Hollywood biographer Donald Spoto, "she was a pixie with a canny charm. Her bubbly, breathless tremolo and her fluttery delicacy were endearing rather than exasperating. There was really no one like her." Spoto was describing a woman who, from her first professional appearance on the London stage in 1903 to her final film, a Western, in 1960, lived a life with more acts than a Shakespeare play, and recast herself as a creative artist, while battling her way out of the debt and despair of the 1929 stock market crash and the death of her beloved husband, producer Flo Ziegfeld.[1]

The only child of a famous circus clown and a widow with ambitions for the stage, Billie Burke was forced into the theatre by her mother, where despite her fears and her lifelong sense of inadequacy she became an overnight sensation — taken first under the wing of Sir Charles Hawtrey in London and later by Broadway producer Charles Frohman, starmaker of Maude Adams and Ethel Barrymore. A Broadway success, Burke set fashions with each of her appearances in plays by Sir Arthur Wing Pinero, W. Somerset Maugham, Booth Tarkington and Noël Coward. She was proposed to by Enrico Caruso and adored by the elderly Mark Twain. Then she met producer Florenz Ziegfeld on the eve of World War I, and in that clash of old world and new, that end of the last glamour of the nineteenth century, Billie Burke's life took a very different course.

As her career suffered under Ziegfeld's management (and the mistaken belief that marriage to Ziegfeld gave her roles that she did not have to work for), and she poured her own cash into Ziegfeld's magnificent, money-burning productions, Billie Burke also discovered that she had married a man who could not leave chorus girls behind. Violent scenes that few would believe her capable of followed, with threats to walk out on the marriage — but Burke was unable to leave Flo. It was more than needing to stay together for their daughter, Patricia. Flo and Billie were a team, the true king and queen of the Jazz Age. And Billie came to the conclusion, when it all broke up and disappeared in 1929, that the great tragic role she had yearned to play on stage was one she had already taken on in 1914, when she married her brilliant, flawed Flo.

I was in New York City in September 2007 to read from my biography of Charlotte Greenwood at a Times Square bookstore when my partner and I, strolling back to the Hotel Pennsylvania, stopped to look at a theatre sign. We paused because the sign in question bears a name that spells the magic of a bygone age — the Lyceum. The oldest Broadway theatre still in use, the Lyceum had just showcased two of the greatest talents of the American theatre, Christopher Plummer and Brian Dennehy, in *Inherit The Wind*. And it was where Billie Burke, under the careful and canny management of producer Charles Frohman, enjoyed many of her biggest successes.

We walked up to the building, only to find its pale grey Corinthian-columned and arch-windowed façade swathed in the plywood cladding that usually means one thing — renovation, restoration or demolition. Luckily, in this case it meant the first two. Through the doorway we could see hard hats in t-shirts, revamping the century-old interior. My plan to go inside, maybe take a few pictures, was dashed by a sign: "Authorized personnel only." As we stood there, trying to see in, a construction worker came to the door. We struck up a conversation about the work being done to restore the theatre, and he asked me how I happened to be so interested.

"Ah, Billie Burke, you say?" he remarked. "You know, there's still a picture of her in the lobby." He paused, having assessed my seriousness from the foregoing conversation as only a true New Yorker can do. Then, looking both ways, like a mustached villain from one of Billie's early comedies, he stood aside and said, "Come in for a look — but *no pictures*."

We entered a jewel-box of a lobby, its double staircase curving up at the back, washed in tones of cream and gold and the sense if not presence of lots of rich brown velvet, the approved fabric of the Edwardian age. Beside the entrance doors, in the original theatre bill display case, was a program from Billie's 1912 hit, Sir Arthur Wing Pinero's *The Mind The Paint Girl*. And there was indeed a picture of Billie, though whether she was smiling or posing thoughtfully, finger to chin, I cannot recall. What came to me was the sudden realization that a history unknown to most passing in the street — unknown to most theatergoers, however devoted and avid they may consider themselves — was still more or less intact in this little theatre on West 45th Street, behind the scaffolding and plywood, where we stood smiling back at smiling Billie Burke, my partner and me and the kindly construction worker. For a moment it was possible to understand something of the grace and charm of that lost world of sophisticated, frothy comedies and high-toned dramas, which Billie had had the good fortune to be a part of and the misfortune to outlive by more than one lifetime. And seeing how far from us that world is, it was possible to understand just how it could have been so forgotten.

You might ask those people passing by on West 45th what they know about Billie Burke, and they would tell you much the same story: bubbly-voiced Glinda the Good, or dizzy Clara Topper, or that silly woman in that movie, you remember.... Her film work has come so close to eclipsing her accomplishments on the stage that it makes perfect sense that these and the world that briefly made them possible are even more consigned to fairytales than her most noted role, as the Good Witch of MGM's *The Wizard of Oz*.

That is why this book is not so much about the Billie Burke most people think they know as it is about the real woman behind the caricature — not so much about that caricature's work in film as the trained actress's work on the stage, which was her first and last love and a source of both misery and joy, much like that other greatest thing of her life, her marriage to Flo Ziegfeld.

Where Billie's film performances seemed to me superlative, and/or where she herself was especially proud of a role in this medium with which she always had a love-hate relationship, I have given these more detailed examination. What I have not wanted to do in this book is allow that stereotype to dominate the real woman. Billie Burke was a superb Millicent Jordan, Clara Topper, and Glinda the Good Witch of the North. But the greatest ingredient in all her acting was herself.

That is why this is the story of that greatest performance of them all — as Mrs. Florenz Ziegfeld, Jr.

PART I
Sawdust, Stardust

CHAPTER 1

"A shy, wistful sort of moppet"

While she was hardly as obsessed as that most famous of stage mothers, Momma Rose, Mrs. William E. Burke was no slouch: without her prodding, the world might never have had that iconic figure of twentieth century film culture, Glinda the Good Witch of the North.

"I was a shy, wistful sort of moppet," remembered Billie Burke, future sorceress of Oz, "who never in this world would have got ahead had it not been for my mother."

It was Blanche Beatty Burke, Billie said, not herself, who made the fateful decision that her daughter was going to be an actress — or else. And once having made a decision, Blanche was never one to back down, or let anyone else do so.[1]

According to her granddaughter, Patricia Ziegfeld Stephenson, Blanche Hodkinson, to use her first married name, had had hopes herself of becoming an actress. She was certainly a woman with a powerful sense of self-dramatization, with the need to control that often accompanies a theatrical nature. "She was a managing type," remembered her daughter; "everything she did and said was predicated on the hypothesis that, if arrangements were only left to her, everything would naturally turn out all right." Drama also infused her official history of her family, which continued down to the obituaries that appeared at her death.

According to Blanche, her mother Cecilia Flood Beatty had been a belle of New Orleans, accustomed to ordering her writing paper and her linens from Paris, a gracious plantation chatelaine who as a widow was known to obsessively spend time in the Senate gallery in Washington, D.C., taking notes on all business of the day. Billie even recorded in her memoirs that she had met a former slave of her grandmother's named "Cousin Lucy" in Washington.[2] Talking to a reporter in 1908, flush with the vicarious success of Billie's first big Broadway triumph, *Love Watches*, Blanche went even further, declaring that her daughter was "descended from the two first families of Virginia," yoking Billie's father to the story of grand family origins.

The 1850 Census, and Blanche's descendants, tell a less glamorous story. "We always heard they were from Ohio," said William Stephenson, Billie's son-in-law, and census records support this. In the 1850 Census Blanche Beatty, aged 6, is shown with her father, John A. Beatty, "printer," and mother, Cecilia, and several siblings, living in Zanesville, Muskingum County, Ohio. Their neighbors were a laundress, laborer and various tradesmen — a far cry from white-columned Louisiana plantation houses at the end of cypress drives. Furthermore, both John and Cecilia are themselves shown as having been born in Ohio in the early nineteenth century. As was the practice later on when film studios managed the lives and destinies of their stables of stars, for some actresses (like Merle Oberon), elegant origins were invented, while for others (like Joan Crawford), hard-luck childhoods were spun from thin air to accentuate the roles studios gave these women to play. Thus Billie's fictional origins were perfectly matched to her stage persona: the carefree grace and indulgent luxury erroneously believed to have epitomized the Old South matched the grace and luxury she exhibited in personality and wardrobe on the stage and off it. Who would not believe her a daughter not of rural Ohio but of antebellum Louisiana and Virginia? (In fact, it was John Beatty, Blanche's father, who had some grand but distant ancestry: his descent from the Asfordbys of Lincolnshire and New York gave Billie a bloodline to the early Plantagenet monarchs of England; John was also descended from several prominent Dutch settlers of New Amsterdam.)[3]

Though petite and lithe, with a clear complexion, chestnut hair and black-browed green eyes that gazed at the world with an insouciant questioning directness, Blanche was no beauty — her best feature, as her daughter politely points out, was the way she carried herself, as if all the world were a stage and herself the one player in it: "she had a Look," wrote Billie, in a sort of blanket effort to give her mother distinction of appearance as well as of character. (Another feature of which she was proud, according to Billie, was made clear one day when Billie returned to Burkeley Crest to find Flo Ziegfeld and Blanche lying beside the pool in the sun, Blanche arguing with Flo that her feet were far prettier than his.)

But Blanche Beatty's was not a Look guaranteed to make theatergoing swains swoon in their boxes. So she went about the business of asserting herself through the one avenue available to her — marriage — and even then she seems to have bided her time for an opportunity that would take her as far away from Muskingum County as possible. In 1865, aged about 21, Blanche Beatty married an Englishman named George Hodkinson. Blanche's age — very close to old maidenhood in the notions of the time — and her choice of a foreign-born husband, smack of a personality eager to have a different life from that of her working-class Ohio family and friends. A woman so determined to better her situation would have the patience to wait for her ideal, or what approximated it, and Blanche Hodkinson had all the will-power, if not necessarily the patience, that she needed.[4]

Moving the family to Washington, D.C., Hodkinson gave Blanche four children — Florence, Blanche, George and Grace — with a few of whom Billie Burke was still acquainted

Blanche Burke and daughter Billie, ca. 1889. The strength of the former and the dependency of the latter are clearly displayed. Private collection.

in later life. When or how — or whether — Hodkinson died is a matter of conjecture, but by June 1880, Blanche (claiming to the census taker that she was 32 years old instead of 36) was living at 819 Fourteenth Street in Washington, a few blocks northeast of the White House. Billie claims her mother was working as a clerk at the Treasury Department, but the 1880 Census, taken just three years before Blanche met future husband William Burke, shows her "keeping house" and taking in boarders. Among these was a woman, Julia Bomar, who worked as a Treasury Department clerk and her brother, Cyril, a Congressional page — but no evidence that Blanche herself worked in a government capacity.

More significantly for Billie Burke's identity, though we do not know why or how, was the presence in the household of a New Hampshire–born gentleman named William H. Appleton, who was employed as an examiner at the Patent Office. Why this gentleman's surname, years later, is included among Billie Burke's given names is unknown, but may point to some sort of friendship with Blanche — perhaps it was Appleton who with his government connections helped Blanche get boarders, or assisted her in obtaining the Treasury Department job she is alleged to have had when she met Billy Burke. Billie, who remembered so many people from her earliest childhood, never refers to Appleton in any of her published writings.[5]

Blanche's crucial year, Billie tells us, was 1883. Sometime in early January, Blanche went to Pittsburgh to visit friends. Billie does not say exactly how her mother came to be invited to a party for J. A. Bailey, partner of circus impresario P. T. Barnum. Blanche had no theatrical background or exposure, and she was not to show much interest in it even after her marriage to a star of the circus circuit. Perhaps Blanche simply went to the circus for some light entertainment, and to her surprise left it in love with Billy Burke. She would not be the first or last woman to do so. "All the girls thought he was perfectly wonderful," Billie wrote, and there was certainly something about Billy that set him apart from the average clown.

Born in Knox County, Ohio, on October 23, 1844, William Ethelbert Burke had first wanted to be a chemist and in his teens worked for a druggist in Frederickstown. According to a biographical booklet published by Barnum & London in 1882, while he sold smelling salts and bromides Billy had the drugstore staff and customers in stitches, but already as a schoolboy he had had a reputation for bringing the house down: "A grotesque attitude or a peculiar grimace from Billy was sure to create an uproarious laugh in the school-room that resulted in a reprimand from the teacher, who was often holding his sides and straining every nerve to repress his own impulse to laugh outright at his amusing pupil."

Yet his happy-go-lucky nature also had a serious streak. Less than four months after the start of the Civil War, the eighteen-year-old Burke enlisted as drummer boy, on August 11, 1862. By late December of that year, Burke was a participant in the Christmas battle of Chickasaw Bayou, the first engagement of General Sherman's Vicksburg campaign. Thirty-two thousand Union troops fought 15,000 Confederates commanded by General John. C. Pemberton near Vicksburg, Mississippi, which ended with a minor victory for the Confederates.

According to his daughter, Burke only fought for a few more months, when he was discharged in April 1863 due to medical disability. In fact, Billy took part in another famous battle, that of Arkansas Post, in January 1863. Seriously wounded, Burke was then honorably discharged.

Despite her childish pleading, Billie Burke could not get much out of her father about his war days. Like many veterans who have seen direct combat and spilled blood of their own, Burke was obviously not keen to share memories of the experience, especially with a young daughter. Many men on both sides of the conflict emerged from the Civil War broken and bitter, but not Billy Burke. His wounds healed, and Billy Burke did what could only be expected of such a congenitally cheerful person: in 1865, two years after his discharge, he joined a minstrel troupe, and his career as clown began.

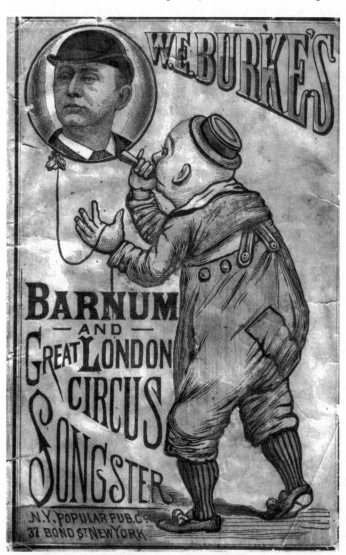

Cover of the biographical booklet on Billie's father, the popular Barnum & Bailey singing clown Billy Burke, published in 1882.

It was not a career without risks. Burke almost died a clown before he had begun to live as one: while he worked with James M. Nixon's circus, the ship the company was sailing on came close to destruction in a storm off Galveston, Texas. The shipwreck was followed by another one on the Red River, in which Burke lost his wardrobe but luckily not his life. He also managed to escape a yellow fever epidemic in Shreveport, Louisiana. His ability to sidestep disaster and keep smiling as if it were not really happening, was among several character traits that he would hand down to his daughter.[6]

Billie Burke recounts her father's devotion to Dan Rice, perhaps the most famous American clown who was not only a friend of Abraham Lincoln's but was the model for that embodied *Zeitgeist* of the USA, Uncle Sam. According to Billie, her father modeled himself after Rice in his habit of quoting profusely from Shakespeare to suit a comical situation. Like Rice, he donned costume and face paint that did not entirely conceal the real person underneath — the 1882 biographical booklet featured a sketch of Burke painted as clown, inflating a balloon that bore in its reflection Burke's unpainted face, gazing off in the distance like a soulful *artiste*.

In many ways he was an artist, using comedy to put across a complex combination of emotions, much as his daughter would do in time. There was a winsome quality to Burke's style that would also be associated with his daughter's stage and screen presence.

"I am told he was witty and clever with satirical pantomime," Billie recalled. Instead of dressing up as a tramp or buffoon (which was, ironically, her future husband Florenz Ziegfeld's favorite garb for costume parties), he wore all white with a ruff around his neck, white face paint, and pink paint outlining his mouth, with black teardrops below his eyes. But he was no sad Pierrot. Perhaps most emulative of Dan Rice, besides exchanging jokes with the audience and quoting Shakespeare, Billy Burke sang popular songs not in parody but straight, in a strong, bright baritone voice — songs written for him, such as "I'd Like It All Over Again," Irish-themed ditties like "The Maguires" and "Paddy Duffy's Cart," the comic song "The Baby's Got A Tooth," and dramatic recitations of John Greenleaf Whittier's poem "Barbara Fritchie."

Many of these songs and poems were funny but many more were on the wistful side, more proof that Burke was not just a funny-looking guy who busied himself with sight gags but a performer who grounded his act with emotional sincerity. Billie remembered that when her father took the ring, not just the audience but all the other circus folk under the tent — the trapeze artists, lion tamers, and the other clowns — stayed still and listened. And her father, claims Billie, was capable of entertaining more than just unsophisticated rubes in the American regional backwaters. Though he had studied no foreign languages, Burke was somehow able to bring his meaning and methods across to audiences in a half dozen foreign tongues, which would come in handy when his European tours began.[7]

Much to the dismay, as Billie records it, of her Beatty and Hodkinson relatives, when Barnum & Bailey's circus left Pittsburgh after that 1883 show, Mrs. Blanche Hodkinson of Washington, D.C., had eloped to New York City to become Mrs. William Ethelbert Burke. As Blanche often told Billie in later years, when moved to disgust by provincial American ways: "God deliver me from Jeffersonian simplicity!" If Blanche had wanted color and action in her life, she got it: by eloping with and marrying a clown, Blanche Hodkinson had shunted off any trace of the simplicity she despised. And as the couple's marriage certificate indicates, they really did get married in a hurry, only eleven days into January 1883 (the ceremony was presided over by Dr. George Hendric Houghton, Rector of New York's Episcopal Church of the Transfiguration, a parish that specialized in attending to the religious needs of theatre people like Billy Burke, who because of their "immoral" calling were excluded from regular churches.[8]

But after this marriage, what became of Blanche's children, the youngest of whom, Grace Hodkinson, was only 11? Perhaps this is a source for some of the families' dismay on hearing of Blanche's and Billy's marriage. All Billie records is that her mother joined the tour until it was apparent she was pregnant and needed to be in a quieter setting—perhaps Grandmother Beatty or the Hodkinson relatives took her in. In the nation's capitol, on August 7, 1884, Mary William Ethelbert Appleton Burke was born, a few months shy of the birthday of another feature of Washington, D.C., the marble obelisk of the Washington Monument on the Mall. The child's father, still on tour with the circus, telegrammed Blanche with characteristic tongue in cheek: "I don't care whether it's a boy or a girl, but does it have red hair?"

Red-bearded J. A. Bailey, who Billie says was quite fond of Billy Burke, sent an even kookier wire to the recovering mother: "I will make you a firm offer of one million dollars cash for the baby." Though she undoubtedly got the humor, canny Blanche knew her child was worth more than that.[9]

For the next several years, with Billy Burke on the road most of the time, Blanche and Billie lived between quiet, orderly Washington, where they stayed with Blanche's mother, Mrs. Beatty, and near New York City, the latter to be close to the center of Billy Burke's work—so close, indeed, they lived at Sheepshead Bay, not far from Coney Island and Manhattan Beach, where Billy Burke performed.

At some point during this period, Billy started his own circus, which his daughter describes as a "small affair." The little company did not do well. Billie says she was eight years old in 1892 when she, her father and mother set sail for England, where Billy Burke hoped to do better business, but in fact her father is listed in various advertisements in the *New York Times* as late as summer 1895, when Billie was just shy of eleven. In December 1894, Billy Burke, "Barnum's Famous Clown," is listed among such entertainers as Jo-Jo the Dog-Faced Man and George the Turtle Boy, "the most marvelous freak before the public," at Huber's Museum on 14th Street. In June of the following year, Burke was listed as "principal clown" in a circus production at Manhattan Beach, under the direction of his mentor, Dan Rice. Billie is said to have attended her first four years of school in Sheepshead Bay, which, if she started at five and ended there at nine, brings us only to 1893. Perhaps she was taken out of school to join her parents on tour.[10]

However fuzzy Billie was in chronology (and she would remain so, either by accident or choice, for the rest of her life), she did remember the voyage. The Burkes sailed second class, and Billie remembered being so cold she wore mittens the entire time. She was also badly seasick—not a happy maiden voyage for a girl who as a woman would travel first class across the Atlantic on the greatest luxury liners several times each year. "I had dreamed of Kings and Queens and Princelings," Billie wrote later, possibly echoing her mother's hopes for such a change of situation, "of glitter and panoply, and instead there was merely the chill smudge of Waterloo Station and the crisp cackle of Cockney voices."[11]

Billie tells us that in London, Billy Burke produced a show called Billy Burke's Barnum & Great London Circus Songsters, in the advertisements for which Billy was billed as "America's Greatest Clown." But for all the hoopla, like Billy's variety show in New York, the London show did not play long. Blanche's managing abilities, which were to prove so effective for her daughter, seemed to be of little use for her husband— indeed, it is possible it was Billy Burke's relaxed approach to his own career that focused Blanche on their daughter and her star possibilities. Burke settled into music hall gigs, singing in costume, and made a good enough living for the family to move into their own flat, albeit in what Billie remembers as not the best part of London — it was, she recalls, the sort of domestic situation where the landlady brought the family's meals on a tray and a pail of water for their baths.

Perhaps dislike of this flat sent young Billie wandering through the streets in search of the new and strange, which is what she found when she met one Rev. Mr. Kirschbaum at St. Margaret's Church, Westminster, where Henry Purcell had once been organist and where Sir Winston Churchill would be married in a few years. This was where Billie was, as she describes it, officially christened. She had never been baptized — perhaps a legacy of her parents' peripatetic lives, or the fact that entertainers were not welcome in most churches — and when Kirschbaum agreed to carry out this lapsed rite of passage, "I told the handsome curate that I wanted to be named 'Billie,' for my famous father."

To add to the strangeness of this memory, Billie does not say that either of her parents were present for the ceremony. Did the Rev. Mr. Kirschbaum go through the motions of a pretend baptism merely to humor the insistent ginger-haired girl?

The mystery is exactly what the Burkes called their daughter before this. Newspaper and other sources suggest she was called Ethelbert, after her father's middle name (such was the name she gave when she married Florenz Ziegfeld in 1914), and Billie indicates in her memoirs how unhappy she was with the thought she might be nicknamed "Bertha." An article from 1908 claimed that Billy and Blanche wanted a boy, and were so sure they would get one they advanced him the name William Ethelbert Burke, Jr. "[S]o the young lady was taken to the altar and christened William Burke, Jr. — and somehow the name seems to suit her." Billie, however, stated she was never taken to the font at all before making the effort herself. She says the Rev. Mr. Kirschbaum asked her for all the names in her family, then suggested "Mary" to add to the bunch, as that was a name he loved. "And that is how the name of Mary William Ethelbert Appleton Burke was registered at Westminster Abbey," Billie recalled. Which leaves us, perhaps forever, the question of who Mr. Appleton was to Blanche Burke, that her daughter's name should commend him.[12]

CHAPTER 2

The Education of an Actress

What formal education Billie had began in earnest in London. While Billy Burke, on his nights off, was teaching Billie popular songs and swinging with her on his swivel chair, Blanche was laying bolder and more serious plans. Billie was sent to the Misses Baillies' School where she did poorly at math and well at music, despite having to practice in a freezing room with one of the teachers prodding her for her mistakes at the piano with "a cold, raw, red finger."

She only seems to have visited her father backstage once, to see him work with a comedy mule—like his hero Dan Rice, Billy Burke had a way of charming the most recalcitrant animals. This persuasiveness did not extend to his wife, however. Billie confesses she had had no interest in the theatre as a profession, no aptitude for it apart from "a trick of mimicry" she inherited from her father, and a great deal of fear of the prospect of showing oneself and one's abilities (or lack thereof) before a large hall of strangers. But Blanche had no such doubts. "[T]his determined woman decided that I was going to be a great actress," Billie recalled. Or a famous opera star or dancer. The very randomness of Blanche's plans for Billie—that she be famous, no matter how or what—seems to have irked Billy Burke as much as it frightened his daughter. Perhaps this was because it was Blanche's way of offsetting her husband's professional setbacks by exploiting their daughter's potential star power. This clearly concerned Billy, because as Billie remembered, he insisted that she make her own choice about what she wanted to do with her life, not fall in with Blanche's own plans.

Blanche was not daunted by her husband's or her daughter's resistance. She took the young girl to see what she considered the best exponents of the theatre—Ellen Terry and Sir Henry Irving in Sardou's *Robespierre*. She only succeeded in scaring Billie. Blanche then ordered acting lessons, elocution lessons, dancing lessons. Singing lessons brought such enthusiasm from the teacher that she offered to send Billie to Italy for opera study. But opera study would take years of hard work before a yield on the investment, and Blanche "wanted quicker action." In the meantime, puberty was setting in for Billie and men began to pay her attentions that differed considerably from the innocent demonstrations of affection she was used to from her father's circus friends.

"Yes, I began to experience that kind of thing early," Billie wrote. "I have no false modesty about it; a good many men have reached for me from time to time." When she got older she came to realize that Blanche was probably aware of the uses of sexual attraction in furthering an acting career, and even suggests in her memoirs that her mother turned her toward the stage specifically to exploit it. Billie's "adorableness" (read "sex appeal"), which she herself eventually did everything in her power to develop, was certainly to become the main attraction in all her early stage work.[1]

Such as it was, Billie's education was interrupted for long periods when she accompanied her father and mother on tour. "It was the custom," she tells us, "to play Paris in the spring, Germany in the summer, Russia in the autumn and London in the winter." She did not always go along with her parents on these tours, but on at least one of them she remembered the clowns and troupes she met, including the Russian clown Durow (which of the Durow brothers, Vladimir or Anatoli, whom she saw she does not say) and the Danish clown Adolph Frederik Peter Olschansky (not William as she writes in her memoirs). She never met but always wondered about circus stars of an earlier day who were friends of her father's, such as Robert Sherwood, the Barnum clown who had actually stepped out of the sawdust circle and shaken hands with Queen Victoria in 1888. The Queen was amused, but Sherwood retired that year. As it did her father, encounters between the zany liberalism of show business and the stodgy conservatism of the so-called respectable world outside the theatre or circus tent always fascinated her.[2]

Billy's European tours were successful, though it was Blanche who "managed both my father and me as if we were delinquents likely to drop a bomb or squander the family fortune if we were not constantly supervised." As soon as Billy Burke had registered the family at a hotel, he and his daughter cleared out of the place for a few hours while Blanche, head wrapped in a cloth, scrubbed the place down — a habit Billie herself was to adopt to the amusement of her daughter and husband.[3]

Billie later regretted having slept or stumbled through some of Europe's most famous museums and historic places, but if the adolescent was being harried by her mother to add art appreciation to the program that was to make her a famous actress, it is easy to understand why the technique failed. Billie's one interest in art at this time of her life was when she watched her father sketch "quite good" charcoals of the cities he toured.[4]

For all her energy, Blanche was the last person to lead a future actress to the stage — for all her pliancy, Billie had a will to match her red hair, and reacted mulishly to Blanche's overeager handling of the reins. Life stepped in to effect the desired transformation. Billie does not betray realization of it, but it was during two years when she was boarded with artistic London families, while her parents were on an extended European tour, that she learned the most from life and society that later went into her technique as actress. She lived first with the family of journalist William Beatty-Kingston, a reviewer for *The Times* and other periodicals who took on music, books, theatre, and wrote of the society and crowned heads as well.

The Beatty-Kingstons lived in a manner that at first confused Billie and later became her key to understanding and displaying on stage the complex personality of London's "good" society. Mrs. Beatty-Kingston was a large lady with auburn hair who ran her home along the grand pattern, with a stuffy butler to match. But then at table she would sit down holding her fat pugs, one under each arm, her daughters carrying their dogs to the table as well, and tea was livened by these animals' feasting on saucers of milk while their human guests sipped tea. There was also a parrot that had been taught to screech greetings to the eldest son of the house, earning a hail of muffins from the boy. This was the same house, muffins littering the floor, that had a grand piano lavishly plaqued in silver with the memorial that Franz Liszt had once played it. Standing near this same piano, aging but revered opera soprano Adelina Patti often came to sing for the Beatty-Kingstons' guests.[5]

Later on, Billie lived with the family of Theodore Roussel, the French-born painter who had studied with James McNeill Whistler. Besides helping her with her French, which she soon spoke "glibly," it was in this home that Billie would have learned the possibilities of just what to do with her body. Roussel had many painter friends who Billie says clamored to paint her portrait, "chiefly because of my red hair," a waist-length curtain of shimmering Titian-blond tresses. Assuming poses and discovering which to take to elicit the most satisfaction from her audience was better than making faces at herself in a mirror — Billie came to find what worked and what did not in how she presented herself, and she would not forget the lessons.[6]

Blanche saw the blossoming young woman Billie had become, and decided her crash course in the art of graceful speech and movement must be put to the test. She arranged bit part after bit part for her daughter, at various small theatres in London — Billie did not, as was reported later on, make her stage debut in Europe, but in the hardscrabble, noisy venues of London music halls.[7]

"I did *not* want to be an actress," Billie insists, even when, for her performances of "coon songs," she received applause and calls for encores. "I wish I could report that my first real taste of theatrical success, a full burst of approval, inspired me to reach for the heights. It didn't." She did what her mother told her to do, even when what Blanche required of her was "awful and scary." Blanche was not to be opposed. As Blanche pointed out with characteristic bluntness in an interview given after Billie had become a star, "When she says, 'I can't, I can't,' I say, 'Very well, then, if you think you can't, let some other girl have the chance. There are plenty of other girls who would give anything for the chance you have.'" In the face of this kind of pressure, even the strongest personality would have had difficulty holding its own.[8]

Billie went from Birkenhead to Sheffield, where she was part of an act called "The Sleeping Beauty and the Yellow Dwarf." To say she "performed" in this act is stretching the definition of the word: per her description, she had only to lie back on a rock, her red hair arranged all around her. It was the beauty part of the act's title that got her the job, and it was to aid her in getting the next role that came along, which was to launch her career. Composer Leslie Stuart had had great success in 1899 with the musical comedy *Florodora* (not Floradora as Billie and many others spell it), a show thin on plot but thick with beautiful girls. The Florodora Girl was a precursor to the beauties collected and displayed by Earl Carroll and, of course, Florenz Ziegfeld, and they excited all the same attentions — young women wanted to look like them, young men, including heirs to wealth and title, wanted to squire them about or marry them. The American production of *Florodora* ran for over two years (552 performances) and was part of what established Broadway as the "Great White Way."[9]

Stuart was working on a new show which was to be called *The School Girl*, and he hired Billie to perform in it for half of what she was paid for her work at the London Pavilion — five pounds per week. Sensing greater potential, however, Blanche agreed, and Billie watched while Stuart and producer George Edwardes put their heads together over just what to do with the young beauty they had signed on. It did not take them long to come up with an idea. In the second act, she was to sing a syncopated ditty, "Mamie, I Have a Little Canoe."

In the scene, Billie and three other young actresses pantomimed paddling a canoe while Billie sang. Billie seems to have discovered later on that a great deal of discussion had gone on about this song and who was to sing it, not just on the part of Stuart and Edwardes but also with their American co-producer, Charles Frohman. The cast boasted three popular stage beauties, Edna May and Pauline Chase, Frohman's clients, and Marie Studholm, who was under contract to Edwardes. None of these women was to be told that what everyone knew was the show-stopper song of the evening was to be sung by a comparative unknown — they would only discover this in rehearsal, when Billie performed it.

Before Billie had finished, May, Chase and Studholm, always on the *qui vive* for potential upstaging, realized that the red-haired teenager had been given the show's hit, and they threatened to resign. Billie never knew what was done to appease these "offended queens," or what Frohman, Stuart or Edwardes had to concede or promise to get them to go on with the show, but go on with it they did.

"Do not tell me that the English are cold, impassive people," Billie wrote. The audience did more than applaud her, as other audiences had done. They roared, stamped, whistled. "It was like a tidal shock smashing across the footlights after my rather quiet number." Billie ran from the stage, bumping into things along the way, and was caught in the wings by the stage manager. She was sure she had failed and that the audience was out for her blood. The stage manager, Pat Malone, turned her squarely around and told her he would slap her if she did not return to the stage — a hint at how much of a child she was seen to be by management, and an indication of how little sympathy a child performer could expect to receive in those days from same. Billie hurried back on stage and sang the "Canoe Song" again, to even greater cheers. *The School Girl* ran for more than two years.[10]

Suddenly, she was a celebrity — significantly, the event that signaled stardom to teenaged Billie Burke was not the appearance of reviews hailing her great talent (she was never to receive such in London, and not many in New York), but a collection of fetching postcard photos emphasizing that adorableness with which she would always be associated, displayed next to portraits of royals and theatre divas. Billie would never forget the day she strolled past the display windows of a fashionable West End photographer, and found pictures of herself sitting beside those of Lady Randolph Churchill, Queen Alexandra, and sweet-faced actress Gertie Millar.[11]

"London was enchantment then," Billie remembered, "and I was deliciously aware, too, that it was full of interesting Sin." Once called "Copper Knob," a nickname more appropriate for a child actor, Billie was now christened "the American Flapper," a term she believed derived from her hair style, which was basically a pile of hair pinned up as if in haste, with tendrils dangling (or flapping, as Billie puts it).[12]

Billie Burke at left, as Mamie Reckfeller, in her first London hit, *The School Girl*, in 1903.

Even in her most formal photos, wearing velvet edged in ermine or flowered silks and lace, the Billie Burke of this time looks as if she has just come in from a windstorm. How the term "flapper" actually began is a subject of some controversy (and it would come to identify not insouciant young Edwardian women with long hair but insouciant young post–World War I American women with short bobs). But it was a look that went well with the personality Billie was developing on stage, that of a winsome American beauty without a care in the world.

The "interesting Sin" Billie was awakening to had its origins at the very height of English society, in the person of King Edward VII, a genial libertine who had been kept too long from the throne by his mother, Queen Victoria, and developed all the habits of drinking, partying and keeping mistresses that would set the tone for his briefer but far more glamorous reign.

Thanks to Blanche's constant vigilance, Billie knew virtually nothing about this or any other sin, but she learned a few things just by watching a star like Edna May in action. Billie looked on, fascinated, as male admirers flocked to the dressing room of the beautiful Edna, bringing the actress candy which she then good naturedly shared with Billie and the other young supporting players. Billie also looked forward to the nightly appearance of the Maharajah of Cooch Behar, who wore a jeweled turban and reminded Billie of a leopard as he waited outside Miss May's dressing room, diamonds in his hands. The bucks of London waited with him, happy to do so as long as it took for the stage goddesses to change their clothes, fix their hair, and accompany them to

Billie Burke as fashion plate in Edwardian London. These images were displayed in shop windows throughout London, and made into postcards.

any number of fashionable restaurants "for a hot bird and a cold bottle and who knows what sophisticated revelry. I never saw it," recalled Billie. "I went home with Mother, wondering."[13]

Billie soon had her own landed beau, whom she refused to name when writing her memoirs as "he is today a gentleman of some eminence in the Empire." Various pieces of the puzzle her coy recollections present to posterity add up to one Captain

Francis George Stanley Cary, whose family had lived in the pillared seat of Follaton at Totnes, Devonshire, since the eighteenth century. Following the breaking of his engagement to Billie, Cary married in 1912 and has numerous descendants. Frank Cary was in his late twenties when he knew Billie, but he knew how to have fun. As Billie later described in a letter to Nancy Hamilton, Cary could make her laugh like no other man she ever knew. He had a playful, childish, irresponsible streak that she warmed to. Traveling up the Thames to Skindles Hotel in Maidenhead (infamous later as a pre–World War II haunt for adulterers), or riding horseback together or dining at the Savoy, Billie and her captain were a pair of scamps, leaping into unoccupied train compartments and scaring anyone who tried to enter by impersonating the insane. In these years, for Billie life was all a game, not to be taken seriously. Nor, indeed, was show business: Billie records how she and one of her friends in *The School Girl* chorus provoked Edna May by turning to her in the middle of her big song and grinning at her, orange wedges planted in their mouths.[14]

It was while Billie was dining at the Carlton with Captain Cary, fending off his offers of marriage, that she first met producer Charles Frohman.

"I barely knew [Frohman]," Billie remembered, but she walked up to the table where sat a "small, round little man" with "beautiful seal-colored eyes" and a protruding under lip. Frohman, though born in Sandusky, Ohio, spoke an almost broken English, in a sort of telegram shorthand that matched the jabbing forefinger he used when speaking about anything meaningful to him. Billie confidently announced to Frohman that she had heard he was taking *The School Girl* to New York and that she would like to come along with the company. Frohman jabbed at her with the famous forefinger: "You may go. But Edna sings 'Canoe Song.'" Billie could only retreat to her table, humiliated and disappointed. There was no point traveling to New York if she could not sing the song that had made her famous in London.[15]

As it happened, Edna May had another purpose to serve closer to home. After being passed over for the role of Peter Pan in a Christmas revival, Billie got work in the musical comedies *The Blue Moon* and *The Duchess of Dantzic*, which then led her to Edna May's vehicle, *The Belle of Mayfair*, at the Vaudeville Theatre in the Strand. When Edna went on holiday after a long run, Billie was cast as her replacement. The owners of the Vaudeville were a pair of brothers, Carlo and Giuseppe Gatti, whom Billie unaccountably describes as Greek. They proceeded to fall in love with her: they had her dressing room redecorated, sent her flowers and presents, and one of them asked her to marry him, although as Billie apologetically wrote later on, she could not remember which Gatti had made the proposal.

The Gattis had an office at the back of the theatre, from which they could watch the performance each evening. One particular night they had as guest Charles Hawtrey—later Sir Charles—with whom the brothers Gatti were discussing the lease of one of their theatres.

"Sir Charles was one of the magnificoes of the London stage," Billie wrote, an actor-producer who managed some sixteen theatres in London and produced over one hundred plays. "Hawtrey was a large man," recalled Billie, "with big, beautiful brown eyes,"

Billie Burke and co-star Farren Soutar in their 1906 musical comedy in London, *The Belle of Mayfair.*

famed as the best stage liar of his day. His, according to one writer, "was a comedy that expressed with unobtrusive finesse an individual temperament." Born at Eton, where his father served as master of the lower school, Hawtrey was very much the gentleman on and off the stage. He had attended Eton, Rugby and Oxford, and if he was referred to posthumously in *The Times* as a "lazy worldling [who] had nothing but good manners to show for an expensive education," Hawtrey was a hard worker once he found his true métier — the theatre. He first acted on stage at age 23; by 25 he was mounting successful productions and receiving the attention of London's persnickety theatre critics.[16]

It is strange Hawtrey had never encountered Billie at the Savoy Hotel restaurant, one of her usual haunts with her Devonshire beau — perhaps he spent too much time in the Savoy's American Bar, which offered a naughtily named drink, the Hanky Panky Cocktail, of his own invention. But once Hawtrey had seen Billie on stage, he knew he had found something special. He asked to see her at his office; she arrived out of breath, and his first remark was: "Well, Miss Burke, would you be interested in straight comedy?" Billie could hardly keep from shouting "Yes," but Hawtrey, who was born to be a mentor (as he was to Noël Coward, among others), pulled her up short by reminding her that she would miss the dancing and singing of the musical comedy shows she had been doing.

"[C]omedy is dry, hard work," he warned Billie. She would not find the same sort of audience — meaning the adoring young men — smiling up at her from the front row. Billie insisted she wanted to be an actress and would try her best to rise to the occasion. As susceptible to Billie's charms as those younger men, Hawtrey decided she deserved a chance, and offered her a part playing opposite him in a new play called *Mr George*. Thus began Billie's first real lessons in the art of acting.[17]

Working with Billie from morning to afternoon, Hawtrey taught her how to communicate on stage, not just with her audience but with her fellow actors — a big difference from the musical comedy method of playing exclusively to the stalls. He taught Billie what she calls "the drawing-room manner," and yet adjured her to behave as naturally when making an entrance as if she were striding into her own home. Billie learned to move, sit, speak with a grace, refinement and ease none of her earlier theatre experience would have developed in her. In short, Hawtrey gave Billie the air of clever *chic* that was to form her chief charm in her early stage work. Supporting her in this was her first foray into the realm of stage fashion, which *Mr George*, set in the eighteenth century, visited on her with a glamorous vengeance.[18]

The play was a bit of fluff, but it fit Billie on all levels — the story of an American girl come to England who surprises the family who takes her in when they discover Mr. George is actually a girl. (Billie was to play a variation on this theme in *Peggy*, her first motion picture, in 1916.) England discovered Billie Burke both through this play and the one following, *Mrs Ponderbury's Past*. Adapted by Francis C. Burnand from Ernest Blum's *Mme Mongodin*, this was the first of the comedies in which Billie would play a fashionably dressed lady of society. More photos of her appeared in shop windows, wearing the beautiful clothes which would become regulation garb for her.

It was at this period that Billie was selected along with other ingénue beauties to be presented to portly King Edward VII, who had an appreciative eye for pretty young actresses, and slender, increasingly deaf Queen Alexandra. The presentation, less formal than a presentation at court, took place in a garden (Billie does not say where, but perhaps in the gardens of Buckingham Palace), to which all the girls sallied in their lacy dresses and big sun hats. Billie "curtsied so low" to the royal pair, she recalled, "I could have picked dandelions." It was one of the first of many hints that comedy in elegant settings would be a stock theme of Billie's career.[19]

Sometime between Billie's performances in *The School Girl* in spring and *The Duchess of Dantzic* in autumn 1903, Billy Burke had begun to suffer from some malady Billie does not name. To treat his illness, she says, her father had moved to a cottage near Bath, so that he could "take the waters." People who made use of Bath's allegedly wonder-working, sulphur-reeking waters did so for maladies ranging from gout to angina, so it is impossible to guess just what was wrong with Burke. His abrupt disappearance from Billie's narrative after the start of her career may be for any number of reasons, but Billy seems to have reconciled himself to Blanche's plans for their daughter—she says he came to see her in *The School Girl* and in *The Duchess*, but he died on October 6, 1906, before *Mr George* went into production. Billy Burke had often assured his daughter that "I will see my baby's name in lights on Broadway yet." Had he lived a few months longer, he would have done so, because the first hints of renown for Billie Burke in London were about to bloom into stardom in New York City.[20]

A rare soulful image (ca. 1906) of Billie in her London musical comedy days.

After their meeting at the Carlton Grill, when Billie had had the nerve to ask Charles Frohman to take her to New York with *The School Girl* and suffered his refusal to allow her to sing the "Canoe Song," Frohman had apparently thought things over. Playwright James M. Barrie, who probably knew Frohman better than most of the producer's clients and saw his best side more often than they, called Frohman "the man who never broke his word."

He also never gave in when he thought he was right, as he did when he insisted that Barrie drop writing novels in exchange for writing plays. This was a quarrel, Barrie wrote, that lasted for sixteen years, yet Frohman "always won, but not because of his doggedness; only because he was so lovable that one had to do as he wanted." Frohman clearly did not see Billie as a musical comedy star or feel that she could make a name in that genre. But in straight comedy, which she had been learning from the master Charles Hawtrey, Billie showed more than promise. The producer who had put the names of Maude Adams and Ethel Barrymore in lights would work the same magic with Billie Burke. First he had to get her.[21]

At the end of December 1906, Frohman was in London, and sent Billie a card asking her in his shorthand manner to come to his office. He had a play, *My Wife*, that was not doing well in London but which he was sure would be a success in New York. "Would you like to go to America?" he asked Billie.

Having been rebuffed by this small, gentle-looking man in a public setting, Billie could hardly believe this offer made in the privacy of his office. She told him that she

Billie Burke, fashion plate extraordinaire (ca. 1907).

was performing with Charles Hawtrey, what he had done for her and what his plans were, and added, "I don't suppose you remember that I was in *The School Girl* and wanted to go to America then?" Frohman only nodded, mildly meditative as a Buddha. It was up to Hawtrey to decide, he said. "Maybe you will be interested, say, by August," he told Billie in his softly apologetic voice. Directly after, Billie told Charles Hawtrey about this meeting, and Hawtrey seems to have known it was only right to let Billie seek her destiny in New York, though he wanted her for *Mrs Ponderbury's Past*, his next production. He admitted he was not sure the play would be a hit, but he hoped Billie would act in it and "we'll see how things work out." Billie respected Hawtrey all the more for his fine sense of generosity — he had, after all, just developed her, trained her in all his techniques, and here was a Broadway producer threatening to whisk her away to New York.

As it happened, *Mrs Ponderbury's Past was* a success, running till summer, when it closed for the season. Billie hints in her memoirs that Hawtrey, with his reputation for charming the ladies, had shown more than a few signs of being interested in her, which scared her in a way she did not find unpleasant — after all, this was the girl who had "started early" in the art of charming men. Whether Hawtrey's attentions ever led to anything more than longer-than-necessary embraces on the stage is impossible to say, but clearly Billie's mind was not on Hawtrey or London. Nor was Blanche's. When Frohman, ever patient, approached Billie again, she agreed to go off to New York to act in *My Wife*, at what she records was to her then the astonishing salary of $500 per week. "Mother and I joyfully accepted," she recalled. She assured Hawtrey that she would be back in London by the spring. "I think you are going to be a very fine come-

Charles Hawtrey (ca. 1907), Billie's mentor and co-star in *Mrs Ponderbury's Past*, Billie's final London role before heading for Broadway in 1907.

dienne," Hawtrey told her, patting her hand. Go to America, he advised, make a pile of money, and then come back to him, "and we will find something fine to do together."

But Billie Burke never returned to Charles Hawtrey. She had just taken out a forty-eight-year lease on a small house in London's fashionable St. John's Wood district. She had Hawtrey planning out her future stage career, and she had more than one handsome suitor, one of whom could have given her a title.

But New York and America took hold of Billie Burke. For the next three decades, they would not let go.[22]

CHAPTER 3

Toast of Broadway

"New York amazed me," recalled Billie, after she arrived there in the hot August of 1907 with her mother and all the baskets, boxes and bundles that constituted Blanche's idea of proper travel accoutrements.

Each night, Billie emerged from the brilliant lights of the Empire Theatre and marveled at the velvety dark blue sky above the city, studded with a million diamond stars. This had not been possible in smoky London, but as Billie points out, the stars inside the Empire were pretty dazzling, too. She knew she was lucky: it was not the fate of every young actress of twenty three, untried on Broadway, to be starred opposite John Drew, "First Gentleman" of the American theatre.[1]

Charles Frohman had made John Drew a star, or so claims the hagiographic biography of Frohman produced by Isaac F. Marcosson and Frohman's brother, Daniel, a year after Charles' tragic death on the *Lusitania*. The son of Louisa Lane Drew, a famed child actress who for thirty years ran Philadelphia's Arch Street Theatre, and of the short-lived but celebrated actor John Drew, Sr., Drew Junior first stepped professionally on his mother's stage in 1873, aged 20, acting in a "comedietta" called *Cool as a Cucumber*. That would be his style from then on: cool, dapper, worldly, wise. He developed into a comedian of superb flair, in everything from workaday drawing room comedies to the demanding comic roles of Shakespeare.

Drew had been managed by Augustin Daly since 1875, performing in his Fifth Avenue Theatre when not touring the country and the European continent, playing before both the crowned heads of Europe and the crowded pits of regional "opera houses" throughout the United States. Charles Frohman became Drew's new manager much as he had become Billie Burke's, through a sort of drawn-out courtship composed of enigmatic first meeting and subsequent offers of big salary. Over cards (Frohman being an expert player) and dinner (Frohman being an expert diner), and being told by everyone that Frohman was "the coming man," Drew told Daly he was leaving him in October 1892. "With the acquisition of his first big star," states the author of Frohman's biography, "[Frohman] laid the corner-stone of what is the so-called modern starring system." And Drew paved the way for Maude Adams, his niece Ethel Barrymore, Billie Burke, and other early stars of the Broadway stage.[2]

If Charles Hawtrey was a big man, Frohman was a little one. Sitting in his sedate office in the Empire Theatre Building, at his little desk surrounded by Gothic appointments, he looked more like an attorney than a theatrical producer, except for a few characteristic differences — he hated wearing laced shoes or a watch. Somebody could always be asked what time it was, and if a watch-bearing acquaintance was not present, Frohman had a special clock in his office that chimed tunes from his hit shows when striking the hour. He solved the fractious issue of shoes by putting his small feet into comfortable slippers that he could jump into and out of as needed. He also hated to carry money, and when handed the bill in a restaurant he passed it on to his brother Daniel or some other companion to pay it, reimbursing them liberally later on with a similar disregard for cash.

These were a few of the many childlike qualities Frohman had — Billie remembered him sitting in the dark during rehearsals, "fingers interlaced across his middle like a kewpie," murmuring tentative phrases of suggestion to his director or to the actors, like a well-behaved little boy. But for such a quiet man, Frohman had a cutting wit, which, again, was less deliberate cruelty and more like the undiplomatic observation of a clever child. Once, says Billie, Frohman made a suggestion to the English actress Mrs. Patrick Campbell, who turned to him and airily announced: "You forget that I am an artist." Frohman winked at her and replied, "Mrs. Campbell, I'll keep your secret." Billie also saw Frohman enraged numerous times during their seven year relationship, yet it was the sudden and almost comical rage of a boy: "He would inflate himself, pigeon-like, turning red and purple in the face," she remembered; his temper seemed to add inches to his diminutive height.[3]

Frohman had a number of useful theories about what attracted audiences which today serve as the foundation not just of effective theatre but of marketing ploys (stupid husband, smart wife) used in modern television commercials. Americans, he told Billie, love to see a woman triumph over men; and they also needed to believe that he or she, John or Jane Q. Audience member, could actively contribute to save the day for the hero or heroine if necessary, could feel they might cross the footlights and make a difference in the outcome of a play. He would have loved the interactive theatre of the future.

Aside from Frohman's abbreviated but useful coachings, Billie was assisted by her mother, "another martinet," who went over Billie's lines at home to make certain she was word perfect, becoming irritated enough to throw the script at her when she forgot. Billie reports that her mother also coached her in just what nuances and inflections to use when delivering her lines. Having left behind Hawtrey and London, Blanche was not about to let her daughter do anything but succeed in this new opportunity. (Billie seems to have developed from these sessions a sort of penciled short-hand to show herself where in her lines she should adopt particular emotive expressions: happy faces, sad faces, and a whole set of hieroglyphics in between.) When opening night came, on August 31, 1907, Billie knew her lines perfectly, and she was aided in another matter: controlling her nerves. The opening night nonchalance of the other performers, notably Drew's, kept her settled and serene.[4]

Drew's playfulness was just what Billie needed. Drew teased her during their love scenes by feeling up and down her arms for her vaunted elbow dimples. He also tested her dramatic discipline by whispering nonsense to her at crucial moments during the play. Billie got him back on occasion, as when she was required to pull a note from her handbag for Drew to read, and instead retrieved every possible ridiculous toy she could find in the shops of New York, forcing Drew to ad lib until the note finally appeared. Drew says little about Billie in his memoirs except that she was "acclaimed as a charming actress and a beautiful woman" in her role of Beatrice "Trixie" Dupré, the ward of Drew's character, Gerald Eversleigh, who fall in love with each other and marry. He adds that Frohman, in a bit of Barnum publicity that would influence Billie's own self-generated press in years to come, gave out to the papers that the clown Billy Burke had been Drew's old friend of many years' standing, and before his death had made Drew promise to take care of Billie — a blatant fib that would, however, not do *My Wife* any harm at the box office. How better to attract audiences than to "reveal" that Billie Burke was not only playing the ward of her real-life guardian, but falling in love with and marrying him?[5]

According to Billie, on opening night Drew took more than twenty curtain calls; and it gradually dawned on her that *My Wife* had made her, an unknown young woman who had only gained a following in London music halls, a star. "I was petted and congratulated," she wrote in her memoirs, and what pleased her most was that she had been accepted by an American audience — "my own people."

But Billie's success was no surprise to Frohman. In June, before Billie had set foot back on American soil, he had told a reporter he was "confident that Billie Burke, who will be Drew's leading woman next season, will greatly please New Yorkers," noting that Billie was "delighted with the prospect of playing in her native land." Frohman's PR style was as quiet and brief as his conversation, but he knew that publicizing Billie's desire to please her countrymen was a patriotic touch that was sure to warm theatre goers to Billie before they even saw her perform.

Detail of silver souvenir spoon, one of many items inspired or endorsed by Billie Burke as her fame spread in America. (Photograph by Les Hayter)

No photograph and no review can recreate just what it was that Billie brought to the stage. While critic George Jean Nathan could claim to have seen Billie all the way from her beginnings in London musical comedy to leading lady on Broadway and never knew her to play anything but a bubbly airhead (*vide infra*), we have to give Billie's immense fan following the benefit of the doubt.

As a young comedienne, she had a sparkle and verve that gave her the impression of being forever youthful, a sort of permanent child. She had something of beauty though she was not conventionally beautiful. Her acting ran the gamut from winsome to forlorn, but nothing deeper. It did not need to be. These qualities and others are a textbook example of the sum being greater than the parts. Add to the list her flowing hair, fiery red in an age of angelic blondes and demure brunettes, and her blue eyes, which she had learned to do many things with boarding with upper class families and attending high society balls in London. She had a physical grace that is commented on even in the most negative reviews, making her an ideal model for the slim-waisted, lace- and bead-dripping gowns and ostrich fans of the Edwardian era. And she had that trilling voice, which was neither her real timbre nor her natural manner of expression, but which matched perfectly the sprite-like characters she played.

The young woman who first strode onto the stage of the Empire Theatre that hot late August of 1907 caught the eye and ear much as a brightly plumaged bird might do, one that curiously cocked her head at her fellow actors — especially at Uncle Jack — but who never seemed one of them, and might fly away at any moment: an early echo of the self-absorbed Billie Burke of the Hollywood years. What male audience members, especially, saw, both those with eyes for women and those without, was the total embodiment of the pretty, charming, pleasing and naughty little witch a woman was supposed to be in those days before the winsome Victorian age, living on for a few years after the Queen's death in 1901, was replaced by the more sardonic desideratum of the reign of Edward VII and the even harder-edged feminine ideal born during the boozing and spending of the 1920's.[6]

The *New York Times* critic (probably Adolph Klauber) who covered *My Wife* was not so warmly welcoming toward Billie as her gaga American audiences. "In the role of the volatile young lady ... she was wholly pleasant," he wrote, "though in no way remarkable."[7] It should be remembered that *My Wife* was up against a good deal of competition that season. Billie was aware of it and lists in her memoirs such productions, running concurrently with *My Wife*, as *Under the Greenwood Tree* with Charles Cherry, *The Fool Hath Said There Is No God* with E.H. Sothern, *Rosmersholm* with Minnie Maddern Fiske, *The Grand Army Man* with David Warfield, and Donald Brian and Ethel Jackson waltzing into a hit with *The Merry Widow*. Mary Pickford, a pretty blond Canadian girl formerly named Gladys Louise Smith, made her debut that season in *The Warrens of Virginia*. (And would form some hard opinions about Billie, based more on her own insecurities as an actress than on anything Billie ever did to her, in her later years.) Frohman, who had the energy to rehearse up to a half dozen plays at a time, was especially busy that year, producing *When Knights Were Bold* with Pauline Frederick, *The Ranger* with Dustin Farnum and Mary Boland (later to figure in Billie's history), Raymond Hackett's debut performance in *The Toymakers*, Ethel Barrymore in *Her Sister*, Maude Adams in *The Jester* and George Ade's play *Father and the Boys*. Also on that season was a revue called *The Ziegfeld Follies*, produced in the New York Roof — known as the Jardin de Paris — featuring such stars as Grace La Rue, Emma Carus, James Manley and George Bickell. *My Wife* ran for 129 performances at the Empire Theatre, which compares very well against the paltry 44 performances of *Under the Greenwood Tree* and the 39 of the *Rosmersholm* revival. (And indeed, with the rest of Billie's future plays as a star.)[8]

As in London, stardom brought Billie the attentions of male admirers. And despite being guarded not just by Blanche but by Frohman, "my other duenna," she fell in and out of love "as regularly as I washed my hair." (According to an article published twenty years later, it was in this play that Flo Ziegfeld first caught a glimpse Billie.) But she was also courted in ways less dangerous in the eyes of Blanche or Frohman by some distinguished older men, among them Mark Twain.[9]

Billie entered Twain's life just at the time when his world seemed to be falling to pieces. Twain's beloved wife, Olivia, had died suddenly in Florence, Italy, in June 1904; the *New York Times* on the seventh of that month reported the grievous news that a distraught Twain knelt beside Livvy's coffin and "speaks to no one." Then in 1909, his favorite younger daughter, Jean, died during an epileptic seizure. Twain never recovered. His writings from this period till his death are dark, complaining, nearly paranoid, often confined to letters he wrote but never sent.

"With me," Billie notes, in the years 1907–1908, Twain was "gay and amusing," a gallant show Twain must have gone to some pains to display specially for Billie. His mourning had not ended his love for the theatre, and he first met Billie after a performance of *My Wife*, a play which, with its May-December romance, would have been sure to appeal to him. "He would shake that beautiful shock of snowy white hair," she remembered, lean his head against hers, and say, "Billie, we redheads have to stick together." Billie kept up with him even when she was on tour. If she was playing Philadelphia or some other city close enough to New York to travel there of a Sunday, Billie would always come to Twain's house on lower Fifth Avenue for dinner when invited, which was often.

There weren't many bright spots in Twain's life, and it is charming to think of the grieving old philosopher enjoying a few happy hours in the company of the playful young actress. In return for her friendship, Twain offered Billie some valuable advice about life. On a photograph Twain inscribed to Billie in December 1907, which she reproduced in her memoirs, Twain gave her a motto she would hold to for the rest of her career: "Truth is the most valuable thing we have — let us always economize it." (That this was also Blanche Burke's motto would only add more authority.)[10]

CHAPTER 4

Halcyon Hour

In her memoirs, Billie lavishly recreated the tone and tempo of this period — that time before the first world war mowed down a generation of bright young men, when the names Gould and Astor and Vanderbilt meant something in New York society, when millionaires kept "cottages" of marble and gilt at Newport and rich men drank champagne out of a beautiful actress's slipper. Tastes and smells she experienced then never left her, as when she recollected her introduction to a peculiar beverage offered at an afternoon tea at the home of socialite Frederick Townsend Martin, author of *The Passing of the Idle Rich*. Martin's house was swamped in chrysanthemums, and "Freddy," who had a way of purring over Billie like a cat, gave her a cup of hot tea, into which he directed her to pour rum from a carafe — her first time for that particular "mixed drink."

That cup of tea and rum was woven in Billie's memories with the scent of the hundreds of chrysanthemums, so that the combined bouquet of rum and of this flower always reminded her of her first outings in New York high society.[1]

These were the days when a young actress of quality allowed herself to be escorted only to such restaurants as Delmonico's or Sherry's, where Billie learned to eat oysters without bearding them (in London she had been told they were poisonous left intact). These were also the days when the animal lover in Billie Burke took second place to the worshipper of luxurious furs: chinchilla coats down to the ankles, and rare aigrette feathers sweeping from one's hat almost to the ground. These were all paid for by Charles Frohman. All Billie had to worry about was where to live, and in a pattern that was to persist all her life, she preferred to live just outside the sphere of her busy professional world — in New York's "sixth borough," Yonkers, a little less than twenty miles north up the Hudson River.

A reporter who interviewed Billie at this house, located at 10 Delavan Terrace, described it as a "homey one and a half story red granite and wood structure built upon a still green terrace.... There are mullioned windows and ruffled muslin curtains. About it hangs an air of quaintness and quiet," which in most respects could also describe the house in Brentwood, Los Angeles, where Billie spent her last years. Billie liked 10 Delavan Terrace and its surroundings because it reminded her of the cottage she had briefly leased in London's St. John Wood. She seems to have also warmed to its very ordinariness, something that came as a surprise to some of the press who visited her there. One reporter who visited the house described it as oddly bereft of photographs of Billie — he had obviously been in the homes of actresses who could not leave a table or mantelpiece ungraced by their own image, but Billie's was decorated with paintings and elegantly simple furniture, as well as "the handicraft of the Indians." The one celebrity touch was the presence of several photos of Billie's theatrical colleagues and heroes (John Drew among them).

Billie claims in her memoirs that at this time she purchased a beige Italia motorcar, replete with a chauffeur, with her $500 per week, to be driven to and from the theatre in the high style expected of a popular actress, but other sources indicate she had merely brought to Yonkers the same blue Italia she had had in London. (The chauffeur's name was George A. Sentre, possibly the same man who in August 1909 struck and killed a child while driving Billie's car — the first of many such fatal and near-fatal incidents involving Billie and automobiles.) Despite Billie's age (she was in her mid-20s), Blanche continued to meet her at the theatre in the Italia and drive with her back to the safety of Yonkers. Billie, obviously, was still sitting beside Blanche in a car instead of going to parties, wondering about, instead of participating in, "interesting Sin."[2]

Billie's official history as fashion plate begins at this time. For all her later insistence that she wanted to be taken seriously as an actor, at this period she was only interested in how she looked and how she was looked at. "I always thought," she wrote, "that the chief reason for the success I had on the Broadway stage as a young woman was my clothes." In many ways it was, but it was not always because she wished it otherwise. Even as late as 1960, the fact that she could not have *carte blanche* to purchase an expensive dress to wear for a projected appearance in a television show called *Inside Story* (NBC's first videotaped show) turned out to be a deal-breaker.

"She was disillusioned with me," recalls Richard Lamparski, whom Billie had invited to tea, "because she thought I was a producer. I was actually an associate producer — really a sort of errand boy. Once she found this out, and that I wasn't going to be able to allocate money for her to go to Saks with to buy a new frock.... She'd seen it at Saks — I believe it was mauve — and she thought she'd get a deal with the buyer if she mentioned that she would be wearing the dress on NBC. Once she found out that I couldn't provide that for her, that was it. It was 'just have another cookie and be on your way'!"

Billie ultimately did not appear on *Inside Story*. Clothes were still that important to her — above all, they were important to her career. Thinking of his meeting with Billie, Lamparski recalls a comment made to him by actress Blanche Yurka: "She once told me, 'I don't know why I bothered to study acting. I should have studied colors! Jane Cowl [like Billie, another clothes horse] made a whole career out of changing her clothes. I never thought what I was going to wear!'" In Billie's case, for most of her career clothes did not just make the woman, they *were* the woman.[3]

Through the pleasant clouds of popularity and praise, Billie knew she was living in a silken cocoon, full of pleasure and no pressure. There was no motivation at this time of her life, as she clearly recalled later, that would have prompted her to work on her craft and graduate from fashion plate to solid actress. The critics' notices, which on the road were not a lot better than what she had received in New York, inspired no challenge to become something better.

Chicago's Percy Hammond, for example, who could be rough, pulled his punches with Billie by damning her with faint praise of her beauty and grace. Billie could not have cared less. She had "pretty clothes, security and applause," and what did it matter that she didn't always please the male critics who dominated journalism — she dressed more to please women than men. She had her youth and beauty and gracefulness, and she had the pleasure of seeing personal attributes like her hair and clothes being copied and sold in department stores — false ginger curls (inspired by Billie's hastily pinned up pompadour) moved off the shelves as fast as Shirley Temple dolls would do in later years, as did clothing styles made the fashion with each Billie Burke premiere.

She also had fun. On tour in wintry Minneapolis, Billie took advantage of a snowstorm to purchase a sled, which she took down to the streets where children were playing. Sliding down ice hills with these urchins, who seemed to have been delighted more to have an adult playing with them than because they knew she was the famous Billie Burke, Billie recaptured some of her lost childhood, which had been spent indoors with teachers of singing and dancing and fencing instead of playing in the snow. When news of her sledding reached New York, Frohman's company manager was mortified that one of their stars would comport herself in this manner. It was ironically an adventure that, as Billie points out, would in a later period be the very least film studio heads would expect their stars to indulge in for purposes of publicity. Frohman probably did not mind the incident at all — what he wanted, as with Maude Adams, was a star who was also a sort of permanent little girl, a child he could dote on and protect and delight (as well as make a pile of money from), and the more she went sledding with street urchins, the better.

"What I had to do was be as pretty as I could," she wrote, somewhat ruefully, "and as gay as I could on the stage, so I did that." This was what Billie had been guided to do, first by her mother in the London music halls, then by Hawtrey and, at first, by Frohman on the legitimate stage: be not a good actress, or an actress at all, but be *adorable*, a burden Billie Burke would carry for the rest of her life, well past the age when an actress's or woman's main attraction is adorableness.

Not surprisingly, it was in this period that she contributed, if briefly, a bit of slang to Edwardian American English: to "billieburke" meant that a young woman was "behaving adorably." For the time being, anyway, Billie behaved adorably, and did as she was told. The uphill battle to remake herself as an actress of substantial gifts would come in time.[4]

"Billie Burke will appear in 'Love Watches' at the Lyceum Theatre the end of August," Charles Frohman reported in July 1908, "and after a quick tour of the country will open in London the second week in April." The next day, the *New York Times* carried this statement by Robert Schable, a spokesman for Frohman who probably penned the earlier quote and had seen the original play, *L'Amour veille*, in Paris: "It's a charming comedy, most perfectly acted here, and I am sure Mr. Frohman would be proud to have it done so well in New York."[5]

A frequent adapter of foreign plays for the American and English theatre market, Frohman had found in this frail comedy by Robert [marquis] de Flers and Gaston

Poster of Billie as Jacqueline in her 1908 Broadway and touring success, *Love Watches*. This poster was purchased at auction by director and friend of Billie's George Cukor, and given to her in the 1930s. Stephenson collection.

Arman de Caillavet what Billie considered her best play of this period. It was certainly a sample of the kind of light drawing room comedy in which Hawtrey had taught her to shine; and the fact that it was a piece requiring lavish costumes was another plus for Billie.

In the play, which had been updated from the eighteenth century to the present day, Billie acted the part of Jacqueline, "a flower of a girl, whose head is full of sentimental fancies." Jacqueline meets her cousin, Count André de Juvigny, under memorable circumstances — he has fallen off his horse. She falls for *him*, only to conceal her passion until she has to confess it. A roué, André nonetheless proposes and the two are married. The pair live happily until his past catches up with them, in person of André's former girlfriend, Lucie. André promises the jealous Jacqueline he will never see Lucie again, but when the latter arrives and André gallantly agrees to see her home, Jacqueline responds by telling her whole family that she has left her philandering husband and is consoling herself in the arms of another man, Ernest, who has always kept his love for Jacqueline to himself.

Family members arrive at Ernest's house only to be told Jacqueline is not there. Jacqueline, realizing the storm she has stirred and regretting her treatment of André, rushes home to her family to tell them the news. Ernest arrives in hot pursuit, and when André arrives, he is the only person in the house who does not know what has transpired. While Jacqueline waits outside the room, Ernest blurts out the truth, upsetting André and drawing Jacqueline forth to castigate Ernest and declare her love for her husband. André finds amusement in Ernest's disconsolate expression on hearing this, but the plot is tidied up by a *deus ex machina* in form of a young stenographer, who had been nursing a romance for Ernest and now gains his offer of marriage — all of which rings false to anyone aware of the serial infidelity of real *ancien régime* French aristocracy. Clearly, in adapting the play, Gladys Unger was writing more to the coy hypocrisies of the late Victorian age.

Billie knew, even as she drew crowds, that her "acting did not set the Hudson afire." But the New York public (as might be guessed) loved it and Billie (with her "baby-blue voice") in it. According to one critic reviewing the production, "it is delightfully played, Miss Burke passing from the leading lady stage to that of star, with signs of developing talent, an improved method, and no end of appealing charm." Billie was "wistful," "alluring," "bright," "vivacious," "full of life and go" as "the little husband worshipper."[6]

The play would have a 172 performance run, and with admirers' bouquets, adoring reviews cascaded onto the young actress's head, some of which are worth reading at length:

> Bully for Billie Burke! She pouts, she purrs, she gurgles, she stares blandly. She is a kitten, a mouse, a doll that squeaks. Miss Burke's performance was delicious. — Rennold Wolf, *New York Commercial*, 8/28/08

> As the chief instigator of joy and sorrow, Miss Burke is given opportunity to display a versatility she but hinted at in her delightful work of yesteryear in *My Wife*. — *Journal of Commerce*, 8/28/08

> This Little Billie is the best thing Du Maurier never wrote.... In this merry fling from the French, Miss Burke gives you the joy of living right and floods the play with the sunshine of success. She is a creature of infinite variety. — Charles Darnton, *The Morning Telegraph*, 8/23/08

> Miss Billie Burke is the artfully artless.... She is the only actress I have ever seen who can feed a grown-up audience mush and make it ask for more. — *New York Globe*, 8/28/08

Telegrams poured in — everyone from actor William Gillette ("More best wishes than you could shake a stick at") to Billie's officer beau, Frank Carey, in England ("Wishing you every possible success tonight, dearest") papered Frohman's offices with good wishes, and the flowers overflowed.

Billie also received a letter from one of the authors of *L'amour veille*, de Caillavet, a month after opening, which made her happier than all the other missives put together:

> Dear Miss Burke —
> I am sending you the little article which appeared in the *Figaro* about you. I saw Mr Frohman a short time ago who spoke to me of your great success. I hope someday we shall have the pleasure of seeing you play in Paris.[7]

The *Figaro* piece de Caillavet referred to states without equivocation that Billie Burke is every bit as sensational as the young Maude Adams:

> Un de nos confreres d'outre-mer declare que depuis l'apparition de Maud[e] Adams, il y a une dizaine d'années, on ne vit rien d'aussi sensationnel que l'apparition de Miss Billie Burke.

Billie sent de Caillavet an invitation to be her guest at a performance of the play, and was thrilled when he accepted.[8]

Over a month after opening, a critic would write a sort of encomium to everything that made Billie such a box office draw, and everything Charles Frohman wanted his audiences to carry home from a performance:

> There is something beautifully appealing in the sunshiny youth of Billie Burke. Youth in love with loving is a pretty picture to contemplate, especially when you are in the secret and know that the mists of understanding are sure to clear and leave the lovers in enjoyment of the halcyon hour.[9]

Australian-born Cyril Keightley, who was making his Broadway debut in *Love Watches*, was the first of Billie's many attractive leading men, and belonged to the 50 percent she remembered with affection. In his early 30s, Keightley was handsome, reminding Billie of a youthful Walter Huston, and he also had the quirky sort of character Billie adored. She was passing his dressing room one evening and happened to glance in the open door to find Keightley standing in his underpants and a top hat. Billie reversed step, put her head in the door, and told Keightley that while he was a pretty sight, she could not figure out what on earth he was doing. The actor tipped his hat and turned back to the mirror. "I wear my top hat to set my hair," he explained coolly. "Do you set your hair, Billie? I recommend a top hat."

Frohman ordered clothes for Billie that put her other roles to date in the shade. Billie's couturière was the posh London house of Madame Hayward, who put gowns on her back a season ahead of what was being worn in New York, setting off a craze for the light embroidered afternoon dresses and swank evening gowns Billie wore in the play. Two of her costumes for *Love Watches* sounds fit more for a queen than a soubrette: a large plumed hat, long stole and muff, all of swans' down, the stole lined dramatically in turquoise velvet; and a "shell-pink dress in lame embroidered in diamonds and pearls," all sounding as if Gilded Age New York were not quite ready to retreat from history to the novels of Henry James and Edith Wharton. As one article stated at this time: "There can be no better comment on Miss Burke's dressing than that of a dress maker who recently said, 'I always like to see Billie Burke's gowns, as I get such good ideas from them for debutante frocks.'" A little later, MIT student Otto R. Rietschlin was to write to Billie in a way that showed how even males were affected by her gorgeous clothes: "were I a girl your gowns would cause me the utmost envy."[10]

In November, Billie stepped from the stage to the page with an article for the *New York Times* explaining why she played the parts she did and what being an actress meant to her:

> The villains have a much easier task [than] a mere heroine, and when it comes to self-analysis of this sort, I could almost wish, for the time being, that I were one of those bloodthirsty persons — it's so much easier to pick villainy to pieces than it is "lovableness."

Billie would soon find that in the hands of some critics, loveableness could be very easily picked apart. But note this revealing observation from an actress whose future film typecasting made her fans assume she was the same feather-brained creature off screen as on — obviously, loveableness could be manufactured, too: "It's a great mistake ... to think that simply because an actress is a certain way before her audiences she must necessarily be that way when she's by herself in her home life."[11]

CHAPTER 5

"There is only one Billie Burke..."

Popularity brought invitations, and through 1908–1909, Billie was made a permanent fixture in New York society. It was all the best possible advertising Charles Frohman (not to mention Madame Hayward) could ask for.

In November, "Freddy" Townsend had Billie to a reception in the ballroom of the Plaza Hotel, where Billie recited (she does not record what) to such fellow guests as Charles Dana Gibson, Augustus Juilliard and wife, Ethel Barrymore, and a constellation of Vanderbilts, Goulds, Belmonts, Auchinclosses, Carnegies and other *crèmes de la crème*.[1] Some of the parties were like something out of a vaudeville show. In mid–January 1909, Billie attended one such gathering at the Hotel Metropole given by George Kessler, the "champagne king" of New York.

The party's theme required guests to dine in a setting resembling a butcher's deep freeze, with *papier-mâché* sides of beef hanging overhead and glittering cakes of ice at which guests, dressed as butchers, were served steak and wine by waiters and waitresses also got up as butchery workers. Among the entertainers for the evening were, besides Billie, Ethel Barrymore, Anna Held, Blanche Ring, Nora Bayes and De Wolf Hopper, along with other lights of Broadway.

Florenz Ziegfeld was one of the guests, attending with wife Anna Held, but Billie, who claims she never met Flo until New Year's Eve 1914, does not mention noticing him at this affair. Nor is there evidence that he noticed her — Anna Held was still very much the focus of his eyes and heart at this time. (Although in 1927, Flo seems to have confided to a reporter that he first saw Billie in *My Wife* in 1907.) Both Flo and Billie would have to wait for that life-altering meeting till another party five years into the future. In the meantime, Billie had a life-threatening experience ahead of her, one of several instances where her artificial play world of wearing gorgeous gowns for adoring audiences collided with the real needs of an exhausted and lonely woman.[2]

Love Watches was taken on tour late in January. En route to Boston, Billie cut or pricked her hand or finger — neither she nor the newspaper reports are completely clear on what happened. Billie claimed she scratched her finger on a rose thorn (did a fan too hastily push a bouquet at her? Did she injure herself while gathering flowers thrown to the stage?), but several reports indicate she had punctured her finger on a pin. Billie's right hand began to hurt and swell, and the thin red lines of blood poisoning appeared. Undaunted, she went on stage night after night; and the hand got worse. In

Springfield, on January 28, Billie played Jacqueline "wearing a white glove several times larger than she ordinarily wears." In Hartford, shortly before this, a doctor had treated Billie's hand with some sort of ointment or dressing that stung, and she had gone on stage that evening, wearing a sling and carrying a 104 degree temperature. In a piece headlined "Billie Burke Plays A Little Comedy Under Great Difficulties," the *Springfield Republican* reported that many present at the performance "noticed the long glove on her right arm when she first came on the stage, and later they saw the wrist was stiff and evidently tender, for it was favored as much as possible."

Two doctors, the report went on to say, were stationed in the wings, should they be needed. What they should have done was kept her off the stage in the first place. If anyone ever thought of her as a fragile piece of Dresden porcelain — and many did, because Frohman's press insured that was the image that got circulated — Billie now proved she was made of much tougher material: she would not give up. But she was taking a foolish risk.[3]

As the tour ground on, Billie getting sicker, a doctor in Northampton put a poultice on her arm — these were the days when the common cold was treated with bags of chopped onions. When that treatment didn't work, the doctor called in a specialist from Boston. This man's advice was grim: Billie's arm would have to be amputated. The consternation this caused can hardly be overstated. Sarah Bernhardt may have been able to carry on with an artificial leg, but artificial arms, while far improved compared to what had been developed for Civil War amputees, were never going to work for a woman in a Madame Hayward gown.

Billie knew she was risking her life, but she said she would not consider the procedure. Blanche was adamant, too. "Billie will never be any good without her arm," she pointed out, not quite tactfully.

The danger Billie was in, almost twenty years before the discovery of penicillin, was very real. And her condition could only have been made worse by her insistence on going on stage night after night, exhausting herself. It finally took orders from Frohman to get her to rest; to make absolutely sure, he canceled the Boston run out from under her.

"There are many plays, there is only one Billie Burke," he is alleged to have telegrammed. The newspapers reported Frohman's words as "There are one thousand weeks, but there is only one Billie Burke," but what he actually wrote, as can be seen from the telegram pasted into Billie's 1908–1909 scrapbook now in the archives of the University of Southern California's Doheny Library, is far more casual yet far more personal: "That's all right there are thousands of other weeks but only one Billie Burke."

Watched by her doctor, Billie struggled with the pain and the enforced rest. Incisions had to be made in Billie's arm to drain off the pus, and the painful treatment worked: as the infection subsided, both her arm and her life were saved.

Billie remained in her suite at the elegant Hotel Touraine, recovering through February. For six weeks, Frohman continued to pay not only her salary but those of the whole company, and would never let her see the medical bills or know the losses the company had suffered.[4]

❦

Frohman was already busily making plans to take *Love Watches* to London, where he probably hoped to cash in on Billie's renown there as a Hawtrey leading lady a few years before. His idea seems to have been that Billie was already such a box office draw it was the scintillating Miss Burke people were coming to see, not the rest of the cast. So instead of bringing over the American cast, which had proven such a successful team on Broadway, Frohman hired all English actors (save for Billie). Billie confides to her memoirs that she had her misgivings about this plan, but other distractions kept her from doing too much about it. As she prepared for her trip on the *Lusitania*, booked for late April, she was settling in a new addition to her Yonkers household. A mother, May Watson, and her twelve-year-old daughter had moved into the house.

Billie claims she had met May in Charlotte, North Carolina, where May lived with her daughter, Sheridah (called Cherry). One independent source claims that May Watson was an actress who had "stood as sponsor for Miss Burke when she was starting upon her theatrical career," so it is possible Billie and Blanche were compensating May for some financial or other help she may have given Billie. May was known to have friends in Sheepshead Bay, Bath Beach and Bensonhurst; it is likely that Blanche Burke met her when she was living in the locale. The *New York World* reported in July 1909 that May Watson's husband, Thomas, was a well-to-do contractor, who had gone to Puerto Rico for a job. May had gone to visit him, and returned with some unspecified "fever" to Brooklyn, where May formally separated from her husband. She had nowhere to go, which is why Blanche, on hearing the news, arranged to have May and Cherry brought to the house at Yonkers.[5]

The Watsons saw Billie and Blanche off on the *Lusitania* on Wednesday, April 28, 1909. Before the ship had even docked at Liverpool, the Burkes received a wire: May had died. The story was that she had contracted pneumonia at the pier in New York, but the "fever" she had picked up in Puerto Rico was clearly more than a passing inconvenience. Now the issue remained of what was to happen to Cherry. By means of transatlantic telegrams, Blanche closed down the Yonkers house and had Cherry put aboard a liner sailing for Paris, where Billie met her. According to Billie, Blanche later formally adopted Cherry, but she lived with and was supported by Billie till her marriage.

On her arrival, Cherry was thin and delicate, and wearing dowdy black mourning clothes. We don't know her reaction to the events that had swept down on her in short succession, but while it was not every orphan's fate to be taken under the wing of a famed actress who stayed in the best hotels and wore the best clothes, the shift from being plain Cherry Watson of Yonkers to ward of Billie Burke in *Belle Epoque* Paris could not have been easy. It also could not have been easy to find herself in the care of two such vigorous women as Blanche and Billie, who had all sorts of plans for her future.[6]

Billie had been watching Blanche at work for so many years, it was a simple matter to use her tactics when she had a girl of her own to mold and shape. She shared her loftily professional opinions about parenting in an article that appeared in the September 18, 1910 *Washington Post*. "When fate made me the foster-mother of a little girl," runs the article under Billie's byline, "I was at first appalled by my task. There were several disconcerting things about the little girl. First, she was such a big little girl, being 9 years younger than myself. [Cherry was actually 14 years younger.] Second, she was such a grave little girl, with big gray eyes. She wasn't at all as I had conceived all children to be — glancing sunbeams of gayety." Billie's answer to how to deal with this situation was to put herself in Cherry's place, imagining herself watching Blanche die and having nowhere to go, and how she would want to be rescued and by whom. Naturally, she saw herself being rescued by her own gracious self, but when it came to what to do with the child once she had her, Billie reverted to pure Blanche Burke: "Train her as you would want to be trained."

Train Cherry she did. She took her on a tour of France, Italy and Switzerland, exposing her to fine restaurants and foreign tongues. An unnamed cousin of Billie's, a member of the company, was marshaled to take over as Cherry's governess, and soon the skinny girl with braids who had arrived looking like a waif was almost as elegantly turned out as her foster-mother. Billie's first consideration, after teaching her some songs (including "My Little Canoe"), was to cast an appraising eye on Cherry's dramatic potential. "Had she, or had she not, talent for the stage?... When I was satisfied that she had a taste and talent [for it] I knew that her future was in great measure settled." So Cherry, left with relatives while Billie set forth to reconquer London, was kept busy with the full array of music and dance lessons that had characterized Billie's own childhood and for much the same reason: to outfit her for the stage, whether she wanted it or not.

Because so many of Billie's plans for Cherry resemble the education program Blanche had once laid out for her, it is tempting to believe Blanche was behind some of the planning. In any case, Cherry eventually did go into show business, starting with a few chorus jobs and following with a bit part in Billie's second silent film, *Gloria's Romance* in 1916. She was married that year to Chester Monroe Offerman, and after this film and a few turns as a Broadway chorus member, her projected career in show business came to an end.[7]

Whether caring for Cherry and planning her future made Billie forget about the present played a part in what happened next is unknown, but with the London production of *Love Watches*, Billie would find she had a great deal of growing up of her own to do.

If Frohman's publicity is to be believed, Billie used most of her time in Paris to brush up her French, with a view to performing *en français* at some point with Frohman's Paris company. A report from later that summer of 1909, after *Love Watches* was done in London, claims Billie worked so hard at French she had to take a rest in Venice. (More Frohmanesque exaggeration.)

She clearly had trouble with the language she later claimed to read with ease (and there is no audio record of her speaking more than a few simple French words), because another report, from June, announced that Frohman had asked de Flers and de Caillavet to write a play for Billie casting her as a "madcap, dare-devil, irresponsible, unconventional American girl who doesn't speak French at all," though all the other characters would do so. The idea was that once her French improved, the new play could be retranslated for New York and London and Billie herself be the only character who spoke

French. This planned play, of dubious value for the annals of dramaturgy or for Billie's career (though showing Frohman's effort to achieve Billie success at any cost), was never written. And in any case, if she ultimately found herself in need of a vacation, London's demanding theatre critics and not conjugating French verbs would give Billie plenty of reasons for one.[8]

Love Watches was set to open on May 11 at the white-columned Haymarket Theatre, and Billie was right to think that at least her American fans were well-disposed to her. A reporter in London recorded that on the night of the first performance, "[Billie's] floral tributes were as remarkable as they were numerous," overflowing from the theatre to wash over Billie's suite at the Savoy Hotel. A gargantuan arrangement made entirely of roses illustrating a scene from the play was either too big for Billie's rooms or was judged too good for publicity to be hidden away there, and so was given pride of place in the Savoy's lobby. This "amazingly inartistic offering" came from an admiring American who, the journalist added, had also hired two African American singing dancers to amuse her on the *Lusitania* and had thrown a ball in her honor before the play opened. Was this American Charles Frohman? Whoever it was, he had the sort of taste Billie would come to associate later on with that master of expensive excess, Flo Ziegfeld, Jr.[9]

Roses and admirers, however, availed nothing. On opening night, the play was not well received — in fact, there was booing at the end, something new to Billie, who during all her time performing on the London stage had been accustomed only to cheers and applause. Frohman's decision to assemble a whole new cast, instead of bringing over the American one, had much to do with this reaction, because as a few critics pointed out, Billie was not strong enough as a leading lady to carry the play on her own shoulders — attesting to what must have been the considerable assistance of that winning team on Broadway.

The play was also cursed, in a way, by its success in New York — plays which win a high reputation in one country don't always catch on in another, and this one didn't even have its original cast. Billie should have remembered that London audiences were in no way like the easily entertained New York ones and were at once more sophisticated and less inhibited about their opinions. She chose to believe their reaction was because the London public did not care for French adaptations, and that they judged the play "without chivalry and without merit" — though if chivalry was what most mattered to them, they would not have booed a production so dependent on the charms of its leading lady.

As one journalist put it, in London Billie "has not scored a great success as an artiste, but she had had a tremendous success de beauté." She was a stage beauty whom the Haymarket audiences had been given reason to believe could also act, and when they discovered her wanting on that score — unlike the audiences in New York and at regional American houses — they had made their disappointment known.[10]

Most of the reviewers assigned to *Love Watches* took care to keep Billie out of their line of fire, though shrapnel reached her all the same:

> The only plausible reason for the existence of such a type of entertainment is the star system. In the case of an artist like Miss Marie Tempest there is something to be said for her exploitation, but really in all seriousness, Miss Billie Burke, bright as she is in

her own line, is not big enough to be the pivot of a poor play. — *The London Sphere*, 5/22/09

Miss Billie Burke, who has returned to England after making a great success in America, is not a trained actress.... She has developed all the exaggerations of American farce ... and seeks to make little shrieks and grimaces and sudden jumping about the stage take the place of genuine acting. — *The Daily News*, May 1909

The saddest case of all is that of the clever lady, Miss Billie Burke. Not very long ago she was acting at the Vaudeville Theatre, a piquant, versatile, resourceful and clever actress.... Alas! Last night told a very different tale. Miss Burke seemed by a certain fatality to do everything wrong. — *The Daily Telegraph*, May 1909

How 'Love Watches' ran so long in America surpasses all my comprehension. — *The Daily Mail*, May 1909

Many American newspapers were more eager to jump on the London bandwagon than defend the play or Billie, with the *New York Press* reporting that same month, under the headline "Frohman Losing Money," that "'Love Watches' [has] proved an absolute failure in the Haymarket and is withdrawn after a career of something less than three weeks." The *Chicago Journal* of a few months later proclaimed that "Billie Burke would seem to have scored the most pronounced London failure of any American star who has yet visited there professionally," noting that the ticket receipts for some nights totaled no more than about $30.[11]

When Billie might have thought she had seen the worst, her leave taking from London was as fraught with disaster as her performances. The night before departing she was staying at the Carlton Hotel. Just when everyone had settled in for the evening

MISS BILLIE BURKE
Who is starring in her big success, "Love Watches," in London

Billie Burke, flush with the success of *Love Watches*.

the cry went up that the hotel was burning down. Everything was already packed, and Blanche was in the bathtub. Billie grabbed what she could, wrapped dripping Blanche in a coat, and they ran down three flights of stairs to the street, where in the half-light of the summer's evening they got into a car put at their disposal by a friend of Billie's. Once inside, Billie shrieked: she had left her jewel box in the room. Blanche calmed her — she had the box with her, safe and sound. Then Blanche cried out: she had left her corset behind. Billie rummaged through the things she had grabbed and found she had it. "[W]e embraced each other," she remembered, "and congratulated each other on our presence of mind in rescuing our most valuable possessions."

As it happened, Billie's trunks were saved and brought to the Haymarket stage for safekeeping, but this meant she had no change of clothes when she boarded the *Caronia* next morning with Blanche and Frohman, wearing just a light summer dress, no hat (without which a lady was not one in those days), and high heels, and with no nightgown. She had to borrow everything she needed from actress Dorothy Donnelly. Billie was so ready to get back to New York, she could not have cared whether she did so wearing a flour sack. London was never to be the welcoming place for the Broadway leading lady that it had once been for the charming young ingenue.[12]

CHAPTER 6

Soubrette

Resettled in Yonkers with Cherry and Blanche, Billie made arrangements for Cherry to attend the Tewkesbury School near Hastings, and with a similar sense of doing her duty she began to sit for interviews. She gave one to Ada Patterson of *Theatre Magazine* which provides us a revealing glimpse both of Billie's newfound confidence and of her continued dependence on her mother. (It would have been hard for her not to include Blanche in the conversation: she was there the entire time.)

Dressed in the silk kimono that was her preferred at-home wear, like the languid ladies painted by Whistler, Billie received Miss Patterson in the drawing room, and with Blanche occasionally interjecting (maid Thurston and manservant Vassey also hove, if briefly, into view), Billie spoke of her past, her present and her hopes for the future. In contrast to what she later wrote in her memoirs, Billie claimed that it was Billy Burke who urged her to perform at the London Pavillion, because he did not want his daughter to suffer the "drudgery" of working in the music hall choruses.

This was a change from the story she told later on, that Billy did not even agree with Blanche's plans for putting Billie on the stage at all. She also spoke of her fan following from England, describing in graphic detail a possibly apocryphal but no less "grewsome" example of this: a British officer, curiously thinking his gesture a kind one, had sent Billie a photograph of herself which had been carried into a skirmish in South Africa by a fellow soldier who had been killed in the fray — the photograph, found on his body, arrived still spattered with the man's blood.[1]

Then Billie got down to business. "Her future?" wrote Miss Patterson. "She is immeasurably ambitious ... [t]o become the American [Gabrielle] Réjane...." It is significant that Billie sought to emulate Réjane (1856–1920), the French actress famed for her vivacious beauty, which made her equally successful in comedy and drama — Réjane had started in musical comedy and worked her way up to strong dramatic roles (her most famous was Catherine in Sardou's *Madame Sans-Gene*), finally opening her own theatre, a career achievement Billie would aspire to. (She was still talking about building her own theatre into the 1920s.)

This interview was also Billie's first opinion on record regarding the choices an actor must make between real life and the stage. She had already pointed out in the *New York Times* that she was not the same person at home that she was under the proscenium. The previous year, rumors had gone the rounds that Billie was engaged to marry an English peer (typical exaggeration by the press: Frank Cary was a gentleman but no peer), and the confusion was compounded by the story that she was actually engaged to Captain Cary (which she no longer was).

Perhaps it was as much Blanche speaking as Billie when she now announced categorically that she would not leave the stage in order to marry, because "I think when an actress marries she should leave the stage. She cannot be happy if she is married and remains on the stage." Art, she said, must come before one's husband, and she added that if she ever found a man whom she could love better than she loved her art and her career, she would leave the stage behind. "But I have never met such a man," she finished coolly.[2]

For the time being, Billie seemed to be satisfied with the adulation washing over her from beyond the footlights of every theatre she played, and she played many throughout the United States when Frohman sent her on the road tour of *Love Watches*. In February 1909, after she had played his city to acclaim, *St. Louis Times* editor Russell T. Edwards sent Billie a hilarious "Dear John" letter:

> Yesterday, one man wrote verse to you and for several days everyone on the staff is padded-cell raving about you and today I used your name in the weather [stating that the climate was "as fair as Billie Burke"]. Please go away and leave us in peace once more.[3]

That same month, one woman friend wrote to Billie congratulating her on the play but begging her not to "marry that marquis, give him to Princess 'Pat' [Princess Patricia, daughter of the Duke of Connaught and one of crowned Europe's most eligible princesses] and stick to the stage, the public needs you!"[4] It can't be determined whether the marquis referred to is the character whom Billie, as Jacqueline, marries in *Love Watches*, or her unnamed suitor from the British peerage. Used to it by now, Billie found this worship easy to keep in perspective. But her nonchalance was put to the test when she received a proposal of marriage from a most unsuspected quarter.

She doesn't tell how she knew this, but according to Billie opera tenor Enrico Caruso had been watching her, in theatres and across the dining room of the Hotel Knickerbocker in New York. During the Boston run of *Love Watches*, Caruso was singing two of his greatest roles, Rodolfo in Puccini's *La bohème* and Radamès in Verdi's *Aïda* at the new Boston Opera House, which happened to be located not far from Billie's theatre. When not performing, Caruso began taking a box for Billie's performances. He came every night, says Billie, and every time he would toss her a fragrant bouquet of American Beauty roses. Florid notes followed.

Caruso was eleven years Billie's senior, and had made his New York debut in 1903. By 1909 he was at the top of his powers and if short and increasingly pudgy, he was always a handsome and charismatic man, with a gleaming bronze tenor trained up from baritone range. He had a reputation for falling into and out of love as quickly as he changed hotels for his various star engagements, which may be why Billie avoided him at first—and with her mother and Frohman watching her every move, there was little else she could do. They only met when a mutual acquaintance introduced them in a restaurant. This was Caruso's cue to call on Billie at her hotel, where, as she remembered, he dropped to his knee and asked her to marry him. Billie was amused and flattered. Caruso, she said, not only sang opera—he embodied it. Calling her "leetle babee," Caruso pursued Billie not just with roses, notes, and proposals, but sang to her, wherever they happened to be, whether walking along the Charles River together or in parks full of proper Bostonians unused to impromptu *al fresco* opera. Perhaps unaware that Caruso had been cited for indecency at the monkey cage of the Central Park Zoo in 1906 (Caruso claimed a monkey pinched the bottom of the woman who subsequently complained — he was fined for the infraction anyway), Billie felt safe enough with him to accept his invitations to dine, where between loving compliments the tenor ate spaghetti like it was going out of style.

For all the pleasure this novel wooing gave her, Billie was careful with Caruso, treating him like a big baby who could not possibly mean what he said. She felt in later years that perhaps she had been too hard with him, though what she could have done to be nicer that would not have only increased the tenor's ardor she does not say. As for Caruso's broken heart, she need not have worried. Once he was back in New York he recovered from his Boston romance unimpaired, leaping into a series of parties for composer Engelbert Humperdinck and pursuing other beautiful young ladies. If his interest signified anything in Billie's life, it was as a sort of dry run for Flo Ziegfeld's hot pursuit of her five years later, when she was not to get away so easily.[5]

One of Billie's distractions from operatic passion was Frohman's offer of the starring role in W. Somerset Maugham's play *Mrs. Dot*. Billie would play Mrs. Worthley, a role originally written for English singer and actress Marie Tempest, who had played it to great success in 1908 (Charles Frohman's first production of a Maugham play in London). Twenty years older than Billie, Marie Tempest was similar to her physically: short, with reddish hair and an easy flair for comedy. These facts would not have been lost on Frohman, who may have been thinking he could groom Billie to carry the Tempest torch in America.

Mrs. Dot would be the first of four Maugham plays in which Billie would star, but none of these would be as successful for her or for Maugham as this comedy of how a rich widow inveigles a man in marriage to herself, despite his being promised to another woman. Billie and Maugham both made a great deal of money off the play, so much so that afterward Maugham would show Billie, when she visited his elegant Georgian house in Mayfair, a small portrait of herself, which had been made to celebrate the play's two hundred fiftieth performance in America. Maugham told her, with a smile, "That is the woman who bought me this house."[6]

Billie considered *Mrs. Dot* one of her best plays, along with *Love Watches* and Sir Arthur Wing Pinero's *The Mind the Paint Girl*, but what interested her most at first was its author, whom she called "Willie." In his mid–30s when Billie met him in 1910, and not yet having come to a resolution about his sexuality, Maugham had a sense of style which Billie saw as "French," attributing this to Maugham's birth and early childhood spent in Paris. (It was actually just his adopted high society manner.) She loved his clothes, his striped trousers and top hats, which added needed inches to his height, but it was his "smoldering brown eyes" that made her "a little in love" with him. He may well have been a little in love with her, too.[7]

Mrs. Dot was written to be a crowd-pleaser, what one London theatre critic called "champagne kind of drama," and during its London run it was but one of three Maugham plays running to acclaim in the West End. What made it such a success was the fact that it had been tailored to fit Marie Tempest's comic gifts like a Bond Street glove: "her tantrums are delicious fun," a critic wrote after the play's 1908 premiere, her performance impressing her audience "forcibly with the fact that she is a great comedienne," wrote another.[8]

Tempest's success was a tough act to follow, but Billie knew she was lucky to get the part, and she played down Miss Tempest's history in the lead role by adopting an insouciant attitude to the whole endeavor. She later believed this nonchalance had much to do with making the American production a hit, as of course did her fashion show costumes: "a chiffon affair draped over white ince and bordered at the feet with skunk fur," another with "a court train of lace falling from the shoulders to the floor [with] a hat of Nattier blue brocade and pink roses, with long streamers of black velvet coming from under the wide brim." But Billie's airiness may also have contributed to the less than pleasant critical appraisal she received on opening night.[9]

"Several things were proved at the Lyceum Theatre last night," wrote Adolph Klauber in the *New York Times* of January 25, 1910, "one of them being that Mr. W. Somerset Maugham can thank his lucky stars that he was so fortunate to have Marie Tempest play 'Mrs. Dot' originally. And it only goes to prove once again how very much a very good actress may do for a play.... Minus Marie Tempest, or some one just like her (and that some one is not to be found,) 'Mrs. Dot' is an amiable farce."

He went on to skewer Billie on the prongs of facetious compliments:

> Miss Billie Burke is very pretty and very gracious and sweet in roles that suit her youth and lie within the range of an immature experience. But her reputation as an actress is not going to be increased by this appearance as Mrs. Dot. There is no other Marie Tempest in New York, but to be quite truthful there are women who could play the part all around Miss Burke as far as acting goes.

The rest of the cast was given only slightly more praise; one, Basil Hallam, was referred to as "a sort of laughing English donkey."

Klauber, who clearly had had hopes for Billie that had been genuinely disappointed but not altogether destroyed, would write a few days later that Billie "has been projected too suddenly into prominence," but he had hope that with experience and luck "her technical facility may in time come to equal her attractiveness of person." These were harsh words for the beautiful exponent of "sunshiny youth," so adored in her first roles on Broadway. Despite this heavy critique, however, *Mrs. Dot* did remarkably well on tour. Whatever critics had to say against her, like Maugham's frothy play, Billie was a crowd pleaser.[10]

Billie claims in her second book, *With Powder on My Nose*, that she had tried for the part of Peter Pan even before Maude Adams did. But she had never met Peter's creator, James M. Barrie, the weaver's son from Kirriemuir become internationally famous author, until she and Blanche were on holiday in summer 1910, after *Mrs. Dot* closed on Broadway.

A great friend of Frohman's, Barrie often accompanied the little producer to Europe, where they would meet Billie in Paris to dine at the quaintly rustic Pavillon d'Armenonville in the Bois de Boulogne. Barrie seems to have taken to Billie at once. She recalled his quiet drawl, "almost a purr," not at all the broad brogue popularized by professional Scotsmen like Sir Harry Lauder. Barrie was a shy, sweet man, but Billie discovered he had a naughty streak which he shared with Frohman.

At a particular Paris sidewalk café, Frohman and Barrie would arrange their chairs so as to face the area where women would step down from their carriages. Billie sat nearby, grinning, as the two grand men of letters and the stage leaned back as if asleep, their hats pulled down over their eyes, and from under this camouflage studied the female ankles alighting onto the sidewalk, trying to divine whether each pair they saw belonged to blondes, or brunettes, or redheads, ladies of the drawing room or ladies of the street. Billie noted that Frohman never judged in error, while Barrie, "with all his sympathy and deep understanding of the feminine heart," never got it right, seeing the ankles of a cocotte and thinking their owner a meek young maiden. How much of this was because Frohman's judgment was not distorted by romantic feelings for women, whereas Barrie's was, is anybody's guess.

Barrie's tenderness was very much in evidence on another occasion, when Billie happened to be in London. She and Barrie had gone for a walk one afternoon. They had returned to his house, and Barrie showed Billie into his study, which she found neat, small, and shaded. Shelves on every side contained Barrie's own works, including original manuscripts. Tea was served and they chatted. When it came time to leave, Barrie helped Billie on with her jacket, then stopped and quietly asked, "May I kiss you?" Billie boasts she was not accustomed to being asked. (And considering she felt perfectly at home sitting by while two older men tried to guess from ankles whether a woman was a lady or a whore, she was certainly a lot more sophisticated than she pretended to be on the stage or when interviewed by the press.) She gave Barrie her permission. He kissed her "an inch south of my left ear"—a mere peck of a kiss, but enough to unsettle the author who had created Wendy Darling, with her yearning to kiss Peter Pan. And, too, perhaps what started as the kiss of father to child transformed itself in Barrie's heart or loins into something too close to a more primal urge toward this beautiful young woman so trusting as to be with him alone. At any rate, Billie rapidly found herself being shown to her brougham, wondering if Barrie's kiss had really happened at all.[11]

With Cherry in tow, Billie spent the better part of the summer at a farm in Devonshire, where, according to the press reports, she loved to work and play out of doors because "the air in that county did not cause tan and freckles." Neither she nor Cherry, the press was told, could afford those blemishes due to "stage purposes," another indication that Billie's plans for making an actress out of Cherry were still serious. (By the fall, Cherry, under the name Adele Cheridah, would make her stage debut in the chorus of *He Came from Milwaukee*. Her only other Broadway credit is a bit part in *The Girl in the Train*, which opened a month after her debut.) Perhaps the farm was a little too close to Follaton House and Captain Cary, because by September the New York press was insisting Frank had proposed marriage and been accepted. Frohman's office, of course, issued a firm denial.

In any case, the next two Broadway seasons would find Billie playing the soubrette on stage instead of to a real life lover, in three stage appearances two of which were adapted from foreign sources: Frantz Fonson and Fernand Wicheler's *Suzanne*, adapted by C. Haddon Chambers, *The Philosopher in the Apple Orchard*, a short curtain raiser for the Fonson comedy adapted from a story by Anthony Hope (best known as the author of *The Prisoner of Zenda*), and *The Runaway*, adapted by Michael Morton from the comedy by Pierre Veber and Henri de Gorsage.[12]

In all three roles, it was as if Charles Frohman had not demoted but rescued Billie from the Maugham drawing-room of *Mrs. Dot*, where she had played a widowed woman of the world but lacked the requisite depth and experience to carry it off. With these roles, Frohman turned back the clock to the ingénue who had proved so pleasurable and profitable for audiences and producers. Perhaps, too, Frohman was giving Billie breathing space to prepare for the role she considered her greatest stage success, in a part that can almost be seen as a documentary of her life off stage — as Lily Paradell in Sir Arthur Wing Pinero's *The Mind the Paint Girl*.

In *Suzanne*, which opened at the Lyceum the day after Christmas and closed in February 1911 (after sixty four performances, thereafter playing regional houses outside New York), Billie was back in the element she so loved — playing a winsome young woman in a foreign setting, in this case Brussels, and wearing period costumes. While helping her father in his beer-selling business, Suzanne must balance more than bottles as the frequent intermediary between her argumentative parents. Romance enters the picture when a young Parisian comes to work with Suzanne's father to learn about the beer business. Despite being engaged to a local boy selected by her parents, Suzanne falls in love with the Parisian, and any guilt that may have entered her pretty head is dispelled when she discovers that the man her parents want her to marry already has a lady friend and a child. It remains for Suzanne to convince her parents to accept the Parisian as her husband. Which, of course, she does.

Sometime toward the end of January, Frohman decided to use a two person "playlet" developed from Anthony Hope's story, "The Philosopher in the Apple Orchard," for Billie and gentlemanly Irish-born actor Lumsden Hare to perform as a two-person curtain raiser for *Suzanne*.

Though the story is lightweight fare coming from the author of *The Prisoner of Zenda*, it reads as if written especially about Billie. In the sketch, a pretty young girl, Miss May, approaches a philosophically inclined bachelor, Mr. Jerningham, who is reading in an apple orchard, and asks his opinion of her case. There are two men, one of whom might be in love with her. One of them *is* madly in love with her, has proposed marriage, and is approved of by his family, only she does not feel the same. The other is a friend of hers, "fearfully clever — and he's rather handsome. And the girl ... she admires him tremendously," and thinks him the greatest man who ever existed. She would love to be with him.

As Mr. Jerningham slowly reasons his way through her story, she tells him the plot comes from a novel, not from life, but is more desperate than ever to know his final verdict on what the poor girl should do. Should she marry the man who loves her but whom she does not love? Should she try to convince the man she loves to marry her, even if he grows not to love her but becomes tired of her? Mr. Jerningham tells her the answer is simple: marry the man she does not love, because if the man loves her, she'll come to feel the same. As if upset by this answer, Miss May rushes away. Mr. Jerningham goes home shortly after for lunch, only to be told by his hostess that Miss May has departed on the train. She does not tell him she left in tears, nor that she had gone away to marry a man she does not love. He idly comments over his lunch, "I'm really sorry I missed Miss May. That was an interesting case of hers." What he really missed was that he was the man Miss May would rather have married.[13]

The Runaway was Billie's first role of the 1911–1912 season. In this play she acted the part of Colette, a young orphaned French girl living with two aunts, one kind and the other a termagant, somewhere in the country outside Paris. Full of "life and youth and sunshine," Colette has a talent for art, which besides her other charms attracts the notice of a famous painter, Maurice Deloney. Deloney tells Colette she must come to his studio if she ever finds herself in Paris. Crisis arises when the aunts try to marry Colette off to a local rustic — she flees with her bags down the road to Paris, where on being turned out of a hotel because she is too young, at eighteen, to register there on her own, Colette seeks refuge at Monsieur Deloney's studio. Already having succumbed to her charms, Deloney needs no urging to keep her there, but Colette has to use them on the police chief sent to collect her on behalf of her aunts, and then is faced with Deloney's jealous mistress, despite whom Deloney falls in love with Colette, she with him, and the story ends happily ever after.

By the time she played this role of a girl in her late teens, Billie was getting on toward thirty, but somehow was able to convince her audiences otherwise through her girlish looks and her youthful demeanor. She got a better review from Adolph Klauber in this play than she had in *Mrs. Dot*, though Klauber obviously still felt she had a lot of dramatic growing up to do:

> Since she began to appear out of musical comedy she has had no role [than Colette] which suited her so well, none in which the opportunities were as great for personal success. There are possibilities of depth to Colette, heart notes, so to speak, which she does not strike, for her emotions are always from the throat and never seem any deeper. But otherwise she is charming, for she has the prettiness to please the eye and the playfulness, the coquetry, the grace and the ginger to suggest the various lighter mood.[14]

There was some unintended comedy toward the end of the run of *The Runaway*. While the company was playing at the Broad Street Theatre in Philadelphia the automatic sprinklers came on and flooded the stage between acts — whether set off by fire or accident was never explained. The audience was treated to a performance of the clean up crew sweeping up water and sprinkling sawdust, and in the middle of it all Billie emerged to make "a graceful little speech" about the flood, no doubt to keep people from leaving the theatre. The play ended with the actors resuming performance while dodging water droplets falling from on high. It was one of several less than perfect theatrical occasions on which Billie's memoirs choose to remain mum.

CHAPTER 7

Burkeley Crest

Some time over the summer of 1911, Blanche had decided that as New York was to be the center of her daughter's career, it was time she put down some roots.

Yonkers wasn't far enough away from town — now Blanche wanted to move farther out, almost thirty miles from downtown Manhattan, to a property at Hastings-on-Hudson in Westchester County. Built between 1855 and 1868, the house, which stood atop an incline in the middle of fourteen acres of land (later increased to over twenty), was a gabled mansion constructed of rusticated stone. Boasting some twenty-two rooms on three floors (including servants' quarters), the house had a sunny conservatory which Billie was to liven up with a billiards table and a collection of caged birds. The property was christened "Burkeley Crest," playing on Billie's name; the words were emblazoned in bronze, one on one stone pillar of the entrance gate, one on the other. (These bronze plaques are now in the possession of Billie's descendants in California.)

Burkeley Crest cost Billie $60,000; in twenty-first century values, this must be multiplied many times to arrive at a modern equivalent value — a few million dollars might come close. Burkeley Crest was proof positive that whatever critics had to say about her work, ticket sales were hot and Billie Burke was making very good money.[1]

Billie believed she owed Burkeley Crest, at least in part, to Maxine Elliott, sister-in-law of Shakespearean actor Sir Johnston Forbes-Robertson and considered one of the most beautiful actresses to ever walk the American stage. Billie's salary from Frohman continued, despite her growing popularity, at the same $500 per week he had offered to induce her to leave London and Charles Hawtrey several years before. To his credit, Frohman paid for all Billie's clothes, which were by now such an extension of her stage persona it would have been disaster (and poor advertising practice) to let her appear in public wearing anything but the best Madame Hayward had to offer. While the couturière bills must have been enormous, and Billie loved wearing the clothes, she did need not just to make a living but put some money away for the future.

Maxine Elliott was not just beautiful but had a head for business, and was known to have torn up and tossed back at Lee Shubert a contract for her brother-in-law which she did not consider sufficiently remunerative. Maxine called on Billie one day and over tea told her how wonderful it was to get what you wanted from a producer — in her case, the cooperative (if not always congenial) Lee Shubert. She must have had some idea that Billie was not making as much money as ticket sales warranted, because she

Bronze signs that once adorned the stone gates at Burkeley Crest. When the estate was sold in the mid–1940s, the new owner gave these to Billie. Stephenson collection.

asked her point blank how much Frohman paid her. Billie told her, "Five hundred per week," and Maxine nearly spewed her Earl Grey on the opposite wall. Then Billie confessed she had the same understanding with Frohman that Maude Adams had — no contract at all, just a shake of Frohman's delicate little hand.[2]

"Why Billie, that's terrible!" Maxine gasped. "I happen to know that Lee would be happy to give you fifteen hundred dollars a week *and* ten per cent of the gross."

Clearly, Blanche had not been paying as much attention to matters financial as she once had done. But Billie did not need her mother to work her up into a frenzy over how vastly underpaid she was. She marched into Frohman's office the next morning, and spoke to Alf Hayman, Frohman's money man. Billie gently suggested that as the cost of living was going up, she should be getting more money. It was when she mentioned Maxine's name that Hayman hit the ceiling. "A Shubert spy," he groaned. Then Billie told him how much the Shuberts were paying Maxine, and watched while Hayman began to "rant around with a face as red as a geranium." He growled finally that he would go talk to Frohman about it, but that Billie was to stay away from the Shuberts — who, along with Ziegfeld, the Frohman company despised — and especially hard-headed Maxine Elliott.[3]

Then "C.F." summoned Billie to his Gothic office. Billie's face must have fallen at his first words: "Give you five hundred a week to live on." But that was not all: "Then we put away a thousand a week for you. In bonds." And pay her ten per cent of the gross.

"And that," Billie wrote later, "is how I began to make money, thanks to Maxine Elliott, the most beautiful woman I ever knew."

What she did not know then was that in less than thirty years, following the stock market crash and the meltdown of the Ziegfeldian dream, that money Charles Frohman salted away for her would come to mean far more to her than even Frohman could have imagined.[4]

"I think it was the year of *The Mind the Paint Girl*," wrote Billie, "that something dawned on me, something of what the theater could really mean." From this year, 1912, Billie began to consider herself real actress material. But she was also playing a part which, unlike most of the others she had performed over the past several years, not only fit her abilities perfectly but also allowed her to draw the most on her own experience.

"Such roles as I have played are the sort I know about," she had written four years earlier, "the people I've impersonated are real, live, breathing people to me." Billie knew women like Lily Paradell, the music hall beauty at the heart of Sir Arthur Wing Pinero's play, best of all, because she was very like herself.[5]

Unlike the scenario painted by Pinero in his 1912 play, not every Gaiety Girl yearned to marry a lord of the realm, nor was England crawling with lords eager to give up their place in succession or society to marry a Gaiety girl. There were plenty of angry fathers to step in before their sons led a theatre star to the altar, and plenty of jilted theater stars who, having been incautiously proposed to, could be counted on to sue their erstwhile fiancés for breach of promise. Scandal, sometimes in the durable form of natural children, was the more scandalous result. But solid marriages of actresses into the peerage did happen, the most famous of which was that of Denise Orme, the stage name of Jessie Smither. Born a year after Billie, pretty, working-class Jessie performed as a music hall singer, starring at the Alhambra and Gaiety Theatres in the early 1900s. In 1907 she made a secret marriage to Sir John Reginald Lopes Yarde-Buller, 3rd Baron Churston of Churston Ferrers and Lupton, bearing him six children. Three of her four daughters married back into the peerage, and the fourth, Joan Barbara Yarde-Buller,

Billie as Lily Paradell, London chorus girl pursued by viscounts and millionaires, with William Raymond in Sir Arthur Wing Pinero's 1912 play *The Mind the Paint Girl* (Sarony).

married Prince Aly Khan, becoming the mother of the Aga Khan IV. To top it all off, after divorcing Lord Churston and having contracted a second marriage with one Theodore Wessel, Jessie pursued the already married and financially exhausted seventh Duke of Leinster, who (having contracted his first marriage with actress May Etheridge) divorced his American-born second wife to marry Jessie in 1946. Her sister Eileen Orme also later married into the peerage.

There had been suggestions for some time, usually in jest, that the English peerage, short on chins and long on noses, could do with an infusion of healthy commoner blood to refresh the gene pool—they had already been marrying American heiresses without snobbish qualms in order to resuscitate many a family exchequer. Pinero had great fun with the whole subject in *The Mind the Paint Girl*. As if recommending a new system of eugenics, he has one of his characters say, "Why, Mar, these tip-top families ought to feel jolly grateful to us.... It's my belief that the Pandora Girls will be the salvation of the aristocracy in this country in the long run." This was social commentary not always appreciated by critics or by conservatives, but made a statement that everybody recognized as valid, along with the more romantic sentiment that love should know no social boundaries.[6]

Pinero's play is titled after a song made popular by a beautiful music hall star, Lily Paradell, who is the brightest of several lovelies who perform at the Pandora Theatre in Leicester Square. Like the Florodora Girls, these women draw men to them like moths to flame; but unlike many of these women, Lily, insecure in her newfound wealth and popularity, wants the moths to flutter only so close. Jerome Kern set Pinero's lyrics to a jaunty tune:

> When you pay my house a visit,
> You may scrutinise or quiz it
> But you mustn't touch the paint!
>   Brand new paint!
>
> Once you smear it or you scratch it
> It's impossible to match it;
> So take care, please, of the paint,
>   Of the paint!
>
> Chorus:
> Mind the paint! Mind the paint!
> A girl is not a sinner, just because she's not a saint![7]

The two worlds these women lived in—as professional entertainers on the one hand, women who were admired and emulated for their style and manner, and on the other regarded by "good society" as something not far above professional prostitutes—are encapsulated in this song. *The Mind the Paint Girl* is not just a snapshot of changing post–Edwardian mores but a mirror turned to the audience themselves. No English traditionalist wanted to think about a common music hall singer being pursued by a besotted viscount, as Lily is by Lord Farncombe, let alone stand by as the chorus girl makes the young lord wait on her hand and foot. But the shocking spectacle only drew them to the theatre all the more.

"*The Mind the Paint Girl* ... had not been a success in London," Billie points out in her memoirs, and she admired Frohman for risking it on Broadway. New York fell in love with the story of Lily Paradell, and the play gave Billie "ravishing clothes" to wear. But ravishing clothes were not the only reason why Billie did so well. Lily, like Billie, is a beautiful and talented girl who, starting from nothing, was a star built up out of a few talents, striking physical beauty, and a propensity for attracting young men to the theatre, just to see her, no matter the play she was in. Like Billie, Lily is used to getting her way, accustomed to and flattered by stage door johnnies and their diamonds and roses, which Lily leaves scattered over her elegant drawing room to be assessed by a mother as domineering as Blanche was to Billie. The similarities go on: Lily's house in London's Bloomsbury district has a conservatory built out over the front portico, like Billie's at Burkeley Crest; Lily's picture, like Billie's, appears on everything from candy boxes to packs of cigarettes. (In his 1922 novel, *The Beautiful and the Damned*, F. Scott Fitzgerald even places a photograph of Billie as Lily Paradell on the bedroom wall of his hedonist alter ego, Anthony Patch — an indication not just of the kind of man likely to fall for Lily but the kind who fell for Billie as well.)[8]

Like Billie and other successful actresses, living in a time when for most actresses the only way to succeed was to submit to being managed, if not actually hounded, by men wanting a piece of the action financial or otherwise, Lily is often treated like a commodity, a source of "brokered sexuality" for both her admirers and her managers. Since Billie's first successes in London, photos of her exploited what can only be described as a kind of kittenish sexuality, peeping out from her furs and feathers, coy yet seductive, a delicious creature rendered temporarily inaccessible by her armor of laces and frills. Billie went a bit further for Pinero's play, as she described to a reporter in the far off 1950s: she made one of her entrances wearing nothing but a negligee and slippers, "and I always heard a few deliciously shocked comments, 'She isn't wearing any stockings.'" (Emphasizing her feet the more, Billie claimed she "rouged my heels and toes, to make them look their best.") But far from always being on the receiving end, as would also come to characterize Billie in time, in the first act Lily writes a check to an admirer who has gone bankrupt at the gaming tables. Billie would admonish Flo Ziegfeld for the same vice and, too, and she also wrote checks when his own funds ran thin.[9]

The Mind the Paint Girl opened at the Lyceum Theatre on September 9, 1912, with Pinero in the audience, and was a critical as well as commercial success for Billie. "Lily Paradell, risen from the squalid surroundings of a shop in Gladwin Street to the luxurious perfumed surroundings of chief girl of the Pandora Theatre, is, as might be inferred, a creature of some complexity, a mixture of sunshine and tempest, with vulgarity forcing its way in moments of excitement through the veneer of artifice and manners." So wrote critic Adolph Klauber, in a typical summing up. But having been so hard on Billie in all her other performances, Klauber had nothing but praise for her now:

> Miss Billie Burke, having previously distinguished herself by the most varied and alluring exhibition of comedy acting which she has yet given, made a truly splendid revelation of emotional powers hitherto unsuspected. It is possible to congratulate her most heartily on this performance, which from start to finish is suggestive of an understanding of the character, a grasp of its meaning, and a very varied and admirable technical proficiency in conveying its various moods.[10]

Billie believed her breakthrough had everything to do with the fine direction of Dion Boucicault. The New York–born son of actor and director Dion Boucicault, Dion

Jr. specialized in comedy and was known to be a taskmaster for whom no detail was too small to be perfected. His careful direction reminded Billie of Charles Hawtrey's methods. His integrity and his respect for the drama impressed and inspired her: he "started a flame kindling, an urge to play some of the finer, harder, more glorious parts."

Billie realized she had become lazy, contented with herself, happy to play roles that required little of her except that she be pretty and well-dressed. As a result, critics had seen Billie Burke as "a cream puff." She had never considered whether she even had talents worthy of being developed—till now. "I had accomplished something really worthwhile," she wrote. "I was enormously set up and encouraged and determined to do the best I could from that minute on."[11]

The play ran in New York for 136 perform-

Billie as Lily Paradell in Pinero's *The Mind the Paint Girl* (1912) hands a check to Bernard Merefield, one of her gambling-poor suitors. This was an act Billie was to reprise in real life with husband Florenz Ziegfeld (Sarony).

ances, for Billie a Broadway record at that time; it was adapted as a novel by Louis Tracy and published by Edward J. Clode, with several Sarony photographs of Billie in crucial scenes from the play. English dramatist Alfred Sutro came to a performance and promised Frohman that he would write a play especially for Billie.

Feeling that she had grown as an actor, Billie was eager to tour all over the country and through Canada, but Frohman's complicated and heavy imported English sets anchored her to New York. Billie was disappointed but knew that "now that I could make some serious representations about being a dramatic actress," it was vital that she take on another challenging part, working with a director like Boucicault. She approached Frohman with her concerns and asked for another serious role. Not unlike his heavy sets, Frohman dragged Billie's aspirations back down to earth. He had no such play for her, but he did have another Pinero comedy, a revival of *The Amazons*, which he very much wanted her to perform in. "I argued with C.F. for the first time in my life," Billie wrote, but argument was useless with Frohman. For Billie, it was back to having fun on stage, this time wearing not Madame Hayward gowns but knickerbockers.

Billie played one of Lady Castlejordan's three daughters, who have been brought up as boys to help salve their father's disappointment at never having produced any male children. The girls in drag end up having secret romances in a confusion of "boys" kissing boys right under Lady Castlejordan's nose. Jerome Kern composed incidental music and songs for the play; Billie sang "My Ota Hiti Lady" to the pretend mandolin accompaniment of co-star Shelley Hull.

She got strong reviews, not least because she had never before appeared in pants or played a pants role — again, she was singled out for her costume more than her acting. "[I]t may be said at once," wrote a reviewer of the "Titian-haired star," with something of a leer, "that Miss Billie Burke is an eminently pleasing Tommy Beltrubet, both as to manner and — ahem. She figures well in the role." The play, which opened at the Empire Theatre in April 1913, ran till June and had nowhere near the success of *The Mind the Paint Girl*. And "it did not advance me one inch in the direction in which I wanted to go dramatically," Billie recalled, with obvious disappointment.

This bit of comedic fluff did nothing to harm Billie's popularity, which was what Frohman probably had in mind all along. But not long after *The Amazons* closed, he had another offer for Billie that was to provide all the challenge she wanted.[12]

CHAPTER 8

Mr. Ziegfeld

In late autumn of 1910, W. Somerset Maugham arrived in New York City on his first trip to America.

"His principal object in visiting this country," ran a blurb in the news, "is to study American audiences," and indeed, one of the most perspicacious remarks he made later on about what he had learned of the differences between American and English theatre shows he knew early which side of the Atlantic buttered his bread: "[T]he theatre is a habit in America; whereas, in England it is a rare event. An American lives, usually talks, in a highly vitalized dramatic or comic objective fashion perfectly suited to the medium of the theatre. An Englishman, repressing, sometimes never expressing, himself outwardly, is not essentially a character for the theatre." He also planned to see Billie perform in *Mrs. Dot*, with the touring company, as well as John Drew in his play *Smith*, then running on Broadway.

In a long interview a few days later, Maugham noted that what he principally found impressive in American theatre was a higher standard where plays themselves were concerned, plays by "educated men" who were a cut above what audiences had been used to a half century earlier. He pounced on the reporter when it was suggested that if Maugham wanted to study the American drama, he could always read the plays he was interested in without bothering about traveling all the way to America. "A play simply doesn't exist in book form," he replied. "It only exists in the persons who act it." He admitted that he was enjoying himself so much in New York he didn't want to risk "faring worse" by going farther afield (which meant leaving the gilded precincts of the St. Regis Hotel), but did plan to travel to Philadelphia to catch Billie in performance.[1]

Frohman had asked Maugham for a new play in 1912, and while casting about for a subject Maugham remembered a story his aunt had told him about her paid companion, a young woman who had given up a quiet job of serving tea and walking the aunt's lapdogs to join her brother on a rough and tumble farm in the Canadian bush. The shocker, according to the aunt, came when news reached home that the woman had married her brother's hired hand. To add some local color, Maugham spent a winter on a farm in what he described as "savage parts" (it is not known exactly where Maugham stayed, but the setting of his play is Dyer, Manitoba, near Winnipeg) where he "gathered all sorts of material for a dreary, sordid tragedy after the manner of Tolstoi." Frohman had commissioned him to write something uplifting, but he was fascinated as much as repelled by his experiences in Canada, and set about writing what became *The Land of Promise*.[2]

The play opens in the shuttered English drawing room of the deceased Miss Wickham, for whom the gently bred Norah Marsh has worked for ten years as paid companion. In a time (1914) when women were already venturing out into the workplace, albeit mostly in low-paid labor in factories or as secretaries, it would have chafed feminist modern sensibilities that an intelligent, strong-willed woman like Norah should feel that the only work she could get was that strange job of half-equal, half-servant, part-nurse and part-bridge partner, that constituted being a lady's companion. But for Norah, who plays the piano, speaks French, and is conscious of being a lady, there is no question of going out to work with her hands. And she considered herself lucky to have found "a place" in a civilized home, with a George III teapot and lovely garden, and an elderly lady to look after who when not bossing her could be thoughtful and perceptive.

But now her employer has died, leaving her nothing in the will, which troubles Miss Wickham's nephew if not his avaricious wife; and Norah can't face another ten years as companion to another elderly woman, in the same round of civilized toil. Her brother, Edward, has gone out to Canada and set up a farm, and gone enough native to have married a rough-edged but efficient Canadian woman, Gertie. Norah asks "Eddie" if she may come join him on his farm in Manitoba, is happily welcomed, and sets off for the colonies.

The play follows her disenchantment with Edward's rough life on a failing farm, her tussles with his homespun and caustic wife, and finally her desperate effort to escape the farm by marrying one of Edward's hired hands, Frank Taylor, an uneducated but sensitive soul who applies frontier laws of male dominance to the pretend marriage more from habit than desire. Significantly, Norah finally earns his respect only when she turns his rifle on him and actually pulls the trigger (the gun is not loaded).

Before long, Norah has been tamed to a degree by her surroundings, learning she can do many things besides play the piano or speak French and enjoy doing them, but she has also changed Frank's life in ways he appreciates, bringing order and charm to their humble shack. Frank has also become more generous toward her, which he demonstrates when she receives a letter from one of her friends back in England, offering her a place with a highly recommended elderly woman who will be kind and pay well. Frank suggests that Norah go back and take the position, especially as a wild mustard infestation has ruined his farm and will force him to board up the shack and hire himself out to more fortunate farmers. This is when Norah has her chance to show generosity — the nephew of her ex-employer has sent her a check for five hundred pounds, more than enough to save the farm. So she decides to stay in Canada, as Frank Taylor's wife, and the plot resolves.

Maugham was experiencing another sort of snowy prairie at this time, one that he carried with him long after he left Canada — the sobering recognition that he was homosexual, accompanied by the fears of exposure and personal and professional disaster, that usually went along with that self-discovery. As a gay man who genuinely cared for women, it was natural for him to turn to one to help him in his losing effort to deny his true nature. Maugham was in love with an actress named Sue Jones, who was going to America that September of 1913. Maugham would be in New York earlier for rehearsals of *The Land of Promise*, and hoped to get together with her there.

Miss Jones's subsequent behavior has a good deal to do with the next big chapter in Billie Burke's life, because what did not work out as planned for Maugham did work out as unplanned for Billie.

Arriving before Jones's ship had put into port, Maugham did all the romantic things — selected an engagement ring, considered how to ask for her hand in marriage. When Jones arrived, she informed Maugham she was headed for Chicago and couldn't spend even a day in New York. A month later, Maugham caught up with her in Chicago, had supper, and Maugham asked Jones to marry him. "If you want to go to bed with me, you may," Jones replied, admiring but not accepting the ring, "but I won't marry you." But bed was not really what Willie wanted from Sue.

It was in this state of rejection that Maugham returned to New York and rehearsals, vulnerable and full of longing and, possibly, with his pride out of joint. The misery increased when, just before the Christmas day opening, Maugham read a newspaper headline announcing that Sue Jones had married none other than Angus McDonnell, a son of the sixth Earl of Antrim, earlier that month. After returning the engagement ring to the jeweler, Maugham salved his wounds by making himself available to squire Billie about New York City. They dined and danced, and he clearly adored her and was pleased to be seen with her. As he confessed in an interview a few days into 1914, "I feel myself an American playwright in the possession of such a splendidly attuned, keenly intelligent actress of fine range for the leading part as Miss Billie Burke — a type I wish we had more of in England."

Did Willie entertain designs on Billie, as he had done for Sue Jones? On the face of it, a Maugham-Burke marriage looked like a match made in heaven — both were successful, she in his plays and he writing roles for her; both were wealthy and unattached; and perhaps Maugham sensed in Billie the same strength beneath the surface glitter and stage whisper softness that Flo Ziegfeld was to lean on in time to come. Maugham could have given Billie the children she wanted, allied to a respectable family in England — still something of an ideal for her, that nation of quiet-voiced ladies and gentlemanly men. When it came time to confess his homosexuality to her — as he did to wife Syrie in the late 1920s — it is unlikely Billie would have been as upset as she was when, shortly after her marriage to Flo, she discovered his dalliances with women from his *Follies* productions. But maybe marriage to Maugham, as to any of the other suave gentlemen who wanted Billie, was too easy. Billie had to fight for what she loved to fully enjoy it.[3]

Billie received glowing reviews, including a positive critique from the *New York Times*. Though *The Land of Promise* hadn't much depth, per Adolph Klauber, the play remained "a wholly pleasant thing. The same word describes Miss Burke's share in it." Yet Billie was not as satisfied with her part as she had hoped. As she confesses in her memoirs, the overall dreariness of the production depressed her, not to mention the lack of elegant costumes — that passion for fashion to which she would always be susceptible. When Frohman, perhaps sensing that Billie might not take to the play's bleak prairie atmosphere, tried to talk Maugham into lightening up the second act, the playwright said no — he had made enough of a name and enough money to refuse even Frohman's entreaties.

"The change of character was perhaps too sudden for me," Billie recalled. (She also claimed she was having trouble with getting the Canadian accent down pat — meaning a North American accent, quite at variance with her mid–Atlantic "British" accent; she needed a coach from Montreal to help her.) And her discomfort with the character of Norah comes through in Klauber's review, in which he refers more than once to Billie's breathless, talkative manner, as if she had already adopted the chatter-box style of her later character work in films: "Repose of any sort she utterly lacked." Was it also Maugham's wordy script? Billie would not have been the first actress to trip over some of the playwright's lengthy soliloquies — Irene Vanbrugh had difficulties when she played Norah in London, as Fay Compton did with her part in *Caesar's Wife*. Or was it because something had happened between playwright and actress? A kiss, a pro-posal turned down by her, or by him, that strained their emotions onstage as well as off? As with so many other topics that were not easy for Billie Burke to remember or write about in later life, she is silent about what really discomposed her about her part in *The Land of Promise*. Perhaps, too, Billie was already sensing that serious drama was not her forte — certainly it was not where her strongest gifts lay.[4]

Like *The Mind the Paint Girl*, *The Land of Promise* should have been toured, par-ticularly in Canada where it was mostly set, but for one fatal drawback. It was not that the sets were too heavy, but that a few humorless people in Canadian government were a bit too taken with what Lenin termed "administrative ecstasy"; feeling the play offered such a bleak impression of rural life in Canada that nobody would want to immigrate there, they gave *The Land of Promise* the cold shoulder before it had even crossed the border. In what must be one of the mercifully few times border officials have ventured into the realm of theatre critics, William D. Scott, superintendent of the immigration service, was quoted in the Edmonton *Journal* on April 4, 1914, as saying, "[The play] gives an altogether incorrect conception of the conditions in Western Canada." A female member of the immigration service posted to London went a step further: "No Cana-dian man would dream of ordering his wife about.... If there is one thing Canadian men do well, it is the way they treat their wives."

What these bureaucratic censors were missing, of course, were the facts of Maugham's play (which it is doubtful they had read). The fact of the matter is that when Norah gets to her brother's farm she finds it is her sister-in-law, not her brother, who rules the roost. Frank Taylor's treatment of Norah can be seen to be as much the teasing of an intimidated man secretly in love with a feisty woman as assertion of male dominance over a defenseless female. Given Superintendent Scott's successful efforts to keep black immigrants out of Canada, it is perhaps not surprising that he felt the nation's dignity was at stake should Maugham's play ever make it on the boards of Toronto or Winnipeg. It is interesting to note that Billie seems to have agreed that the play gave a warped impression of life in the Canadian wilds (about which she knew exactly nothing) — but perhaps she was just as glad not to have to tour in a show in which she did not feel she was at her best, visually or dramatically. At any rate, the poor advance press discouraged Frohman from introducing the play north of the bor-der, though years later it was toured through Canada without any trouble.[5]

Frohman saw no reason, Billie remembered, to cry over spilt milk. He had another play already up his sleeve, a bright if lightweight comedy called *Jerry*, by playwright and songwriter Catherine Chisholm Cushing (author of the song "L'amour, toujours l'amour"), which he believed would serve as the perfect starring vehicle. Rehearsals began before *The Land of Promise* had even closed. If Maugham was feeling unsettled about his love life, Billie was "frustrated and bewildered" by her career. They were the perfect pair to paint the town red.

Billie loved going to dances with Willie, whose fox trot she pronounced as expert as Sir Johnston Forbes-Robertson's. On New Year's Eve of 1913, Billie gave a going away party for Sir Johnston and his wife, actress Gertrude Elliott, who were sailing for Europe the next day. Willie was with Billie that evening, when Billie's manager Victor Kiraly suggested they drop by the Astor Hotel's Sixty Club, where a costume ball was underway. It was already 1914, 2 A.M. into the new year, to be exact, when Kiraly phoned over to the Astor to announce that Billie and Maugham were en route. When they arrived, Billie gowned in her usual splendid fashion, she walked down the staircase to the ballroom on Maugham's arm.

"At the foot of the stairs," she wrote, "stood this man." She thought he was Italian — his erect bearing and dapper style made her wonder if he were perhaps a prince or a diplomat, though he was not wearing the decorations or orders that would support this impression. (Billie was not alone in seeing Flo as "foreign looking": future Ziegfeld publicist Bernard Sobel likened him to Florentine magnate and art patron Lorenzo de' Medici "the Magnificent.") "He had a Mephistophelean look," Billie recalled, and he, besides her playwright escort, was one of the few gentlemen present wearing full evening dress instead of a costume, enough reason to earn her notice. They looked at one another, then Maugham guided Billie to the ballroom, where they began to dance.

As Billie once told a reporter, in summer 1909, "[N]obody can make love like the American man — when he gets started." Though they had crossed paths on a few occasions already, in forty-six-year-old Florenz Ziegfeld Jr., thirty-year-old Billie Burke had met an American man whose love life needed no starting. And she didn't know it yet, but with her greatest lover she had also discovered her greatest and most tragic dramatic role, unlike any she would ever have the chance to play on stage or screen.[6]

He had come to the ball that New Year's Eve dressed as a tramp, his signature fancy dress costume, and he had come with a woman who was not his wife — his ex-wife, French comedienne Anna Held, was there, too, dressed as the Empress Josephine (another famously jilted beauty). She had been glaring at Ziegfeld and Lillian Lorraine, the other woman; when Lillian exited the party after a spat with Ziegfeld, Held transferred her glare to Billie. She had been around Flo Ziegfeld long enough to know what would happen next.

Born in Chicago on March 21, 1867, Florenz Ziegfeld Jr. was the first of four children, three sons and a daughter, born to Florenz Ziegfeld Sr. and his wife, Rosalie. Some biographies of Ziegfeld have assumed he was Jewish, based apparently on a stereotyping reading of his surname, but such was not the case: Florenz Sr. was the son of the Lutheran mayor of Jever, capital of Friesland in lower Saxony, facing the North Sea, a man who also served as an official at the court of the Grand Duke of Oldenburg (probably Paul Friedrich August, d. 1853). Florenz Jr.'s mother was Rosalie de Hez (or Gez), a Catholic born in Belgium who was a grand niece of General Count Etienne Maurice Gérard, a Marshal of France who served both Napoleon and, after the restoration, Kings Louis XVIII, Charles X and Louis-Philippe. Rosalie's family was already in Chicago when Florenz Sr. arrived. The couple married on May 17, 1865.[7]

Florenz Sr. may not have had a technical right to place "Dr." before his name, but he did study music from an early age with Carl Johann Christian Stiehl (royal director of music in Jever) and later at the Leipzig Conservatory, the school established in 1843 by Felix Mendelssohn, where he joined the circles of musical lights such as Ignaz Moscheles and Louis Plaidy.

While he may have been a talented musician, Florenz Sr.'s main interest was the propagation of music education, a dream he pursued through a number of failed ventures (including a conservatory that burned down in the Great Fire in Chicago in 1871), until he finally managed to set up and maintain the Chicago Musical College, which is still functioning under the auspices of Roosevelt University.[8]

Music may have run in this family like water down a steep hill, but the stream got diverted where Florenz Jr.—*Flo'chen* to his mother and Flo to his friends—was concerned. Billie would remember how his one party piece at the piano was a "crashing crescendo of arpeggios," which he performed like a pro, only to stop there with a bored sigh.[9] Flo attended Brown Elementary School, forcing ground for so many famed names (Lillian Russell, Eddie Foy and Edgard Rice Burroughs), then Ogden High School, working for his father at the Musical College. Flo wanted something different out of life from his father's round of Bach, Beethoven and Brahms, which his family seem to have been willing to indulge, sending him at age sixteen to a Wyoming cattle ranch. Flo became fascinated by the spectacle of Buffalo Bill's Wild West Show—according to one chronologically problematic legend, he won a shooting match with Annie Oakley, according to another more likely account, Flo responded to a challenge from Buffalo Bill Cody and proved such a superb marksman Cody hired him—compared to which the fusty Victorian frills of his parents' home became too small, too pedestrian, to contain his fantasies. Billie believed that the "bold, bright colors of the West" had much to do with inspiring Flo's creative imagination, noting that the most vivid special effects in his Broadway shows were recreations of the spectacular sunsets he had seen out west as a teenager. It is easy to visualize the rangy young man, born and bred amid the concrete of Chicago, standing in rapture as the flames of a Western sunset kindled, flared and died down beyond the dark horizon.[10]

According to Billie, Flo became a favorite in Chicago society, with a debutante and sometimes two on his arms—the wealthy mothers and fathers of these young women were to come in very handy in the near future. Now named treasurer and director of the Musical College's board—administrative positions dependent on slow democratic processes which it is scarcely possible to believe he endured as long as he did—Flo saw his chance to shine when the World's Fair came to Chicago in 1893. Dr. Ziegfeld was elected to the board of commissioners for the international congress of musicians for the event, along with Theodore Thomas, and planned a program of American and European music. Billie claims her father-in-law was director of music for the Fair itself, but while this was not true, Dr. Ziegfeld had considerable clout and ambition, offering programs to educate audiences in the music of the Old and New Worlds. At this time he also produced a nightclub, called The International Temple of Music, which was housed in the Trocadero, some distance from the Fair grounds and not connected to the World's Fair. The venture was not successful for a couple of reasons — competition from the World's Fair, and lack of interest on the part of ticket buyers in the mix of popular and classical music the program offered.

This was where Flo stepped in. Using a mix of vaudeville and popular music, dancers, jugglers and beautiful girls, he managed to turn the show around. But his real success came when he discovered and made famous the German strongman, Eugene Sandow, by inviting Chicago society ladies to come backstage and feel the beautiful blond Sandow's muscular arms.

The show expanded as Flo took to being an impresario in a big way, creating ever more outlandish stories about Sandow's superhuman strength to gain press attention and ticket sales. He took Sandow to New York, where Flo became a frequent patron of such restaurants as Tony Pastor's and Koster & Bial's, and where he began to collect the wealthy friends, like Diamond Jim Brady, who were to back his future projects. He also met Charles Evans, who with co-star William Hoey had had great success with the Charles H. Hoyt comedy *A Parlor Match*; convincing Evans to mount a revival, Flo went overseas with him in 1896 to find an actress for the part of Lucille. While in London, the two men attended a performance at the Palace Theatre featuring a French actress named Anna Held. For Flo, it was infatuation at first sight.[11]

Anna Held was born not in Paris, as she would have everyone believe once she became well-known, but in Warsaw, perhaps in March 1873, the daughter of a German-Jewish glove maker. The family fled to France to escape one of eastern Europe's frequent pogroms; the father seems to have become an alcoholic, forcing Mme Held and her daughter to work in factories to make ends meet. Anna supplemented this income by singing in the streets. After the death of her father, Anna and her mother went to London to live with relatives, and it was there she gained experience acting in Yiddish theatre before returning to Paris, where she made herself known as a café singer.

Like Ziegfeld, she knew the uses of the daring public act, sitting astride her horse and zipping around Paris on bicycles. She was also extremely attractive in a girlish way, with huge black eyes that she rolled expertly at her audiences, a winsome rosebud of a mouth that she pursed at them, glossy black hair and the proportions of a china doll, replete with a waist as tiny as corsets could make it. The year before Flo saw her in London, Anna had married and borne a daughter, Liane, to a wealthy South American tobacco planter, Maximo Carrera. His family cut his allowance, he gambled away his money; the child was sent off to a convent, and Anna divorced Carrera in 1897. Carrera was not a problem, but if Anna thought that the convent was the end of being troubled by Liane, she was mistaken, as Flo would be, too, in time to come.

Flo and Anna never married, as Billie and other sources state (they had had some sort of ceremony in New York, witnessed by friends), but their common-law union was a sturdy one. Flo was besotted by Anna, as husband and impresario. He cast her in *A Parlor Match*, in his first venture as Broadway producer and hers as Broadway performer, having her sing her big hit from London, "Won't You Come and Play Wiz Me?," a song the lyrics of which combined everything that made up the Anna Held image: girlish charm coupled with sexy innuendo. The show was a hit and both their Broadway careers were launched.

Flo pulled out all the stops to get publicity for Anna, some of it against her own better judgment — such as telling the press she bathed in milk to keep her fresh complexion, or setting up a contest to see whether Frohman star Julius Steger could kiss Anna two hundred times without flagging, or the outright lie that Anna had chased down a runaway horse on her bicycle and saved a worthy of the Brooklyn magistracy. These were pranks, but they rather than the truth caught on, and soon Anna was a big star, in large part because of them.

There is one Ziegfeldian creation that everyone has to actually thank Anna Held for, because it was she who first gave Flo the idea for the *Follies*. She told him about the Paris revues — shows that offered spoofs of popular current plays or operas or of historical events, interspersed with singing and lots of beautiful girls dancing. Anna also shaped Ziegfeld's taste, toning down his circus barker's affection for overly bright shirts and ties and, on the other hand, introducing him to the lavish gilded furniture and marbles and mirrors with which she decorated her Paris house and their apartment at the Ansonia.[12]

By that early January morning in 1914 when Billie saw Flo looking up at her from the bottom of the Sixty Club's stairs, he and Anna had broken with each other for good. At pains to excuse Flo, Billie claims the relationship foundered in part because Anna, despite her great glamour, was just a "Hausfrau" at home, "frugal, domestic, and maternal" — not qualities that could ever be applied to Billie, who till her dying day insisted that the best way for a wife to retain her husband was to be glamorous from dawn to dusk, powder puff at the ready. But she adds that Anna's were fine qualities which perhaps grated on and finally alienated the man who could not be bothered with bookkeeping or the maintenance of a home or a wife who let her hair down off stage.[13]

Billie had heard plenty about Florenz Ziegfeld Jr. before their first meeting. "His reputation with women was extremely dangerous," she recalled. Even though he must have known that Anna Held was at the Sixty Club party, Flo had brought with him his current flame, Lillian Lorraine, beautiful star of the *Follies* since 1909 and one of the most troublesome of Flo's lovers, a self-destructive woman who when in her cups (which was often) was inclined to make bogus but annoying threats. No sooner had they arrived at the Club but they had one of their now customary disagreements, and before Billie arrived Lillian had flounced out, leaving the way open for Flo to pursue other interests — namely, Billie Burke.

The orchestra began and the master of ceremonies, Freddie Zimmerman, called a "Paul Jones." This was a so-called "mixer dance" to get people who otherwise might not know one another to do so through dancing with different partners. Forming a circle, ladies to the right of the men, the dancers did what in square dancing is called the "Grand Right and Left," clasping hands with partner after partner until the M.C. signaled to stop. Each person then dances with the person whose hand they last held.

Billie was soon separated from Willie Maugham and found herself in the arms of the tall dark man, who smoothly and wordlessly swept her around the room. Curiously, or so Billie thought at the time, with each new "Paul Jones" she always ended up with the tall dark man, and as they danced she noticed Anna Held's fixed stare, "with enormous jealous eyes which followed us around the floor." This went on until her manager, Victor, had to hiss at her that there was a matinee that day, she needed to go home and get to bed. It was then, when a passing acquaintance called out greetings to "Flo," that Billie realized with whom she had been two-stepping. This gave her pause, because of the things she had heard — the good and the bad. She knew about his magnificent contribution to Broadway, the *Follies*, though she had never been to see a production. She also knew he had a way with women; she had heard that having just divorced Anna Held, Flo was having an affair with Lillian Lorraine; and there were rumors about other women, from stars to chorines.

Billie knew all this and feared more, but she was thinking with her heart instead of her head. "It seemed that he had danced me into a glimmering world of swirling emotion," she recalled, "a new country full of awe and delight." She felt a strange oneness with him that she could not shake. She had fallen in love.[14]

As with Caruso, at first it was Billie who kept her distance, Flo who made all the moves. The assault on the fortress that was Blanche's and Frohman's protective guard began with flowers, delivered to Billie's dressing room. Then they met on Fifth Avenue — Billie thought it was by accident, but knowing Flo, it probably wasn't. Billie remembered she was getting out of her car, wearing a sable jacket and carrying a chinchilla coat. Flo was amused, perhaps impressed: "I see you are the most extravagant person in the world," he told her, "next to me." He was, of course, right.[15]

When Flo came to tea at Burkeley Crest, he ended up staying to supper, and he took Billie out to dinner so often during the run of *The Land of Promise* that she put on more weight than was proper for slender Norah Marsh. He invited Billie and Blanche to his apartment at the Ansonia, the thirteen-room flat which had once been his and Anna's home and was still filled with her overdone gilt French furniture. (Had Billie only known then, Flo had installed Lillian Lorraine in an apartment right over their heads.)

Flo charmed Billie by courting not her but Blanche, quickly assessing that she was the source of all decisions concerning Billie's life: he sent Blanche rare fruit out of season, and bottles of pink Champagne, and was as much the gentleman as an exacting woman like Blanche could ask for.

Blanche evidently sized up Flo as well, because before long she was telling Billie she felt Flo could advance her career far faster than Frohman — speed still being Blanche's watchword. Billie was, after all, getting older — she was nearly 30, which in Blanche's day meant more than just skirting the boundaries of middle-age. How long could Billie be presented as a sweet young romantic lead? Was Frohman the right manager for her at this time of life? Blanche must have considered these and other factors as she sat thinking at Burkeley Crest, pondering where to go and what to do. No doubt this was what prompted her warning to Billie that it was time for her to make her up mind about what she planned to do with her life.

Billie admitted later that she knew her mother was wrong about Frohman, and the facts support her. Billie was lucky in having Frohman as her manager for one very good reason: he respected and cultivated her dignity as an actress, and he had carefully assessed what she had to offer as one. Frohman may be accused of many things, but he was developing Billie carefully. He eased her into the sort of straight dramatic parts, like *The Land of Promise*, and the more challenging drawing room comedies like *Mrs. Dot*, then gave her lighter comedies and farces that did not overtax her (but made money), while looking ahead to testing her in more challenging roles. Where he was taking her as an actor is anyone's guess, but he appears to have had a goal in mind, reached by slow and careful method.

I believe Frohman was preparing Billie for a comedy career by slowly edging her away from drama — not the drawing room variety of comedy but the kind directors George Cukor and Dorothy Arzner later saw as her greatest talent: character comedy. Frohman was, after all, the man who built the careers of Ethel Barrymore and Maude Adams, John Drew and William Gillette. He was as much a master at determining how to shape the raw material at hand as a sculptor who, examining a block of marble, determines how best to liberate the figure trapped within it. But however Billie respected Charles Frohman, she loved Flo Ziegfeld, and soon couldn't imagine life without him.

She was feeling herself pulled between two enormous forces. As she wrote, "You learn, after a while, when you begin to grow up, what an enormous difference there is between mere happiness and your career."[16] When Frohman discovered that Billie was seeing Ziegfeld, he was furious. A sedulous protector of his stars' private lives, he was not about to have Billie get mixed up with a man whose intimate activities were the talk of the town. He called Billie to his office and told her, in no uncertain terms, to stop seeing Flo Ziegfeld. Perhaps playing on her concerns about where her work was heading, Frohman warned her that Flo couldn't produce plays, and would ruin Billie's career. And if she married him, Frohman added, *he* would drop her. Billie laughed and said nothing was less likely than that she would marry — she had already told reporters that if a woman wanted a career, she could not be married, that the two were incompatible. Yet even as she repeated this to Frohman, she and Flo were already having prearranged meetings in what they believed were secret places, including Grant's Tomb in Riverside Park, overlooking the Hudson River. It was a cold place in which to conduct a love affair, but it seemed a safe enough place away from Frohman, reporters and all sorts of other spying eyes.

Charles Frohman, the great Broadway producer and star-maker, whom Billie defied to marry Flo Ziegfeld in 1914. Frohman later died on the torpedoed *Lusitania*. Photograph ca. 1910.

But Grant's Tomb was obviously not private enough, because Frohman either found out they were meeting there, or Flo had been unwise with his drinking pals and said too much — there was no such thing as secrecy in the theatrical circles of New York City. (And there is evidence Flo had bragged about Billie once too often.) To show they meant business, Frohman and Alf Hayman came to call at Burkeley Crest one winter afternoon. Their grim appearance on the doorstep unsettled even hard-headed Blanche, who hurried upstairs to tell her daughter about the unexpected visitors.

Like characters in a gangster movie, Frohman and Hayman paced Billie's sun room awaiting her, still wearing their heavy winter coats and smoking their cigars while they tossed clicking billiard balls back and forth across the pool table. There was nothing friendly about this call, which shows that whatever his adorable qualities toward James M. Barrie or John Drew, Frohman could be a bear when crossed. This was a proprietary visit to impress on Billie that her owners had had quite enough of her bad behavior and were about to jerk the leash. And so Billie found them when she came downstairs, their dark clothes and somber expressions in stark contrast to the flowers and parakeets.

As Billie recalled later, the first thing she asked them was whether they thought by appearing without warning they would surprise Flo on the premises — a sarcastic bit of sparring which Frohman brushed aside by throwing her an ultimatum: "This has got to stop," he told her, tossing another ball across the billiard table. Then, in grim duet, Hayman joined in as both men traded off reporting all the bad news they knew, probably a lot they only guessed at, and probably a lot that was based in fact, about Flo Ziegfeld: Lillian Lorraine, Anna Held, lots of other women; his spendthrift ways, his gambling, his debts. Responding to the increasingly heated atmosphere, the birds began to hop about their cages and shriek.

"I defended Flo," Billie remembered, "and I defended myself the best I could," pointing out that her love life was of no concern to either Frohman or Hayman. This was her mistake, and she knew it: of course her love life mattered to her manager — given a perfect storm of Flo Ziegfeld as lover and potential manager, and a baby that might keep Billie off the stage, and a myriad of other factors that could affect her stage career, not to mention an alliance with so dicey a character as Ziegfeld was rumored to be, had Frohman *not* been concerned it would have been astonishing.

Hayman then dropped the bombshell that Charles Frohman had only hinted at in his earlier conversation with her: if Billie married Ziegfeld, Frohman would no longer work with her. This was the consequence Billie had surely feared, as well she might: she had left Charles Hawtrey and London for Charles Frohman and New York, and if Frohman left her, where to go then, whatever promises and plans Flo offered her?

Frohman and Hayman left as silently as they had arrived, leaving Billie standing amid the flowers and the now quiet birds. She wanted Flo more than ever, but she had to make one last effort on behalf of her career: she had to "be true to my work in the theatre ... to be a good actress," which is what she wrote in a desperate note she sent to Flo, in which she asked that they break off their relationship.[17]

Later that day, while Billie was at the theatre preparing for her evening perform-ance, Flo arrived and got her to agree to come to dinner with him. As they ate, he pulled her note from his pocket. "This seems pretty definite," he said. Then he pulled out something else — his tickets to sail the next day for Europe. If Billie really wanted to break with him, surely it was all right for him to leave town and never see her again? It was classic Ziegfeld, this either/or, yes or no, you love me or you hate me test. If Bil-lie had been asked to preside over the judgment of Solomon she could not have been put in a more difficult position. In forcing her to make a choice, Flo was not being any more fair than Frohman had been. Frohman, to whom she owed her very career, had said: marry him and we quit you. Flo, whom she loved but who was still an unknown quantity, was telling her: marry me or *I* quit you. She was, in effect, trapped solidly between the two.

As so often, Billie took refuge in her mother: she told Flo she could not decide without Blanche's blessing. So they both drove up to Hastings after dinner to lay before her Flo's demand and Billie's uncertainty. It was so late when arrived at Burkeley Crest that they had to wake Blanche up, but she had already settled her mind on the issue. She had no objection at all to the marriage. "It's the best thing for you to do," she told them, which in Blanche's language meant that it was also what she felt was best for Bil-lie's career. So carried on that momentum, Flo and Billie decided to marry the next day, right after Billie's matinee.

The brilliant, witty, infuriating, loveable Flo Zieg-feld, Jr., in 1929.

After saying yes, Billie felt a strange combination of relief and concern. It seemed to her wonderful, magical, to be Mrs. Florenz Ziegfeld, Jr. Billie Burke would never feel dif-ferently, even when she saw the full extent of what she had tied herself to: not just a man she loved but his infidelities and his other habits that so threatened her and their daugh-ter's security. But she also realized that she had given up some carefully cultivated, specially unique part of what made her Billie Burke, the stage beauty of her generation, every man's dream girl whom no man had yet captured. When she gave in to Flo's repeated efforts to convince her to marry him, had she taken the motto off her and Flo's secret sepul-chral meeting place — "Let Us Have Peace" — too much to heart? Was it peace she had really gained, and at what price?[18]

CHAPTER 9

Mrs. Ziegfeld

On April 11, 1914, Billie prepared for her Saturday matinee as she normally did, but she remembered being "frantic and frightened" all morning. No wonder. Before the evening performance, she would be getting married, in full face of her manager's disapproval and his threats of dismissal. That she got through the comedy of playing rollicking young Jerry at all that morning shows she had either matured both as actress and woman, or had grown to be more adept already at what would become, as Flo's wife, her lifelong modus operandi: shuffling harsh reality under a silken carpet.

Billie was a little over two weeks into the run of *Jerry*, which had opened at the Lyceum on March 26. The play was preceded by much publicity, including the all-important details of Billie's wardrobe: "In one of the acts Miss Burke is to appear in blue pajamas." (It goes without saying that these pajamas—which were not blue but pink, and which in one scene Billie doffed naughtily behind a screen—became all the rage after opening night.) The play was something of a first for Billie—her first time as an American actress to act the part of a girl who was actually American. Jerry is "an unmannerly young girl ... who says 'Go to the devil' on all possible occasions," wrote one critic, "and who has set her heart on one Montagu Wade of Philadelphia." Jerry gets him by taking him away from her aunt, to whom he was engaged, and when he tries to flee she attempts, or rather pretends, suicide.

It was rumored that in order to give Billie more of a starring part, the role of the hapless aunt, played by Gladys Hanson, had been pared down. It is unlikely this surgery was necessary, because on opening night, at least, Billie seems to have chewed scenery from first act to last. "Not that the comedy revolves too much around Miss Burke," wrote a critic. "Indeed, one leaves the theatre with a confused impression that she has been revolving about the comedy and rather distracting the attention from the work of Catherine Chisholm Cushing, who wrote it."

> As Jerry, Miss Burke is very much herself—only more so. It is as if she had made note of all her graces and mannerisms which in seasons past registered in laughter or applause and had set out to repeat them in double measure.... Jerry is Billie Burke to the nth power, Billie Burke laid on thick, Billie Burke very much overdone.

The review continued to note that "while much of the play is written and acted in the key of comedy, Miss Burke's part is entirely in the key of farce," probably the worst epithet that could be tossed in the face of a legitimate theatre actor.[1] Audiences, however, loved Billie's Jerry, and on April 8, Frohman announced his plans to take the show to London for the remainder of the season and into the next.

On the day of the nuptial event, Billie's nervousness was subsumed into the excitement she normally felt on a performance day, but there must have been an edge to it nonetheless. In her memoirs Billie recalls how, between the acts, she stepped out of her stage costumes and tried on various dresses from a fashionable couture house, unable to decide which one she wanted to be married in. Her fixation on what she would wear was one she turned to in many stressful situations — it may also have been a way to stave off the facts of what she was about to do, and perhaps even a way of confusing herself with the prospect of trying on costumes for a performance not in life but in the theatre: the consequence of her actions might be easier to avoid thinking about too much if she imagined it was all part of a play.

Jerry came to an end, the orchestra vamped, curtain calls were taken, and the play was put to bed till evening. Billie having selected her wedding dress, Blanche came to get her at the stage door with the car. The rest of the plan clicked along like clockwork: they met Flo at Sherry's Restaurant, then drove on to Hoboken, New Jersey. Had Frohman been in the country, it is reasonably certain they would have been discovered and stopped by this stage, but he was safely in London, and Hayman and his crew seem to have been otherwise engaged. Nobody stood in Billie's way.

Not long after they arrived in Hoboken, in the storage room of a Lutheran parsonage, filled with ladders, baby carriages and assorted flotsam and jetsam of church bazaars, Flo and Billie were married by the Rev. Conrad Engelden, who from start to finish could not get their names straight.

> "And now, Flo," Rev. Engelden said to Billie, "you stand here."
> "He's Flo, I'm Billie," she replied.
> "Then you stand here, Bill," the reverend said to Flo.
> "I'm Flo, she's Bill — I mean Billie."

The marriage certificate continued the uncertainty: Flo's name is spelled "Florence," while Billie is called "Ethelbert Appleton Burke." No wonder the poor reverend had so much trouble telling who was who.[2]

When they emerged from the parsonage, Billie had ceased to be just Billie Burke. She was now Mrs. Florenz Ziegfeld, Jr., and the impact of this seems to have rendered her, for the moment at least, speechless. On the ferry back across the Hudson, Flo was concerned enough to question her silence; he put an arm around her and asked, "Is my wife happy?" Billie doesn't record her response. She was happy, but she was also haunted, as she would be for years, by the sense that she had started down a completely new and twisting road, where she could not begin to guess what lay around the next corner. She had, in effect, fallen into her own Land of Oz years before Judy Garland was to do so; and like Dorothy's, her first steps down Flo's Yellow Brick Road were hesitant and fraught with misadventure.[3]

Before leaving for London, Charles Frohman had hung up his hat in Billie's dressing room and said, "Don't be foolish while I am gone." Without Alf Hayman to play bad cop, this was Frohman's way of chiding his favorite star to not do anything rash where Ziegfeld was concerned. But Frohman sometimes displayed incredibly bad timing; in this case, the horse was already long out of the barn.

As Billie waited for her cue between acts that evening of her wedding day, she couldn't help but look at the hat and feel a pang. She had naively hoped that the news would not hurt him too much. It did, of course — she had misgauged the enormity of her disobedience to the man who had, in many ways, created her. According to Billie, Frohman's telegrammed response to hearing the news was the last direct communication she ever had from him. "Send me my hat," came the terse demand.[4]

No question about it, Billie's marriage to Flo Ziegfeld left everyone stunned. Not one of her friends approved of what she had done. And Flo had his own opponents to contend with. Even before the wedding, on hearing that Flo and Billie were an item, Lillian Lorraine had chased Flo to the rooftop restaurant of the New Amsterdam Theatre, and amid the startled diners threatened to drop her fur coat — the only garment she was wearing — if he did not keep away from Billie. (Given Lorraine's promiscuity, it is unlikely many males present had not already viewed her charms.) Billie did what she could to wrap Flo's life in her own packaging, taking care of one piece of the past that it lay within her power to change: she removed all of Anna Held's gilded furniture from the Ansonia apartment, redecorating the rooms in cool Neoclassical hues. With the bright gilt went some of that troubling memory from New Year's Eve at the Sixty Club, when Billie had been caught in the full glare of Anna's great jealous eyes. But it did little to remove the sense that there were other women in his life besides herself. As she would increasingly discover, they were impossible to erase with new draperies and Boraxo.[5]

Frohman was not yet finished punishing Billie. Instead of keeping *Jerry* on Broadway, where the play was doing solid business, and shipping it to London as he had planned, he sent it precipitately on the road in May. Billie's first stop was Chicago, where Flo joined her, and together they spent time with his parents.

Billie had already met Dr. and Mrs. Ziegfeld at her wedding supper in New York, but now she got to know them better in the setting of their own fringed and ruffled Victorian home. She especially liked Mrs. Ziegfeld, a diminutive lady whose Gallic features Flo favored, but she was brought up short when Rosalie insisted on sharing old family recipes with her — all the soups, fritters, sauces and pastries Flo had loved since childhood. Mrs. Ziegfeld suggested Billie learn to make all these things to keep Flo happy (not guessing how little a fritter stacked up next to a fresh new *Follies* chorus girl.). If Mrs. Ziegfeld had tried this tactic on maternal Anna Held she might have had a more salubrious result: Billie, who could not even brew tea on her own, had to use all her dramatic wits to squirm out of culinary commitments but seem grateful for all the advice. Her genuine appreciation was evinced when she later reprinted some of Mrs. Ziegfeld's recipes — with two or three favorites of "Flo'chen's" — in her self-help manual-cum-memoir, *With Powder on My Nose.*[6]

When *Jerry* closed in Chicago, the newlyweds returned to New York, where they spent the rest of the summer at Montauk Point and Fire Island and getting things domestic set up at Burkeley Crest and at the Ansonia. It was from this time that Billie could say she ceased to be ignorant of Flo's tidal relationship with money, because it soon became clear that his cash flow was out to sea. By her birthday in early August, his present to her was a rose plucked from her own Burkeley Crest garden, wrapped in the last cash he had: two one hundred dollar bills.

Somebody needed to keep working, so when Frohman ordered her on the *Jerry* tour of seventy-two one-night stands, Billie gritted her teeth and bore it. Ever thoughtful where Blanche was concerned, Flo set her up with a map of the United States and a handful of flag-shaped pushpins, so she could track where Billie was at all times. Billie, however, could not always be sure of Flo's coordinates, particularly those that related to matters of the libido, the beginning of a state of vigilance that would not let up until Flo's death eighteen years later.

Flo joined her in various cities along the way, often with a jewel in his pocket which she knew he could not possibly afford. Making for more unease, it was not always clear to Billie that these jewels were for her. And one night, at one of the hotels they were staying in together, Billie happened to catch Flo leaving the room of an especially pretty chorus girl. When she asked him what it was all about, Flo gave her an excuse that was to become all too convenient and familiar — he was just doing business. Billie would write with some confidence, "Flo never pursued any woman," and it is possible she was right. All the Great Ziegfeld had to do was cast a glance at a young woman hoping for Ziegfeldian glorification, and she would naturally approach him unbidden. But it was the too-warm reception Flo gave such women after they arrived that was to cause him and Billie so much future trouble.[7]

Billie was far too busy touring to devote much time to pondering the deeper layers of the situation, but as rumors always do, stories reached her while she was in San Francisco — Flo having returned to New York — of certain activities he had been engaging in with other women, which sounded decidedly not like business meetings. These she swept under the carpet at the time and, to a degree, later on when she came to publish her memoirs, much to the chagrin of those who knew Flo and what he was capable of.

Bernard Sobel, who worked as Billie's press agent and was asked by G.P. Putnam's to write Billie's biography, was a good friend and admirer of Billie's but descried the way she soft-pedaled Flo's promiscuities when she published her own memoirs. "A whole volume could be written about his carelessness with heaven knows how many women," wrote Sobel. Flo was, he said, "the perpetual predatory male from caveman on." Billie had not been Mrs. Ziegfeld more than a few months before she realized her marriage was not an achievement to rest against but something more like a battle position she would have to constantly defend.[8]

Throughout the winter and spring of 1915 Billie toured *Jerry*, missing Flo when he wasn't with her and resisting the suspicions raised by "do-good" friends in New York and their stories of his erotic exploits. Her relationship with Frohman remained chilly — he could not forgive her marriage to Flo — but she had signed a five year contract with him in late October 1914, and he had for her a "new American play in which she will be seen in seven different characters," went one newspaper report. "One of the parts to be played by Miss Burke will be that of a clown." This is intriguing because, aside from the obvious echo of Billie's father, this proves that Frohman had plans to challenge Billie as an actress. For all his anger, he had not given up on her — on the contrary, he was giving her another chance. Perhaps Frohman was beginning to understand that far from being just a pretty face, Billie, with her gift of mimicry, had the makings of an outstanding comedian and character actress.[9]

In the meantime, Frohman and most of Broadway was distracted by events that penetrated even the most spangled precincts of American theatre: the outbreak of world war. On June 28, 1914, a young Serb nationalist named Gavril Princip had assassinated Archduke Franz Ferdinand and his morganatic wife, Sophie Chotek, in Sarajevo, where the Habsburg prince and heir to aged Emperor Franz Josef of Austria-Hungary had decided to pay an ill-advised visit. The Balkans had always been regarded as the powder keg of Europe, with Russia, Germany, Austria, Turkey and a welter of allies and adversaries plotting and scheming for control of the region. The murder of Franz Josef triggered Austria to demand that Serbia punish the offenders. Serbia moved too slowly, upon which Austria declared war, which in turn tipped the other dominoes: Russia jumped in to defend their Slav brothers (who were really nothing more than the keepers of what the Romanovs saw as the corridor to their real goal, conquest of that old Russian desideratum, Istanbul). Treaties and agreements made years before, many tied in with the arms race that had begun in the early 1900s, dragged the other European powers into the conflict that came to be called, erroneously, "the war to end all wars."

Despite sharing a grandmother they had both adored, King George V of Great Britain and Kaiser Wilhelm II of Germany became mortal enemies. And on April 22, 1915, the German Embassy in Washington, D.C., issued a warning:

> TRAVELLERS intending to embark on the Atlantic voyage are reminded that a state of war exists between Germany and his allies and Great Britain and her allies; that the zone of war includes the waters adjacent to the British Isles; that, in accordance with formal notice given my the Imperial German Government, vessels flying the flag of Great Britain, or any of her allies, are liable to destruction in those waters and their travelers sailing in the war zone on the ships of Great Britain or her allies do so at their own risk.

Frohman may never have even read this warning, though if he did it is unlikely it would have made much of an impression on him. He had been having a bad time of late—health-wise and business-wise. He had hurt his knee in a fall and his leg was never really right afterward, and as his biographer wrote later, "The great war, on whose stupendous altar he was to be an innocent victim, affected him strangely. The horror, the tragedy, the wantonness of it all touched him mightily." This sounds like the exaggeration of posthumous biography—Frohman was not known as a great humanitarian, and it is more plausible that he was more worried about what the conflict would do to theatre receipts. Something like this would have seemed crucial enough to motivate him to risk the dangerous voyage to London.

Passage was booked on the RMS *Lusitania*, the Cunard luxury liner Billie had sailed on a few years before. Alf Hayman had urged Frohman not to make the trip, but Frohman shrugged him off with the fateful joking retort: "Well, Al, if you want to write to me just address the letter care of the German Submarine U 4." He was still joking when the ship sailed on Saturday, May 1, 1915. A friend asked him if he wasn't afraid of U boats. "No," replied Frohman, "I am only afraid of the I O Us."

Six days later, just off the Old Head of Kinsale, Ireland, German submarine U-20 spotted the liner and fired. There was an explosion and the ship began to take on water, listing so severely starboard that the portside lifeboats were all but useless. Besides

Frohman, a number of other celebrities were on board the *Lusitania*, including Rita Jolivet, an actress Frohman managed. Everyone had just had lunch when the ship was struck. When Rita, having donned a lifebelt, found him, Frohman was on deck talking to Rita's brother-in-law, George Vernon. An Englishman named Captain Scott joined them, then left to get more lifebelts. Frohman was smoking a cigar and didn't seem perturbed. The ship began to tilt, and Frohman calmly told Rita to hold to the railing, so as to save her strength, as if coaching her for an especially daunting dramatic role.

As the four huddled together grasping the railing, surrounded by the screams and death-throes of passengers and the metallic groanings and explosions of the sinking ship, and the cold waters rising higher, Frohman smiled at the others and quoted a line from his most immortal production, *Peter Pan*, in which Peter and Wendy are trapped on Marooner's Rock, and only Wendy is able to escape: "To die will be an awfully great adventure." (Other sources, including Billie, have Frohman saying: "Why fear death? It is the most beautiful adventure of life.") The ship went down in eighteen minutes, and only Rita survived to tell the tale of Frohman's last adventure. Frohman was not yet fifty-five years of age.[10]

Billie was on tour with *Jerry* when she heard of the sinking. According to one report, she had been about to go out on stage when, with poorest possible timing, Flo sent word that Frohman had died on the torpedoed liner. She managed to get partway into the performance, then had to walk off, collapsing in tears.[11]

A funeral of size and scope to match Frohman's standards took place on May 25 at New York's Temple Emanu-El. Crowds overflowed the sidewalks of Fifth Avenue, and within the Temple a galaxy of show business stars converged to pay their respects: Blanche Bates, Hazel Dawn, Marie Doro, Louise Drew, George M. Cohan, David Warfield, Lew Fields were among Frohman's many celebrated friends and colleagues in attendance. Frohman's brother Daniel asked that no flowers be sent, but they came anyway, from Billie as well as Ethel Barrymore, Ann Murdock and others. Sir Johnston Forbes-Robertson sent a laurel wreath on behalf of English actors in America. Frohman's pallbearers alternated between actors and writers: Edward "Ned" Sheldon, George Ade, Augustus Thomas, and E.H. Sothern, Otis Skinner, William Faversham, and John Barrymore, to name a few.

Frohman stars who, because of the grueling tour schedules he had put them on, could not make it to his funeral, made efforts to memorialize him in whichever towns they were performing. At an hour corresponding to that of the 11 A.M. funeral, Billie arranged for services at a synagogue in Tacoma, Washington; Maude Adams and John Drew made similar arrangements in the far-flung outposts where they were touring.[12]

Charles Frohman was gone, but Billie was still under contract to his brother, Daniel, who had expertly taken the reins, and was very different from his brother: less an artist than an administrator, and one who wielded an iron will. And if Billie thought she had had tussles with the one brother over what she could and could not do as a Frohman star, she had more than met her match in Daniel. She would discover just how uncompromising the Frohmans could be when she found herself being courted by the new entertainment medium that was to deliver a body blow to the theatre world that had made her a star.

CHAPTER 10

Movie Star

Film as we know it had its beginnings on April 23, 1896, when a moving picture was shown for the first time in the United States at Koster & Bial's Music Hall in New York City.

The subjects of this maiden voyage into the uncharted cinematic sea, now incredibly tame, were then considered quite novel — two girls doing an umbrella dance, a pair of ill-matched comedians boxing, some footage of surf on sand. A descendant of the penny arcade peep cabinets which had cheaply entertained working class customers, by 1903 film was a going concern — this despite being held in contempt by most stars and producers of the legitimate stage. In 1900 film rose to fill the entertainment vacuum following the struggle for better wages between vaudeville actors and managers (and ended up killing vaudeville in the next three decades). Movies were cheaper than live theatre, and they didn't make any demands on the ticket buyer, who did not need to possess any special theatrical sophistication and usually didn't.

Film's move to Los Angeles from New York, its home base, had as much to do with avoidance by independent producers of the long arm of the Motion Picture Patent Company, a much-disliked trust which regulated exhibition and production via taxes on use of equipment and rental of films, as it did the sunny Southern California climate. Los Angeles wasn't even the preferred locale at first: many an independent tried Cuba, Florida, or San Francisco. But L.A. won out, thanks to its consistently agreeable weather, its varied terrain so useful for location shots, and most of all, its close proximity to the Mexican border, over which a producer could flee to escape subpoenas from the trust. By 1913, the film industry as such had become so entrenched in the sleepy suburb of Hollywood that the area was carved off from Los Angeles to become a city of its own. This was just two years before Billie, having ended her tour of *Jerry* in Los Angeles, was approached first by Thomas H. Ince, the director, who had a film studio in Santa Monica, and then by Jesse L. Lasky, president of the "Jesse L. Lasky Feature Play Company" (merging with Famous Players in 1917 to become Famous Players-Lasky), and offered a job in the "flicks."

She received a smooth letter from Lasky which many a beginning film actress would have killed for. Dated June 18, 1915, the letter refers to Lasky's partner, Samuel Goldwyn, with whom Lasky has discussed signing Billie on as a featured player in the firm. A meeting between Goldwyn, who ran the New York office, Flo and Billie was planned for August, when Billie "will then be able to ascertain just how many weeks you can devote to pictures," given she was considering a new play. In the meantime, Lasky added, leaning on Billie's conscience along with flattering her outrageously, "we shall be busily engaged in helping to preserve for future generations of theatergoers Miss Billie Burke at the height of her career."[1]

But by even listening to this — which was not hard to do when she was told she would be paid $140,000 for one film — she was playing with fire. The news of Lasky's overtures made it into the papers, and at the Frohman offices hell broke loose. Alf Hayman, used as the hatchet man before, rose to the occasion again. Billie received an angry telegram from him, telling her that if she signed with any film company before the Frohman office met with her in New York, "we will not continue with you for another season." Increasingly conscious of her status as Ziegfeld's wife, Billie assumed a nose in the air attitude that was (per her own admission) to worsen with time. She fired back: "Any more irate telegrams from you and I will sign immediately." Hayman then lobbed his biggest missile: the Frohman office would have *none* of its people in motion pictures, "and this means you." The special treatment of the Charles Frohman era had ended. For Billie, and for the Frohman office, the mutual appreciation society was over.[2]

En route to New York after *Jerry* to meet with Alf Hayman, Billie had a lot to think about. She had to sever her connection with the Frohman office — something up to now she had only occasionally threatened to do, while still full of misgivings about whether it was wise. And she was thinking of what had happened to her young marriage because of the cross-country *Jerry* tour.

She could have no doubt that left to himself, Flo was susceptible to other women. That she thought she could change this by marrying him, as seems clear from her later comments on the subject, shows she knew what she was getting into by becoming his wife, even as it shows she was naïve enough to think Flo could be tied down to any one female for any length of time. As had been the case since before they were married, Billie the glamorous leading lady, who had rarely had to make choices any more significant than which necklace to wear with which frock, was suddenly being called on to make decisions that might affect the stability of the shared life she had committed herself to when she told Flo "I do." Billie was thus in the thick of crisis when she returned to New York. And unlike all the other times she had returned triumphantly from tours, when she had been met with roses and attention from the Frohman office, she was met by no one. And Billie found out, to her immediate dismay, that Flo had rented a yacht on which, certain of those informative friends had hinted to her, he had had the sort of parties a man normally gives up once he has been married.

But again, there was little time to think about all of this. She had to prepare for the dismantling of the structure that had supported her since her first appearance on Broadway. After it was over, there was no happy ending. "I am through," she told Hayman at their chilly meeting. "I am going to do a picture." And so, because of her insistence on making a film, she was removed from the Frohman roster and from the company of all the stars Charles Frohman had discovered and nurtured over the past three decades.

Assuaging her hot temper and eager to vent at Hayman for the petty humiliations and efforts to control her before and after Charles Frohman's death, did nothing for Billie's peace of mind. Besides qualms about abandoning her management and turning herself over to Flo, Billie was worried about something else: that spending time in California making films might be as dangerous for the Ziegfeld marriage as the *Jerry* tour had been. Now she had to think with head and not with heart. As her manager, Flo stood to make money off her work, money that was not a regular commodity in his erratic producer's line of business. Thus he could hardly be expected to dissuade her from accepting the part in Ince's film, and probably actively urged her toward it; and with her on the other side of the country, how much easier to keep renting yachts and having fun, so Billie's "friends" could tell her all about it. So off Billie went to Hollywood to make *Peggy*, which would be the first of her over eighty motion pictures. And she pushed the stories of Flo's yacht parties as far under the carpet as they would go.[3]

Thomas Ince offered Billie $10,000 per week, and like many actors trained for the stage, Billie expected to start working from sunrise to sundown the moment she arrived, to justify such a high salary. Such was not the case—not, in fact, for three months. According to Billie, Ince took off for Catalina Island, playground of the rich of Los Angeles, and Billie still got her $10,000 per week for doing nothing. She had brought out to California her mother, Cherry, a young cousin named Dudie, and her cook, maid and chauffeur, all of whom enjoyed the enforced leisure at the house Billie had leased at the beach at Santa Monica.

One probable reason for the delay was likely the construction of a complete Scottish fishing village, which Ince had erected near the ocean, and a chapel that was still standing into the 1940s, at the end of Topanga Canyon Road, all on property belonging to Ince's production company and pre-dating his more famous Inceville by several years, as the Scottish setting for the film demanded. Dressed in jodhpurs and carrying a riding whip, Billie appeared in dozens of photographs with Ince and her fellow actors, most of them looking as if they were about to burst out laughing—the days of high-stress film sets were yet to come—a few of them showing her and Ince in deep conversation, as if *Peggy* were an Ibsen psycho-drama. Perhaps Billie was punch drunk with the dangerousness of what she had done: chucking Daniel Frohman, who would surely have no reason now to speak well of her to any of his Broadway cohorts, let alone recommend her for any stage work.[4]

Peggy was set in Scotland, but Peggy herself came from somewhere else altogether—the film was originally called *The Devil's Pepper-Pot*, and for good reason. "Peggy is a hoydenish American girl," wrote the *New York Times*, "who is invited by her uncle to visit him in Scotland." This uncle, Andrew MacLaren, "the biggest man in the little mountain hamlet of Woolkirk"—as the working script for the film describes him—is at the wee kirk that Ince built, on the Sabbath no less, when Peggy comes racing up the road in a cloud of dust, "and even a novice at watching the animated stories must know as soon as a close up of the young preacher ... is flashed what is going to happen in Reel 5."

In both *The Amazons* and *Jerry*, Billie was celebrated for wearing either trousers or acting hoydenish, or both, so she was in her element as Peggy, though at thirty-two she was almost twice the age of the character she was playing. But she gave the role all

Film director Thomas Ince made so much of having signed Billie Burke for her first film (1916) he circulated this image of himself offering the contract to her on a velvet cushion. University of Southern California Cinematic Arts Library collection.

Above: Billie depended on her directors to an extraordinary degree, and can be seen here in the midst of the set of *Peggy* (1916), her first silent film, in intense discussion with director Ince. Billie played the hoydenish American relative of a dour Scottish Highland family. University of Southern California Cinematic Arts Library collection.

Right: Ince wrote the lyrics for this song, flavored with skirling bagpipes, to publicize Billie's role in *Peggy* (1916).

she had, as "one of the wildest and most alluring witches that ever went around stirring up trouble," who thought her uncle's village synonymous with "a prayer meeting and long whiskers." *The New York Times* thought she did well: Billie and the movies were "kindred spirits." And considering this was her first film, Billie was commended for sailing through "with all the camera knowledge and assurance of a screen veteran."[5]

While still making *Peggy*, Billie was asked by Thomas Ince if she would be interested in a five-year contract with him. It was a fantastic opportunity, and Billie knew it. "I would have become one of the first motion picture stars," Billie declares in her memoirs; she was convinced that accepting Ince's offer would have set her on the road to cinematic fame. Under Ince's guidance, she could well have developed into an entirely different actor than the one we know. She had the petite charm of Mary Pickford with a savoir faire, wittiness and womanliness Pickford dared not display for fear of destroying her image as the sweet American girl. Billie could have gone the way of Gloria Swanson, for example, who also started out in comedies and graduated to the romantic dramas which made her Hollywood's queen of glamour.

Yet it was not to be. For all the thrill of the opportunity, Billie's situation, had most people known the facts, was full of unthrilling misery. Had Billie been more secure in her marriage (still less than a year old) — had the leased yacht on the Hudson been merely for innocent recreation, and the visits to chorus girls and actresses merely business as usual — Billie could have felt she really was Mrs. Flo Ziegfeld and made this next big step in her career with a sense of ease. She could have left Flo about his business and carried on where the winds were taking her. After all, she had given up the Frohmans for Flo. But marriage to Flo had shackled her in ways she would only gradually come to realize. She was not free to choose what was best for her. She had to choose what was best for *them*— the irony being that "them" was not always uppermost in Flo's set of priorities.

These priorities haunted her again during the making of *Peggy*. Her friends back east began to tell her that Flo had been seen with Olive Thomas, a beautiful *Follies* girl who at 21 could have been the 48-year-old Flo's daughter. Of working class Pittsburgh origins, the stunning Olive had won a contest in 1914 as "The Most Beautiful Girl in New York City," modeled her way to the cover of the *Saturday Evening Post*, and was hired by Flo for the *Follies*. It was her appearances, however, in his more risqué Midnight Follies in the New Amsterdam Theatre's roof garden that made her the sex symbol she became. Almost impossibly beautiful, with her large blue eyes, chiseled nose, pert childlike lips and flowing auburn hair, and a fresh youthfulness not yet spoiled by her drinking habits, Olive Thomas was mesmerizing on stage as well as on screen. She became a film star after signing with Triangle Pictures (the studio that helped make Gloria Swanson a star) in 1916, and she made over twenty films with that studio in the course of her brief life.

Billie knew enough about Olive to know that "she was one of the girls Flo rolled twenty-dollar gold pieces with on the roof," referring to the contests he staged with his *Follies* beauties for the delectation of the roof garden's male patrons. It's not clear just what Olive meant to Flo at this point other than as a cute girl who had a winning way with powerful men — we only have his distraught reaction to her death in 1920 to go by.

But each new dispatch Billie received from her caring friends in New York drove her to new levels of frenzy. In her memoirs, Billie characteristically blames her temper on her red hair, but she does admit that what she chiefly suffered from those months away from Flo and the scenes of his merriment was "a sense of bitterly outraged justice," as well as the morbid curiosity that goes along with suspicion. She finally came to a conclusion: that she could not accept Thomas Ince's offer of a five-year contract, and this doubly upset her, because it meant admitting to herself that if she had to work in California for five years, her marriage would disintegrate. Being away from Flo for a matter of a few months had been threat enough. She knew, however, that she had to make a choice. And "I chose my husband over my career," Billie states in her memoirs.

That was the one resolve she was able to keep — but not so her temper. When Flo came to see her in San Francisco after *Peggy* was wrapped, she flew at him in a fury. While he sat calmly smoking in a chair, for two days Billie Burke, the witty, elegant, always composed stage beauty of Broadway became a wild-haired fury, shouting at him, weeping, breaking china and tearing down the draperies when he either didn't reply at all or did with the infuriating riposte, "The trouble with you, Billie, is that when you accuse me you always pick the wrong girl." Given how many women Flo went through, it was probably possible to wrongly pick one at random as his current lover.[6]

When Billie left San Francisco, she did so alone — Flo had gone ahead to New York. She knew now it was impossible to engage him in argument or discussion, which put her in some ways in an even worse position than before — it was the classic *Gaslight* plot, where the woman's fears are not just dismissed but regarded as in some way insane, and ultimately used to undermine her own grip on reality. She sensed that the only way to save her marriage to this man was to maintain proximity to him. Yet she also really had to work, now that she had thrown over the Frohmans and rejected Thomas Ince's movie contract. Flo, ever the gentleman even when at his most caddish, stepped in and arranged for Billie to make a film in Florida called *Gloria's Romance*.

On the face of it, *Gloria's Romance* was a unique next step for Billie in her film career. The film was a twenty part series that followed the adventures of a young heiress who, having driven her car off into the ocean, has to get back to Palm Beach through swamps full of alligators and Indians.

One of the lobby cards for this film shows Billie in a tattered evening gown parting swamp grass to peer out across the water in terror — it was the Perils of Pauline transferred to the Everglades. None of the movie studios of the time was involved in this venture: it was produced by *The Chicago Tribune* in an effort to stimulate subscriptions. Flo had evidently leaned on some Chicago friends for this, notably the *Tribune's* circulation manager, Max Annenberg, who possibly for the first time in newspaper history combined the departments of circulation and newsprint marketing with production design and casting for film.

Annenberg and Flo went the rounds as the former assured Flo that Billie would be properly, even luxuriously, featured in the series and given all possible perks, and

Flo demanding more, always more. Annenberg offered $75,000—Flo demanded double, and got it. Annenberg offered glamour galore, including a sick-bed scene which called for Billie to be draped in jewels—Flo demanded more gems, and got them. Eventually, Billie was paid some $175,000 for her work, which lasted from autumn 1915 to spring 1916, including a powder-blue Rolls Royce with gold initials on the doors, Cartier gems she was allowed to keep, and a Palm Beach mansion she was permitted to use for a time after the series had wrapped. Billie convinced Jerome Kern, who had composed music for *The Mind the Paint Girl* and *The Amazons* a few years before, to compose the score for the series, which ran on two reels; Kern also conducted the orchestra at the film's New York premiere.

Gloria's Romance was the first and only serial ever to have a Broadway premiere, and it was a colossal failure. But there were dividends for Flo. Through this film, Flo had his first taste of Palm Beach society and a way of life (and several wealthy Palm Beach ladies) he soon found he could not do without. He also met Joseph Urban, who had designed Marjorie Merri-

Billie as Gloria in *Gloria's Romance* (1916), the first movie serial ever screened in a Broadway playhouse. It was accompanied by live orchestra conducted by Jerome Kern, who also composed the music—and it was a flop.

weather Post's palace Mar-a-Lago and would become designer not just for Flo's *Follies* productions but for the improvements Flo lavished on Burkeley Crest.[7]

For Billie, while she came out of this project the winner financially, Palm Beach was the start of a new chapter in marital trouble for her. "I felt that my marriage was safe for a little while," she wrote later. But she really knew it was not, and she knew something else: that her position as Mrs. Ziegfeld had never been safe, not even from the first months of marriage. As she wrote to Flo shortly after they began their annual peregrinations to Florida, "Dear old Palm Beach. It's broken up many a home. I hope we will survive it."[8] She knew that as long as Flo produced the *Follies*, and socialized with rich society women in Palm Beach who were eager to add a Flo Ziegfeld charm to their bracelets, she was cursed to be ever on the *qui vive* for the next Ziegfeldian romance.

With Olive Thomas now being pursued by Mary Pickford's brother, Jack, Flo was able to tell Billie that "everything was now straightened out," that there was nothing more to worry her. She knew better, because she loved him, and it was her business now to be detective as well as wife and lover.

Ironically, it was another pretty girl who saved the Burke-Ziegfeld marriage from cracking apart. Some time that early winter of 1916, probably on location in Florida, Billie conceived what she called her greatest Ziegfeld discovery. In her bedroom at the Ansonia apartment, she gave birth on October 23, 1916, to a little girl, her first and only child. The Ziegfelds seem to have been expecting a son, because the New York firm of Gebrueder Mosse provided almost $500 worth of blue nursery outfittings. (Or was this because blue was a favorite color Billie and Flo shared?). Regardless of gender, the child was treated like a princess from her first post-natal scream, blue bassinette notwithstanding. They named her Florenz Patricia Burke Ziegfeld, but she was always known as Patricia to the world and Patty to family and friends.

With that same irony that now attended everything Billie did, it was not Flo who was first to see Patricia after the birth but Irving Berlin. Patricia believes this was because her father had grown restless waiting outside Billie's room and had gone up town to look in at the Century Theatre to see rehearsals of his and Berlin's new show, *The Century Girl*— if so, Berlin evidently considered Billie's welfare far more worth checking on than Flo, who anyhow did not like to be around anything smacking of doctors, nurses, blood or pain. When Berlin came into Billie's room he had a sad look on his face. "What do you know," he told her moodily. "[Lillian] Lorraine got married"—not the kind of subject Billie, after her struggles in childbed, wanted to hear anything about. But two days later, Berlin made up for it with a song called "You've Got Your Mother's Big Blue Eyes": "If you're half the lady that your mother is," ran the lyric, "I'll be mighty proud of you...."

If Billie's ideal of being a lady was to be strong in the face of potential marital failure, to weather the storms of husbandly infidelity with as little self-pity as possible, and try to look deeply into the psyche of the complicated man she had married, then she fulfilled the role. To quote her and Flo's press agent, Bernard Sobel, "She sustained the illusion that a lady could do no wrong." This was more than sustaining an illusion, which suggests that Billie put off the proper lady mask when no audiences were there to watch. The image of the perfect Victorian lady that Billie had cultivated so carefully was certainly a defense mechanism, but in films like *Dinner at Eight, Merrily We Live, Topper* and others, the proper lady routine, carried to a fault, served as

The cover of Bertrand Brown's song "Baby," commemorating Patricia Ziegfeld's birth in 1916. The artist Maud Tousey Fangel sketched a loving Billie kissing her perplexed-looking infant daughter.

source of endless comedic material for the character parts that gave Billie her second film career.

Like everything to do with her and Flo, the production that was their marriage was over the top in the effort it took to hold the structure together. Young Patricia was not just the glue, she was a part of the structure itself. It was because of this child that Billie could afford to let the man she loved and admired have his fun — within reason.[9]

CHAPTER 11

"...you love others so much, too..."

Isak Dinesen once wrote that nobody outside a marriage could know or judge the mechanics of what brought and held two people together, and such is the case with the union of Flo and Billie.

Flo was a loving husband who appreciated his wife and the comfortable nest she created for him, but who had the signal failing of being unable to resist sleeping with other women. Billie traded professionally on a persona of fragile, delicate beauty and a charm cultivated expressly for the pleasure of men, but was in reality a scrapper who had to fight tooth and nail to hold on to Flo, whom she loved with an almost unconditional passion. Where parts of these two repelled, other parts attracted, with enough centripetal force to make it impossible to break them apart. This much we can guess. All the archived telegrams and letters, diaries and newspaper clippings will never tell the whole story that was this couple's fabulous, fractious union.

Florenz Ziegfeld was indeed what Bernard Sobel called "the perpetual predatory male." He could be totally in love with his wife and yet have affairs that were not completely concealed from her, as if the temptation to test her love for him was greater than the need to avoid hurting her. Billie was increasingly willing to put up with whatever it took to remain near him. She wrote, not with sarcasm but with rueful adoration: "At Burkeley Crest, we revolved like little moons around Flo's sun, avoiding the heat when we could." Flo was the center of everything that mattered to her, or she would have been able to leave him on any of the occasions when her frustration drove her close to doing so.[1] But as Sobel also points out, this was not the selflessness of a weakling. Billie Burke was no put-upon little wife happy to let her career go down the drain to serve her lord and master. "[Billie] rivaled Ziegfeld as a personality," he insisted.[2]

Billie was not weak and not the fragile violet she often played as actress, as her frequent explosions at Flo and her couple of serious efforts to leave him prove. Unlike Anna Held, Billie was born with fighting instinct in her blood, probably an inheritance from her stalwart mother, but based also on the fact that she knew what she had as an actress and a woman, was in a position to make choices other women could not attain or afford, and had had more than an inkling of what Flo Ziegfeld was like before she married him. Perhaps, as when a woman will marry a man she senses is homosexual, believing she can change him, Billie married Flo because she believed she could transform him into a faithful, prudent husband and father. She soon discovered there was no changing him. But Billie Burke always went after what she wanted. And she wanted Florenz Ziegfeld, whatever she had to do to keep him.

In his memoirs, Sobel decried the dithery tone of Billie's published recollections, knowing better than most people how undithery she really was. "She was a realist," he insisted. He especially respected her view of Flo, which he demonstrated by reproducing a letter she sent him that, to his knowledge, Flo had never seen. Billie had just read an *Atlantic Monthly* article titled "The Well-Tempered Mind," dealing with the age old question: what is happiness? Billie was especially struck, per the letter, by a quote from the epistle dedicatory to George Bernard Shaw's 1903 play *Man and Superman*, in which the playwright brought the oft repeated tale of Don Juan into the modern age:

> [The joy of life can be defined as] being used for a purpose recognized by yourself as a mighty one — the being thoroughly worn out before you are thrown on the scrap heap — the being a force of Nature instead of a feverish, selfish little clod of ailments and grievances, complaining that the world will not devote itself to making you happy.[3]

This was, Billie insisted to Sobel, part of what made her husband great. Flo's eccentric side sometimes overshadowed "his finer and greater qualities."[4]

It is clear from Billie's letter that the eccentricities she refers to include Flo's extramarital excursions. It would take her years, till long after Flo was dead, to come to terms with the whole arc of his life and career, to really see the man she had tried so hard to figure out while he was alive. She knew it was far too easy to write Flo Ziegfeld off as a randy character, a permanently unzipped fly, a producer out of caricature who had his way with chorus girls on his desk top when he wasn't installing them next door to his wife and child, who lied to a faithful wife and dragged her name along with his when the scandals he could not keep under wraps erupted into fodder for lurid newspaper accounts. There is plenty of evidence to support this image, at least in its larger outlines. But as Bernard Sobel and, later, Dr. Richard Ziegfeld (in his magisterial study *The Ziegfeld Touch*), tried to make clear is that if Ziegfeld was guilty of anything, it was a fatal generosity, and that this was less a learned habit than a congenital flaw programmed into his DNA, which it was in no one's power to alter. Generosity is the key not just to his greatness but to his less admirable characteristics.

For Billie as for so many people who knew him and countless others who only knew him through enjoying his productions, Ziegfeld was a sort of magician, a purveyor of pleasure in all its manifestations. Since his first days as a showman, touting Sandow as the world's strongest man, and Anna Held as every man's ideal woman, down to his masterful assembly of sets, casts, acts, music, colors, dance, stars and costumes known as the *Ziegfeld Follies*, Flo's own sense of who he was, of his own existence even, seems to have been tied, like vital organs shared by conjoined twins, to others' enjoyment of what he created. He was thus the antithesis of the conventional portrait of the big-spending, philandering Broadway or Hollywood producer. This conventional bad guy dislikes authority but has no problem wielding it over the heads of those dependent on his whim. He is selfish and self-centered, and he lets nothing and no one stand in the way of what he wants, whether it be lucre or a new pretty girl. He uses people and when they are sapped of whatever drew them to him in the first place, he discards them like wastepaper. It is his own happiness and satisfaction that interest him, not that of anyone else. He lives and dies unloved.

Of all the things that Flo can be accused of, selfishness is not one of them. This was a trait Billie was well aware of. Whatever Flo had, he needed to share. His immense energy, which did not lag until he was near death, aided and abetted this tendency. And there is a fine line between sharing the big ideas, the dazzling spectacles and the sort of Broadway *Gesamtkunstwerk* that consumed him, marshalling the many talents and bodies necessary to achieve this vision, which had to be shared with audiences to become real for Flo, and the hot libido that went hand in hand with his grandiose plans, which must also be a shared pleasure or it was no pleasure at all. This was not just the promiscuity it has been written off as, as a function of what made Flo Ziegfeld the creator and innovator that he was.

Of course, it took some time for Billie to realize this. In a telegram from 1920, Billie wrote to Flo with pain behind every word:

> I suppose the fact that I love you is my salvation — and my attraction ... you do love me I guess — but you love others so much too.... I think what's the use and then I remember that I am somebody's mother too — but Oh God I could do with some loving....[5]

Flo was who he was, the genius and the flaws intermingled, never to be sorted out from each other. Billie came to see that to demand an alteration in Flo's pattern was to threaten the structure of what made him creative. So this is what Billie meant when she quoted Shaw's *Man and Superman* to Bernard Sobel — the man Flo realized that his purpose in life, his Superman, was greater than he was, and that since this purpose was to bring pleasure to others in bringing pleasure to himself, he was still that great man even in his more equivocal moments. It is certain that Billie also came to the realization that dawns on many spouses of unfaithful partners: sleeping with a momentary fling outside marriage does not equal loving that person as one does one's life partner. "The dog may stray," she wrote, "but the very last thing he wants is a smashup."[6] In Billie's day, for the woman to have taken this attitude of pleasing self, all caution thrown to the winds, was difficult if not impossible, given the dominant male dynamic of the time and the social and professional complications of a divorce; but Billie must have had other reasons than fear of social ostracism for not taking a lover of her own. One of them, and a major one, as she states, was Patricia. But another must have been this understanding of how Flo ticked, that she claimed she had special knowledge of— and her honorable actions toward Flo must be seen in light of this knowledge and understanding of what was for anyone, let alone a wife, one of the most complicated, fascinating, sexy, infuriating and loveable men of show business.

Billie was as important to Flo as he was to her. Billie knew this but does not specify the evidence: she is content to give us such examples of domestic bliss as the fact that Flo loved to rinse her red hair in Champagne, claiming that it brought out all the highlights (she says she didn't believe it, it was just nice licking up the droplets as they rolled down her face)—which is, actually, the charming act of a man who must love his wife. But Billie does not need to make a list: her memoirs are full of details as to why, with so many beautiful girls at his disposal and a few who even wanted him to leave Billie for them, Flo did not leave her, or she him.

For all her sparkle and sprite-like charm, Billie was not the ethereal sprite she appeared to be. Bernard Sobel, who believed Billie a greater actress than most people, including critic Alexander Woollcott, had ever divined, declared her a specialist in this "artificial guise" of ultra feminine allure. Guise aside, Billie was very much the realist Sobel believed her to be. Many found her decidedly untwittery, sometimes abrupt, even rude, especially after she married Flo and no doors were closed to the wife of the great Ziegfeld. Sobel remembered her pushing her way through a group of chorus girls backstage of *Annie Dear*, the musical play Flo produced for her in 1924, treating them as if they were "the dust of the earth," and hearing that she had required two cars after arriving at a train station, so that she would not have to ride with her maid.

Years later, Hedda Hopper, already annoyed that Billie had been cast in the role of Millicent Jordan in the film version of *Dinner at Eight* (Hedda having played Millicent in the Los Angeles stage version), recalled having made a silent film called *Sadie Love* (1919), of which Billie was the star, during which Billie's queenly airs put everyone's back up. The movie was shot at a private house on the Hudson River, and Hedda remembered Billie's annoyance that she had not been given the dressing room of the lady of the house and instead had to dress with four other actresses, one of whom was Hedda. Hedda said that Billie, undaunted in her bid for star privacy, got her maid to rig up screens around a corner, which the other actresses respected but which to rowdy Hedda was a red flag in the bull pen. "I risked a look to see what was so precious," she wrote later. "I didn't make a very big hit with Miss Burke when I returned to my chums and said, 'Girls, she hasn't got a thing that we don't have.'"

Billie's hard-headedness had certainly been on display when she refused to stop performing in *Love Watches* despite suffering from blood poisoning. She was a scrapper, and Flo needed not just someone who pushed back when he pushed, but who pushed *him*.[7]

Billie was a spitfire, but she was also a nurturing presence. She gave Flo a home, something Marilyn Miller would never have been able to do. The Ansonia apartment had been redecorated and all outward evidence of Anna Held expunged, but she was still there, haunting the place. Burkeley Crest was purely Billie's (though frequently referred to as Flo's, which it was not), and perhaps few actresses of her frenzied touring and film making schedule had the gift of creating so comfortable and sturdy a nest as this house. Flo had a real home there, for the first time since he had left his parents' house in Chicago as a young man, and the fact that he did love his home became evident immediately as he began to decorate and expand the house and grounds.

"Burkeley Crest," wrote Patricia Ziegfeld, "was, technically, a country estate, but it suffered from a severe case of split personality, " with "some of the characteristics of a zoo and some of the characteristics of a medieval fief."

Rambling over twenty-four acres, the estate was at once farm, flower garden, menagerie, and playground for adults and children. Flo filled it with as many exotic animals as he did flowers — at one time this Peaceable Kingdom contained buffalos, an elephant, an Egyptian ass, an army of dogs (Billie loved them, both the tiny lap and large police varieties), a monkey Flo threatened to name "Charles Frohman," lion cubs, and that ubiquitous pet of most normal childhoods, rabbits.[8]

The house contained twenty-two rooms and required, at its height, a staff of fifteen, to which was added Flo's tippling English valet, Sidney Boggis, and a governess for young Patricia. The outside staff was almost as numerous as the indoor, especially necessary since, besides the acres of gardens and waterworks to care for, there were several motorcars on the premises: two Rolls Royces (one of them probably the powder-blue model that Billie got as part of her contract for *Gloria's Romance*), a Dodge station wagon, and Billie's Minerva, a Belgian luxury car that costume designer John Harkrider remembered having had solid gold fittings.

Joseph Urban designed the swimming pool, which Patricia Ziegfeld remembered as a marvel of gorgeous ineptitude: for the Ziegfelds he created a pool replete with a fountain, a stone cherub holding a fish that jetted water. The trouble was that this fountain was literally in the center of the pool, so when one tried to get in some laps one invariably knocked his head on the fountain, or when surfacing for air, got doused by the cascading jet. What mattered, as in all things Ziegfeldian, was how well the thing looked, not how poorly it functioned.

Even Blanche made her personal mark: she had what her granddaughter remembers being a mania for Japanese teahouses. Blanche may have seen one in some fashionable garden and become fixated on it as a piece of outdoor décor in keeping with her daughter's star status — whatever the reason, she erected several on the Burkeley Crest grounds, with a few arched Japanese bridges thrown in for added effect. Not to be left out, Billie had theoretically charming but practically unworkable idea of planting rose bushes all around the tennis courts, so that anyone who had to chase a ball off the court ran the risk of severe laceration. And Patricia had her own folly on the grounds, courtesy of her father: a replica of Mount Vernon, sized down for a little girl, each room perfectly furnished and decorated, for her playhouse. Having started out its life as a prop for the set of a Marion Davies movie, the miniature Mount Vernon was shipped out in a crate from Hollywood and added to the landscape of Burkeley Crest and the stuff of legend that the Ziegfelds' life had already become.[9]

Burkeley Crest may have seemed to some the symbol of conspicuous consumption and lavish living, and it was a reflection of the two people who ruled its little kingdom: Flo the dreamer of big dreams, Billie his glamorous sidekick. But it was above all a canvas for Flo to paint on as he wished, without a thought for backers' percentages or opinions of critics. "He sought beauty everywhere," Billie wrote of Flo, and he sought to put it everywhere, too. And she pointed out that whatever his activities in the theatre and the world that revolved around it, "there was a fine line drawn between his home, by which I mean me, and his adoration for beautiful show girls."[10]

Years before she said it on screen to Judy Garland, Billie was already whispering to Flo in 1915: "There's no place like home." And he, even through the bright laughter of pretty chorus girls, never stopped listening, or coming back home.

CHAPTER 12

"The fine days"

Billie remembered those early years at Burkeley Crest, bringing up Patricia with Flo and discovering what a superb father he could be, as "the fine days." Flo's productions were successful, his name was becoming a byword for all that was most glamorous in the theatre as much as "Ziegfeld girl" was the catchphrase for all that was most beautiful in a woman.

Like a pretty girl, the Ziegfelds' life was like a melody, bathed in the first strains of the jazz symphony that became the Roaring Twenties. But in the middle of all the glamour and gaiety, Billie was not truly happy. "For there was always in my mind," she wrote, "the conviction that I was not being true to myself," that she had not really challenged herself in her theatre work. "I was gnawed constantly by the realization that I must be an actress now or never at all."[1]

She was always able to make movies, and she did so at a regular pace, because they were shot not far from New York and they offered shallow plots that didn't require much from her. In her memoirs, Billie idly guesses that she made a dozen of these silent films; but she actually made sixteen of them, including one based on the original version of *Annie Dear*, Kummer's *Good Gracious Annabelle*, and another developed from Maugham's *The Land of Promise*. Because of her film work, she could not ask for more or better popularity: when studios put up contests for filmgoers' favorite actress, Billie usually came out as top, or nearly so.

But as she was too aware, this work did nothing for her theatre career, and as such, did not matter to her. "I barely remember them" is how she dismisses her film work of this period. In May 1918, she gave an interview in which she gave a more candid assessment. When asked about her films, she scoffed: "The movies? Well, of course, they're not like the stage, are they? Not that they don't do plenty of things for you that the stage does not — they get you everywhere and bring you letters from all the ends of the earth. But they're rather — well, demoralizing." In keeping with how so many theatre stars of the day felt about acting in films, Billie regarded movies as work that was easy, sometimes amusing, rarely fulfilling but high enough paying to make the effort worth her while. Movies were something one did while waiting for the ideal stage role. The irony of Billie's career, of course, is that when she had virtually lost everything else, including the stage, it was film that reached out to save her.[2]

For her first play produced by Flo, Billie chose Clare Kummer's comedy *The Res-*

cuing Angel. Kummer was a New York–born song writer who, like fellow female song-writer-playwright Catherine Chisholm Cushing, contributed a few tunes that outlived their composers. (Flo would produce Kummer's musical *Annie Dear* in 1924, to much success, with Billie in the title role.) Billie lists *The Rescuing Angel* in her memoirs but for some reason does not address the production at any length in her recollections, jumping ahead to what she may have felt was the more prestigious revival of the Dumas-Grundy melodrama *A Marriage of Convenience* in spring 1918.

Or perhaps she was unhappy with the reviews. It was certainly the sort of comedy at which she had excelled in the past and which she enjoyed performing. She played Angela Deming, daughter of a wealthy man whom, she discovers, is down on his financial luck. To fix things up for her father, Angela selects the wealthiest among her suitors (Joseph Whiteley, played by Frederick Perry) and runs away with him. The plot thickens when another suitor, the rich but ill-bred William Hanley (Richard Barbee) discovers their marriage and lets Whiteley know that the only thing Angela wants is his fortune. Angela flees home, followed by the two men, who reveal to her father what she has done. At the peak of the crisis the newlyweds reconcile. The announcement that Angela has inherited from a wealthy uncle ties up the loose ends of the purse strings if not the plot.

After the play opened at the Hudson Theatre in October 1917, the *New York Times* was of the opinion that Billie was "not very successful in projecting that portion of [Angela] which is subtle and subcutaneous," describing her elsewhere as "unsophisticated to the point of wildness, and so far from subtle that countless millions dote on her." This would seem to be saying that Billie Burke's technique could be judged by the dearth of her admirers' sophistication. The point of the review was that Billie was popular more for being herself than for her acting ability, which was usually a characteristic of farce performers or serious actors who, through age or overexposure of their unique gifts, were beloved for their special quirks of stage presence. (George Jean Nathan and Alexander Woollcott were of the same opinion: whatever character Billie played, she was always playing Billie Burke.) For all that she had made her fame essentially playing herself, on this occasion she came across as nervous: "she agitates considerably," was the verdict, and she was unfavorably compared to Lola Fisher's performance, which had had far more depth. "This Angela is a creature wholly cutaneous — which is, of course, to say, wholly cute." The play ran for a month.[3]

A Marriage of Convenience was a happier experience for Billie, not least because as the Comtesse de Candale she was able to wear gorgeous costumes, purchased using a budget that, according to her account, seems to have been endlessly accommodating: she spent $125 on a single handkerchief. Actor and producer Henry Miller, at whose elegant new theatre the production was to play, admired the item but advised Billie to carry it, not use it. (It is notable that the playwright only specified a bouquet for her character in the hand properties list — but Billie, as much perfectionist and spendthrift as Flo, would have her way, even in handkerchiefs.)[4]

Based on Alexander Dumas père's *Un marriage sous Louis XV* and adapted by English playwright Sydney Grundy, *A Marriage of Convenience* deals with a woman, Louise de Torigny, who marries the Comte de Candale as arranged by his family, but who actually loves the Chevalier de Valclos, threatening her marriage (although the mores of the day would have permitted a woman of the upper social orders at least one lover, if not two). The irony is that she ends up falling in love with her own husband.

Henry Miller played the Comte in what one reviewer described as a surprisingly histrionic manner, but he was probably responding to Billie's own enthusiasm, which despite her heavy costumes was also remarked upon on opening night. "Billie Burke swept into the Henry Miller company last night," went the report, "her exuberant ingenuosity subdued by a series of stately Louis XV gowns, one to each of the four acts, and her well-known charms enhanced by them." (Henry Miller was evidently just as splendidly costumed: one of his suits had a waistcoat so thoroughly sequined with paste gems Flo was moved to remark, "Are you supposed to be Diamond Jim Brady?")

It was the perfect Billie Burke play: a period piece, set in a time of imagined dash, gallantry and elegance not yet dimmed by encroaching democracy or merchants who dared present bills to be paid; she could wear gorgeous gowns that were a challenge to manage, the sort of ironic circumstance (suffering for beauty) that Billie was uniquely fitted to enjoy; and the sets were something straight out of the salons of Madame de Pompadour.

A Marriage of Convenience was her first period costume role in America, harking back to her success in London in Hawtrey's period play, *Mr George*. The only problem with the production was that Billie and Henry seemed so well-suited, and she so adorable, it was not just hard to believe they would not come to love each other by the end, but that they had ever been out of love in the first place. Thus the production lacked the tension Dumas intended and Grundy more or less retained in his adapta-

tion. It ran for a modestly successful 53 performances, but Billie was reassured enough by its reception to write later, "At weary last it seemed that I was headed back, importantly, for the theatre." Yet her ideal — that her career and Flo's would "gallop successfully side by side" and still allow them to be the parents young Patricia deserved, remained as out of reach as ever.[5]

For the most part, Billie felt good about her life in 1918. "It seemed to me," she recalled, "that I had again established myself where I thought I belonged — as an actress in well-written, high-comedy plays." She very much wanted to continue her progress by playing Lady Teazle in *The School for Scandal*, but reports of this play being prepared for her would flit in and out of the New York theatre news for a couple of years before fizzling out in the glare of Flo's *Follies* fame.[6]

Costume comedies were always Billie's favorites. Here she receives the homage of Henry Miller in Sydney Grundy's adaptation of Alexandre Dumas's *A Marriage of Convenience* (1918).

Flo, who was supposed to be finding and producing such plays for Billie, could be forgiven for being distracted that year, which with the one following resulted in what Billie regarded as his two greatest seasons as producer of the *Ziegfeld Follies*. But 1918 was difficult for Flo, on business and romantic fronts. For starters, the burgeoning film industry (in which Billie was, ironically, a star) was impinging on live theatre with very real consequences at the box office; stars groomed by the New York theatre establishment were flocking to Hollywood and its easier money and greater exposure. Flo was also caught up in a fight that showed both his basic integrity and his basic naïveté, joining fellow producers Klaw, Erlanger and Dillingham in an alliance to combat ticket speculation.

"Unlike ticket agencies today," writes Richard Ziegfeld, "which are content to add $2 to $5 to the price of a $30 to $50 ticket, speculators in the 1920s sometimes tripled a ticket's price." The cause for concern, he points out, had as much to do with fear of bad publicity as it did that the prices would keep people away from the box office: what if the public thought producers themselves were hiking prices for their own benefit? Some probably did, and there was a significant amount of worry that the best seats were being lost (which normally would be given to critics, financial backers and other personages potentially useful to a show's profitability). There was also, according to Richard Ziegfeld, concern that the public's good faith toward producers might be compromised by the revelation that mob money had its tentacles in the business.[7]

Perhaps the biggest of Flo's challenges in 1918, however, was Marilyn Miller's first appearance in the *Follies*. And once this beautiful woman, whose praises Billie had been singing a few years before, hove into view, neither Flo nor his marriage were ever quite the same again.

After the first few years with Flo, Billie recalled, she had learned to sort through the various women in his life and catalog them according to their threat potential. Most of the time there was nothing to worry about — Billie only saw this much later, after she had schooled herself to avoid the self-torture of jealousy. It was actually not so much the women from Flo's theatre world that she had to fear — it was the society wives, in whose company the Ziegfelds spent so many Palm Beach seasons, and whose husbands Flo often touched for production funds, that she had to watch carefully. Because these were the women, as she points out, whom Flo found most fascinating — he had, after all, cut his teeth squiring Chicago debutantes about town. And they were not women Billie could compete with on the same territory, as she could with other actresses. But there were two actresses who stood out on the field of battle — Olive Thomas and Marilyn Miller — who were, Billie points out grimly in her memoirs, "the ladies I had to be emphatically concerned with." As it happened, Marilyn was by far the worst, and it was ironically Billie's doing that she was ever put under Flo's nose in the first place. Unlike Olive, who was basically passive, Marilyn could be aggression incarnate.[8]

It had all started just after Patricia's birth. While Billie was recovering, she put Patricia in the care of a nursemaid and began venturing out to the theatre again. It was at Sigmund Romberg's *The Show of Wonders* that she caught sight of Marilyn Miller for the first time. She couldn't get over the charm, grace and talent of this "confection of a girl," and asked all her friends who she was. Flo had hardly stepped through the door of the Ansonia apartment before Billie jumped him about "her" discovery. Unstoppable when captured by his own enthusiasms, Flo was not disposed to take anyone else's very seriously, even Billie's — every day, every hour, he heard of star-quality girls that he must audition, meet, see. For almost two years, Billie writes in her memoirs, she pestered Flo about darling Miss Miller and all her gifts of beauty, movement and voice, but Flo had other fish to fry. Later on, after Miller had made such a splash with the *Follies* of 1918, and in Flo's heart, Billie pondered the irony of having been the agent of exchange between these two — Flo the avid pursuer, Marilyn the coy but tough and, ultimately, dangerous prey.[9]

After the 1918 *Follies* opened in June, Flo began to show signs of being more than a little interested in Marilyn Miller. Olive Thomas still mattered to Flo but she had married Jack Pickford in 1916 and was busy making movies — whatever the nature of her relationship with Flo after that is unknown. In any case, the glare around the new favorite, Marilyn, would have pushed Olive into the shade. In her 1949 memoirs, Billie had enough distance to look at Marilyn with kindlier, more understanding eyes than could have been expected of her in 1918. She knew Marilyn had much to offer besides youth. "She was, I think, the vision of perfection," she remembered. Marilyn was a symbol of everything that could be beautiful in the flesh, of everything beautiful in gracefulness. Billie saw her, probably correctly, as Flo's *Follies* girl incarnate, one who fulfilled every one of the details he strove to attain. And yet Marilyn Miller was no fragile china doll. She worked like a dog, always conscious of perfecting her craft, another characteristic that workaholic Flo could not fail to appreciate.

She could also be a demanding, foul-mouthed harridan, as described by Patricia Ziegfeld, who once visited Marilyn's dressing room with her father. It was after a performance of *Sally*, Marilyn's and Flo's big success of late 1920. There sat the ethereally beautiful Miss Miller at her dressing table, still wearing her diamond-studded dress from the finale. She was applying cold cream to her famous face when Flo came to the door, holding Patricia's hand, and asked if they might come in. "Hello, you lousy son-of-a-bitch," responded Miss Miller, and the air was quickly blue with her profanity. It turned out Marilyn hated the beautiful dress — it was too heavy, she could not move in it, she had told him over and over again and you no-good bastard, you never listen to me, etc. Marilyn had to threaten Flo with the cold cream jar before he agreed to give her a less cumbersome costume.

Afterward, as Flo stood leaning against a wall dabbing the beads of sweat from his head, Patricia pointed out to her father that backstage wasn't anything like the front. Flo agreed. It was like looking at the other side of a decked out Christmas tree, "the side with the price tag and the tin showing through." That was the other side of Marilyn Miller, too.[10]

Flo loved her, this impossible, arrogant, highly professional and extremely beautiful young woman, though whether she ever felt the same has never been proven. Adding a keen poignancy to the new affair was the fact that Anna Held was dying. The news had broken in May — perhaps it had even driven Flo to seek distraction in Marilyn Miller. By August, Anna was dead, at age 45, of myeloma, a cancer of the bone marrow. Myeloma was not understood in 1918, and in a last fling with newsprint hyperbole, ghoulish rumors went around that Anna was dying from having kept her corset cinched too tight.

Just as he ordered that flowers which had gone an imperceptible shade past their prime must be thrown out, Flo was unable to bring himself to visit Anna after discovering she was dying. Life, not death, was Flo's specialty, and if there was another major difference between Anna and Billie, it was Anna's European acceptance of this fact of life and Billie's American and Ziegfeldian refusal to acknowledge it. Nor did Flo attend the funeral, which started at Campbell's Funeral Chapel on Madison Avenue and moved on—slowly, as there was "a cortege of thousands"—to a Mass at St. Patrick's Cathedral. But he could not resist planning the entire event—he kept his distance from her corpse, yet honored Anna's memory the best way he knew how: with spectacle. And with Flo, spectacle was never just surface glitter but as sincere a gift of his heart as anyone was likely to receive.[11]

Billie pressed on. Flo's next production for her was Somerset Maugham's *Caesar's Wife*, which opened at the Liberty Theatre in November 1919 and played for 81 performances. Set in the English colony in Cairo, Maugham's plot follows the torments of Violet, the vivacious young wife of Sir Arthur Little, the Consular Agent, who is having a secret love affair with Ronald Parry, Sir Arthur's up and coming young secretary. Violet eventually confesses this to her understanding husband, after the women of the colony begin to figure things out, then gives Ronald up to return to the familiar security of her marriage.

Billie seems to have got her teeth into Violet, who leaps onto the stage in Act I with a comment critical of the other women: "Is Mrs. Appleby complaining of the heat? I love it." One of them responds, "You don't know how exhausting it gets," and as Billie proved, Violet is indeed a woman who speaks before thinking, jumps before looking, is exhausting to all those around her. This is the real tension of a play that ends without a conventional climax—what will Violet do next? Billie played her that way from start to finish, according to Alexander Woollcott. He dismissed the part of Violet as requiring "a decorative and girlish comedienne—Billie Burke, no less," whom he described as performing "in a state of continuous emotional upheaval." Ironically, he claimed, this emotional upheaval failed to elicit audience sympathy for her. Woollcott pointed out that such a feat, through three acts, would be hard for an actress of more solid dramatic gifts, but damned Billie with faint praise by blaming the play: "If [Burke] does not greatly stir you, it would be scarcely fair to say it was her fault."[12]

The real stir came when Dorothy Parker, who had replaced P.G. Wodehouse as drama critic for *Vanity Fair*, penned in the January issue that Billie "is at her best in her more serious moments; in her desire to convey the girlishness of the character, she plays her lighter scenes as if she were giving an impersonation of Eva Tanguay." Eva Tanguay was a vaudeville sensation whose high-energy dancing and hit song "I Don't Care" earned her the nickname "The I Don't Care Girl." Tanguay had performed in the *Ziegfeld Follies* of 1909 and, while not beautiful, had a sex appeal to burn that was far ahead of its time. She was still a big star in 1919, but Parker had made a signal mistake in comparing Billie to her and, further, suggesting that Billie was too old for the role of Violet.

What happened next has become the stuff of Parker legend. Whether it was Billie who objected or Flo, a storm of outrage from the Ziegfeld offices overtook Condé Nast, publisher of *Vanity Fair*, in whose publications Flo placed a great deal of lucrative advertising, and in short order Parker found herself fired. True to form, she didn't go out with a whimper: she placed a sign in the building's lobby requesting "Contributions for Billie Burke," and offered other humorous anti–Billie Burke protests on her way out the door. So loyal were Parker's fellow Algonquin Round Table members and *Vanity Fair* colleagues, Robert Benchley and Robert E. Sherwood, that they also resigned from the magazine.[13]

The title of this silent, *The Misleading Widow* (1919), sounds like the fluff Billie made later on as a character actor in talkies, but it was still in the tradition of the clever comedies of Billie's Broadway stardom.

This incident lent that much more fodder to the commonly held belief that Billie only got good roles, and was not to be given poor reviews or the writer would be fired, because she was Ziegfeld's spoiled wife. She may have been spoiled, but it was unfair to consider her the recipient of roles she did not deserve or did not work hard to do well, as her next foray on the stage would show. As Isabel in Booth Tarkington's romantic comedy *The Intimate Strangers*, Billie found she had depths of maturity to bring to a role that was, in fact, her first part as a "woman of a certain age." It was a maturity she would need for the next tough act of marriage to Flo.

CHAPTER 13

Flickering Star

Billie loved working with Booth Tarkington, the Indiana-born author who, just prior to the production of *The Intimate Strangers* on Broadway, had won two Pulitzer Prizes. He and Flo were born the same year, 1869, but there the resemblance ended. Where Flo's energy went off like fireworks, sending sparks in a million directions, Tarkington's intensity was the dark, quiet, focused kind, which served him well when he was given control over *The Intimate Strangers* by Flo and partners A. K. Erlanger and Charles Dillingham. Erlanger was not completely sure of this and Billie remembered him coming to rehearsals, where he ventured a few suggestions. Tarkington was always amiable, Billie recalled, and "pretended that he had been greatly helped in his work." But he went on with the play in the way he alone had envisioned. This was a steadiness Billie could not help but admire.[1]

The Intimate Strangers opens in a rural railway station near Utica, New York, where William Ames, a successful attorney in his forties, played by Alfred Lunt, and Billie, a lady neither young nor old named Isabel Stuart, find themselves marooned by a storm. As the old station master observes, waiting for trains "does git people kind of pettish with each other," and Ames and Isabel have managed to get off on the wrong foot. They then have to spend the night together on the station benches, to be rescued at dawn by Isabel's flapper niece Florence, played by Frances Howard, who comes swinging in with her cigarette and slang and her sly intimations about the way the couple must have spent the night.

Unable to go anywhere else, Ames accepts Isabel's invitation to stay at her farm, with the intention of starting for the station again next morning. As day and evening progress, however, they grow more attracted to one another, though Ames's businesslike manner prevents him from acknowledging this readily, while kittenish Isabel decides to test the sincerity of his feelings by pretending to be far older than she really is — a strange play on Billie's own renowned ability to look perpetually young. She recollects personages and events of an earlier age. She fakes attacks of rheumatism; she even knits as she reminisces with her elderly Aunt Ellen as if they were contemporaries. As Isabel tells Ames during their Act I sparring, a woman is "only as old as she makes men behave toward her," which is the crux of her test of Ames's affection. If she can prove to herself that her age (never given but somewhere near the brink of thirty) doesn't matter to him, she can in turn bring out the youthful tendencies she senses are lurking under his cool middle-aged exterior. So Ames remains at the farm, being tortured by Isabel's trickery to the point where he locates the family Bible and finds that far from being an old lady, she is several decades too young to have ever been at the 1876 World's Fair. But in forcing him to this, Isabel has made Ames recognize his feelings for her, and to see the pointlessness of reckoning age when people are in love. The play closes with them sitting at the fire, Ames kissing her hand.[2]

When the play opened at Henry Miller's Theatre on November 7, 1921, Alexander Woollcott aimed most of his bullets at the playwright. "'The Intimate Strangers' ranges from utterly charming to rather stupid," he wrote in *The New York Times*. About the actors he felt differently. Lunt he liked, and though no fan of hers, he enjoyed Billie, too, though he professed to be puzzled by something new — the quietude and poise she brought to her role. "She never played with so much understanding and so much quiet charm," he wrote. "Somewhere, out of space, she has acquired a repose and dignity that she used not to have."[3] The play lasted on Broadway for ninety-one performances, a nice number compared to some of Billie's recent runs, and it was taken on the road to acclaim. In March 1922, the *Pittsburgh Dispatch* wrote, "The play is successful in providing Miss Burke with one of the greatest parts she has ever had," while the *Sunday Post*'s W. J. Bohmer opined more pointedly, "'The Intimate Strangers' seems to put Billie Burke's resources to the test of sustaining interest as a middle-aged, unattached personality. There is new music in her voice."[4]

In various interviews she gave during the tour, playing the part of Aunt Isabel moved Billie to share ideas about motherhood, views which were informed by the fact that she had brought Patricia along with her (accompanied by a nurse, two maids, three dogs and Billie's chauffeur Ernest) on the tour. To a reporter in Philadelphia, where *The Intimate Strangers* was playing at the Nixon Theatre, Billie said, "The one remaining problem with which I have to deal, outside of my work, is a small individual named Patricia Burke Ziegfeld, who has ruled my house at Hastings-on-Hudson since she first arrived some five years ago [Patty was actually 7].... It is my firm opinion," she added, in an about face from her last recorded pronouncement on the topic, "that the happily married actress blessed with a family is the better actress"— perhaps her answer to Woollcott's and other critics' curiosity about the new depth in her work.[5] In another piece, titled "Red Curls and Motherhood, and Art and Mud Pies, Mix, Billie Burke and 'Pat' Prove," journalist Louise Landis pronounced that "The Billie Burke of the fascinating childishness and pink pajamas roles has disappeared forever. Marriage, motherhood, and the loss of her mother have created a lovely stranger."[6]

Motherhood was partly what had transformed Billie; another was the loss of her own mother, the rock on which her whole career had been built. Blanche died, aged 78, while Billie was on tour in Baltimore, Maryland, and her obituary appeared in *The New York Times* on February 8, 1922. Blanche had been increasingly ailing but in no way any the less independent, so Flo and Billie had built her a separate house at Burkeley Crest and installed a nurse and maids for her care. She suffered from diabetes, according to Billie, but the obituary does not go into those details, it only tells us the interesting news that Blanche Burke "was a talented newspaper woman and a pioneer of her sex in that profession." As with the claim of an antebellum girlhood on a plantation outside New Orleans, no proof has been found to substantiate this assertion.

(And possibly the obituary writer was confusing Blanche with her mother, Cecilia Flood Beatty, whom Billie claimed was a writer of articles against slavery — again without proof.)[7]

In Blanche's honor, *The Intimate Strangers* closed for three days before the tour was resumed. If the dry reference in her memoirs to her mother's death is anything to go by, Billie was not exactly devastated by Blanche's demise — it is possible her illness was so advanced, everyone knew it was only a matter of time. And, too, it was not Blanche's way to sob over anything. Billie had not been brought up to whimper, even about a loss like this, but to soldier on till the finish. Perhaps there was still ringing in Billie's ears her mother's good-natured but adamant mockery of her weaknesses and the need to confront and conquer them.

After the funeral and Blanche's burial in Kensico Cemetery in Westchester (her grave to be surmounted by a bronze figure of a grieving, scantily clad female), Billie did indeed soldier on, not forgetting "this fine woman who might have made so much of her own life but preferred to give herself to me." Billie now assumed that maternal mantle for young Patricia, who was not as strong as a young child as she became later on as a young woman and whose health gave Billie constant cause for concern. Perhaps in keeping her daughter under watch even on tour, Billie was, besides looking after the girl's health, asserting what control she could over her domestic situation back home, where a storm was brewing that winter and spring that grew into a hurricane named Marilyn.[8]

In late June of 1922, Flo sailed for Europe, hoping to set up productions of the *Follies* in London and Paris; Billie was just finishing up her *Intimate Strangers* tour. She got back to New York, Patricia and entourage in tow, to find the lawn in front of Burkeley Crest "swarming with reporters." What about the divorce? they questioned her. Had she seen Miss Miller's statement? Had she communicated with Flo?

Only gradually did Billie piece together what had happened. It began when news emerged that Jack Pickford, the wastrel brother of Mary Pickford, and now fiancé of Marilyn Miller, had been dishonorably discharged from the Navy. Pickford had been married briefly to Flo's favorite *Follies* girl and sometime lover, the late Olive Thomas, in 1917. While in Paris for film work in September 1920, Olive and Jack went out partying one night on the Left Bank. They returned to their hotel and Olive, probably still drunk, picked up a bottle in their dark bathroom and drank its contents. Whether she knew it or not, what she had ingested was bichloride of mercury, an extremely poisonous topical treatment for symptoms of syphilis, which Jack was rumored to suffer from. In terrible agony, Olive somehow lived for a couple of days, unable to speak or see, before succumbing. She was only twenty-five. Flo was devastated by the tragic loss of a beautiful girl with whom he had been in love, and his low opinion of Jack Pickford was not improved by rumors that Olive had taken out a substantial life insurance policy before her death, from which Pickford stood to benefit.[9]

Flo had recently read in the papers that the Navy brass had discovered that Pickford had been using his access to private records to assure certain rich enlisted friends of his that they would receive bombproof berths on ships. Just after he got to France,

Flo was interviewed, in the course of which he was asked about the Pickford case. He recounted the story, clearly disgusted with Pickford, but made no allegations — what he shared was his low opinion of Pickford. Richard Ziegfeld gives Flo the benefit of the doubt by assuming he made these statements innocently, merely repeating what everyone else already knew. But knowing how Flo felt about Marilyn, and about Pickford, it is not realistic to believe Flo did not recount the Pickford disgrace with a certain relish or that he did not know what effect his published opinion would have — he had created too much yellow journalism himself to think that even an innocent remark would remain as such after coming out the other end of a printing press.

Always ready to cross swords with Flo, Marilyn went on a rampage. She told reporters in Boston that not only was the story Flo told about Pickford untrue, and Flo a liar, but that Flo was hardly to be trusted since he, a married man, regularly had affairs with his chorus girls and had even told Marilyn that he would leave Billie to marry her. There was no reason to include her, but Billie was not left unscathed: "She waves her baby at [Flo]," jeered Marilyn, "like George M. Cohan waves the American flag," a particularly tactless remark just after the war, but characteristic of Marilyn's crudity when angry.[10]

Horrified, and unable to reach Flo, Billie headed for Kennebunkport, Maine, where she holed up with the calm, cool Tarkingtons in their seaside home. And she received a telegram from Flo that somehow managed to end up in the hands of *The New York Times*. The missive was printed in the July 24 edition, a portion of which runs as follows:

> Billie darling, I am nearly insane. For God's sake cable me what it is all about. I am not afraid of the truth, and I swear to God there is nothing to which you can take exception. Wait until I am proven guilty.[11]

The scandal was everything Charles Frohman and Billie's friends had feared for her back in 1914: that Flo was one leopard whose spots could surely not be changed. Billie must have wondered whether she should have listened to their advice. A reporter from the *Times* came out to Maine to interview Billie and found her "pale and tired, and her eyes were red with weeping." Even for a woman trained not to show the slightest weakness in public, this invasion of her private life at a most critical moment was clearly too much. When asked if the rumor were true, that she was planning to divorce Flo, Billie didn't say she wouldn't. "I'll affirm nothing," she said wearily. "I'll deny nothing." She didn't believe Marilyn's accusations, but wouldn't say why.

She had nothing further to say about Flo except to defend him from Marilyn's allegations, but this was probably just bluffing — she seems to have realized that the only way out of the mess was to back Flo all the way. The next day, when she was in Boston, she was even more explicit in her new role as defender of Flo Ziegfeld: "There is no trouble of any kind," she insisted. "Mr. Ziegfeld is coming back to America, but it is not because of anything Miss Miller may have said. I have not the slightest intention of leaving him."[12]

When Flo arrived home, however, Billie was in a very different mood. The moment he came in the door she faced him down. "Let's not try to make this thing up," she told him, "if there is only a slim chance [of being successful]" — that while life could obviously not go on as it had done before, it had to go on in some semblance of a marriage, for Patricia's sake if for nothing else. But Flo, who fell back on humor and assumed that smile that so infuriated Billie whenever he was cornered, played his part like a comic character dropped into a tragedy. He just grinned, dug into his pocket, brought out a $25,000 diamond bracelet from Tiffany's, and displayed the sparkling bauble to Billie as a peace offering. Billie took one look, grabbed the bracelet and threw it. Young Patricia, who happened to be in the room, caught the bracelet as it flew through the air; evidently considering it a spoil of war, she kept it for herself, occasionally letting her mother wear it.

And so, despite this very public evidence that all was not well in the Ziegfeld marriage, life did go on — Flo into planning his next *Follies*, Billie into rehearsals for another Tarkington play, *Rose Briar*. The Ziegfeld marriage had turned a sharp new corner, challenging Billie's equilibrium as Mrs. Ziegfeld. Also challenged, perhaps even more so, was her identity as actress. Because not only was time conspiring to alter the familiar landscape of her career, but Flo was making it even harder for her to accept the changes — inevitable, inescapable — that were coming her way.

"The Roaring Twenties were very pleasant," Billie wrote, as one who knew, "if you did not stop to think." That described her marriage, too.[13]

"As my star flickered," Billie remembered, "Flo's activities in the theater assumed even greater importance."[14] He did not have the time, truth told, to run the *Follies* and be Billie's manager, a fact Billie had already discovered but about which she could apparently do nothing. What she calls her "interrupted career" puttered on; when it ran off the tracks, usually when Flo was distracted at the switch, he did make efforts to put it back on course, though not always in the direction in which Billie wanted to go.

Flo next starred Billie in Booth Tarkington's comedy *Rose Briar*, in which, with an irony she could not then appreciate, she played an heiress who has lost her fortune. To survive, she has to perform as a cabaret singer (shades of Billie's future transformation from leading lady to character actress). At the cabaret she meets a cold society woman, Mrs. Valentine, who hopes to use her to gain a divorce from her husband so she may marry another man, Paradee, who turns out to be the man Rose Briar is herself interested in. Rose plays a double game by agreeing to be the correspondent while at the same time seducing Paradee. She succeeds, and the Valentines decide to give their marriage another go. Billie, gowned in an eighteenth century costume, was featured in an opening "Pompadour" cabaret sequence for which Flo pulled out all the stops: showgirls emerged bathed in Joseph Urban's plangent blue lighting wearing elaborate Ben Ali Haggan outfits, while Billie performed Jerome Kern's song "Love and the Moon."[15]

Despite the fact that she was the showcased performer, Billie's part in *Rose Briar* was not well-received, while that of Julia Hoyt, as Mrs. Valentine, was praised. But Hoyt and the production's gorgeous sets could not ensure a long life: *Rose Briar* finished its run at the Empire Theatre after only eleven weeks.[16]

Billie was not very excited about *Rose Briar*, despite admiring and liking its author, but she was obsessed with another play by a writer she had never met. Born Ferenc

Neumann in Budapest in 1878 to a prosperous Jewish family, the man we know as Ferenc Molnár got his start as a journalist, short story writer and novelist, then began writing plays. His first success was *The Devil* (1907), which was produced in 1908 at New York's Garden Theatre and ran for eighty-seven performances. His next big success on Broadway was *Liliom*, well known as the source for the Rodgers and Hammerstein musical *Carousel*, which played the Garrick Theatre from April to June 1921. Brilliant young actress Eva Le Gallienne had starred as Julie in the premiere.

Billie was convinced that this new part, as Princess Alexandra in Molnár's 1921 comedy *The Swan*, was perfect for her in every way. It was, she wrote, "my chance to return to the theatre in a play of major importance in a role that I could have acted to my credit." Gilbert Miller, son of actor Henry and the new head of the Frohman Company, had made the offer — not an overture likely to have pleased Flo, who seems to have had very different plans for Billie and was, in any case, never a friend of the Frohmans.'

And ironically, it is possible, too, that Flo's vision for Billie's future had much in common with Charles Frohman's, in that he seems to have been preparing Billie for a gradual transformation into a character comedienne.

The Swan is the story of a young princess, Alexandra, whose mother, Princess Beatrice, is hell bent on engaging her to the crown prince of Molnár's Ruritanian kingdom, in an effort to restore the fortunes of her own declining house. When the crown prince shows insufficient ardor toward Alexandra, Beatrice enlists the family's handsome young tutor to take her daughter to the ball and make the crown prince jealous. The tutor ends up in love with Alexandra, and she with him, but duty prevails, and they part at the end so that Alexandra can be married into the royal family. The irony, subtly underscored by Molnár, is that Princess Beatrice, herself descended from arranged marriages, involves the family tutor because the crown prince is not showing the ardor for Alexandra that would have been more characteristic of love marriage than royal marriage.

In her memoirs Billie wrote that of all the parts that she had ever read, this was the one she felt sure was perfect for her, the part she had been "waiting and hoping for." She talked to Flo about it and told him she must accept the offer. Flo didn't hang back to consider — he gave her, as her manager, a flat refusal. Billie's frustrations over the past few years, through the Marilyn Miller incident, the ongoing dalliances, what she considered less than stellar plays Flo had placed her in, erupted in a tantrum; "I shrilled about my career," she recalled. She was so furious she broke all the china on their sideboard.

Billie claimed to know the reason for Flo's refusal to allow her to play Princess Alexandra: "He was jealous of Gilbert Miller," she writes. None of the plays Flo produced for her had advanced her career; none seem to have been roles she really wanted to do. Now here was one that she believed could start her on a whole new path, and Flo, "calm and sullen," stood in the way.[17]

But while Billie reports that Flo later admitted to her, even after Eva Le Gallienne's successful run in *The Swan*, that he was wrong and should have let her accept the part, it is more likely it was not jealousy at all that motivated his initial refusal but the need to defend Billie against herself. The role she wanted so badly to play was that of a young woman, no older than her late teens. In 1923, when *The Swan* went into rehearsal, Billie was thirty eight years old. From a distance, and depending on the lighting and makeup, she didn't look it, but there is a big difference between a married actress with a child pretending to be a virginal eighteen, and how the part could and should be played — by a genuinely young woman, imbued with the authentic freshness of maidenly naiveté and grace. A young woman who, one should add, was also suited to the part dramatically. Le Gallienne, who was in her early twenties when she played Alexandra, was everything the playwright could have asked for. Not only had she been Molnár's first Broadway Julie, but she came from a background of European culture and refinement, was multi-lingual and friend of such theatre immortals as Eleanore Duse, had a fresh beauty and quiet intensity of manner, that perfectly mirrors the qualities of the fictional Alexandra.

For all the new "quiet charm" lauded by Woollcott in *The Intimate Strangers*, Billie's stage presence was not one that would or could rely on the simple mesmerizing glow of presence. She had to be in motion every moment, as attested to in almost every review ever written about her — even the adulatory critiques make note of her distracting hyperactivity behind the footlights. (Her only film role emphasizing an unflustered serenity against a backdrop of frantic activity is that of Glinda the Good.)

What Flo may not have been willing to admit to Billie was that if there was any part she could have played with assurance of success in *The Swan*, it was that of Princess Beatrice, the busybody mother determined to marry her daughter to the son of a king. In fact, if Billie had been able to see it, this role and not that of the ingénue could have started her properly on the path to character acting that she only came to by necessity years later and with huge effort. She was the right age to play Princess Beatrice, would have been more than plausible as Le Gallienne's mother, and could have made much of the role with her Victorian fussiness, her catty asides, her plotting and scheming. But it was only in her later years, on the threshold of old age, that Billie was able to write: "Many a woman has lost out because she insisted on playing the ingénue when she should have played the mother, often the more rewarding part." Where *The Swan* was concerned, she still found it possible to think of herself as an ingénue, despite being nearly twice the age needed for that qualification, and nowhere nearly as versatile as the role demands.[18]

It was becoming clearer all the time that Billie's true gift was comedy, not the searching dramas she dreamed of performing. It is not one of the lesser ironies of Billie Burke's career that when she finally did perform in a Molnár role — that of the Countess Di Meina in *The Bride Wore Red*, the 1937 film version of his play *The Girl from Trieste* — she plays just the sort of role she could have made her own thirteen years earlier. "This was my chance," she wrote of Alexandra, "and I lost it." The truth is, had she been more aware of her real gifts — which did not need to rely on attempts at appearing the ever-youthful beauty of Broadway but tapped her genius for self-deprecating comedy and clowning — Billie would have recognized that her big chance no longer lay in playing the leading lady but in taking on the colorful supporting character roles which age and changing tastes were making her more fitted to play.

Had Billie started playing character parts at this time — and as her skill and timing as a comedienne improved — she might have graduated easily to character roles of real substance, instead of throwaway supporting roles in which she was a curiosity instead of crucial to plot. By trying to avoid the inevitable, she would find herself locked into the dithery society matron roles that were, unfortunately for her ideals, so plausible not despite her efforts to constantly be glamorous and beautiful, but because of them.[19]

When Flo wanted her to star in *Annie Dear,* a musical version of Clare Kummer's *Good Gracious Annabelle,* Billie had no choice but to do the part. Not only was it work, without which she was frustrated and unhappy, but it meant money, and the Ziegfeld household was in need of it.

Patricia was experiencing health problems that Billie, probably accurately, believed were caused by the stress of the Ziegfeld lifestyle. Billie monitored Patricia's health like a zealous head nurse, trying out different diets to give energy or curb allergies, and keeping a stash of medicines on hand despite her on again-off again espousal of Christian Science. (As Billie's son-in-law, William Stephenson, once joked, "She was a Christian Scientist who wore a St. Christopher medal!")[20]

Billie also experienced bouts of severe anxiety about the erratic household cash flow. While she was as much a spendthrift as Flo, unlike him Billie had periodical bouts of depression when the bills piled up. In 1923, Flo and Billie owed money on their electric bill, to the point where, as Richard Ziegfeld points out, they had lost credit with the municipality of Hastings; Flo always had creditors coming at him for costs related to costumes and sets and all other aspects of productions, whether for goods delivered or goods rejected (there were on average as many of the latter as the former). The Ziegfelds were in arrears to their decorator, Elsie Sloan Farley, who refused to do any more work until at least part of her bill was paid. Flo started off 1924 by owing $10,000 in rent for the New Amsterdam Roof Theatre.

It didn't help that the Ziegfelds continued chartering yachts for weeks at a time, and took out a ninety-nine-year lease on an island in the Canadian Laurentians. Renamed Billie Burke Island, the centerpiece of this rustic paradise was Camp Patricia, which boasted a half-dozen log cabins, all of them fitted with plumbing and electricity; a staff of eighteen attended to the needs of the family and their guests. The place could not have been more remote — it took the boatman a dozen miles to bring back supplies in the Chris-Craft. Camp Patricia was expensive, but it was a place for the Ziegfelds to get away from the far greater expenditures of life at Burkeley Crest and New York City. And it was nowhere near a casino, a fact that was to become more important to Billie with time.

The trips to Florida that had started after Billie made *Peggy* in 1916 were also burning through what money the couple had. Billie claims it was producer Charles Dillingham who, with wife Aileen, enticed the Ziegfelds to Palm Beach. Though Billie and Flo were careful to lease a house that was within their budget, this prudence was soon abandoned and they began renting bigger houses to reflect, if not match, the grandiose wealth of their friends. Expensive parties given by these people, and Flo's romantic attachments to a few rich women (one of them Louisa Wanamaker Munn, related to most of what stood for Palm Beach royalty), emboldened the Ziegfelds to do the same, without the endless funds to pay for it all. Billie describes parties which, from the perspective of the more sober late 1940s, was like gazing back through a looking-glass into a wonderland that could not possibly have existed, which hardly seemed real. It all had to be paid for, and that involved another problem that came along with these social circles: gambling.[21]

Flo began to haunt the gambling casino of the Bradley brothers. For a man for whom every part of life was essentially a gamble, Bradley's had Flo as attached to the roulette wheel as an addict to heroin. From occasional evenings Flo began to spend all night at Bradley's, winning or losing thousands of dollars without batting an eyelash, egged on by the huge stakes won and lost by men far wealthier than he. He was, wrote Billie, "determined to break the bank, determined to be the best." This obsession became especially embarrassing for Billie when the Ziegfelds were entertaining, because Flo would disappear for hours on end, and the last thing Billie wanted to tell her friends was that her husband had a gambling problem. She would slip over to the casino on her bicycle and look in the windows at him. He knew she was there, but couldn't even look up to acknowledge her. He would wave her away without meeting her eyes, and she would ride back to their house, crying, "struck by the irony of having survived all I had survived only to lose my husband to a roulette wheel." It got to the point where Irving Berlin, who had saved the day when Patricia was born by writing a song to mother and child, now wrote another one to Billie called "The Gambler's Bride." It helped to see the situation as funny, but when Flo lost thousands of dollars that then could not be used to pay bills, it was not funny at all.[22]

Billie admits to giving way to her now familiar temper tantrums, making threats and smashing crockery, while Flo sat and smiled or pretended nothing was happening. She realized she would have to do something a little more serious than break dishes. After one bout of gambling in which Flo lost more than he won and stayed out till all hours, Billie reserved rooms at a nearby hotel and started the staff packing her and Patricia's things. There had been an argument the night before, Patricia remembered: "Mother was saying things like 'This must stop' and 'Where will it all end' and 'Think of the child.'" Flo retorted that she was making a mountain out of a molehill and suggested she stop "chewing the scenery for a change," which resulted in Billie bolting from the room, furious; Flo followed, slamming out of the house.

When he returned the next morning, not quite recovered from what must have been one of the few times this teetotaler had had a few too many, the staff was lined up, bags were packed and ready, and Billie and Patricia stood waiting for him, their coats and hats on. Flo asked what was going on — Billie announced she was leaving him and taking Patty with her. She headed for the door, Patty and the small army of servants following with the luggage, when Flo jumped down the stairs, took Billie's arm, and asked if he could have just five minutes alone with her. They went into the living room, and in what was a kind of rehearsal for Billie's first talking picture role ten years later, as the wife of madman John Barrymore in *A Bill of Divorcement*, Flo not only talked Billie out of leaving but swore that he would never let his gambling at Bradley's get out of control again.

Patricia wrote, "He never went back on his word," but Billie's recollection of the scene was somewhat different: "I had no more trouble with him *that* year." Flo being

Flo, the problems with creditors would have continued in any case, from some other quarter.[23]

When the prospect of doing *Annie Dear* arose, in 1923, Billie may not have been thrilled with the idea but she and Flo needed the money the show could bring. She also seemed to know a couple of other things: that it meant a great deal to Flo to produce a show that starred his wife, particularly after the difficult patches they had been through over the past few years, and that this Kummer musical comedy was something she needed to do, as much for development of her career as for the fact that she did need the work. "Let's do a musical comedy with lots of comedy," she telegrammed Flo early that year. "If I have a funny face we might just as well use it." It was as if the comic muse which had been knocking at Billie's stage door for so long was finally making herself heard, if still indistinctly, because comedy, as usual, was the thing Billie turned to as a last resort.[24]

Some people still think Billie performed in the *Follies*—an error she, for all her loyalty to Flo, was quick to correct by pointing out that she was a *legitimate stage actress*—but if they do, it is likely because of her starring part in *Annie Dear*. Because Flo took Clare Kummer's little pastel of a plot, in which a runaway bride is reunited with her groom, and turned it into a *Follies*-worthy extravaganza.

Billie played Annie Leigh, who has fled the rough embraces of her fiancé, a wealthy mine owner named John Rawson, and taken a job as maid on an estate in Long Island owned by another metal magnate, George Wimbledon. Rawson turns up but without his beard, so Annie doesn't recognize him, and it all works out in the end when they are reunited. What Flo did to jazz up this story, besides providing the most lavish of sets and costumes and a score by Sigmund Romberg and Harry Tierney, was to insert a ballet in which Billie became the boy in a sketch titled "Little Boy Blue's Search for the Crock of Gold at the End of the Rainbow." By the end of the ballet and discovery of the crock of gold, Billie encountered Cloud, Moon, Rain, Wind and all the other friends and foes of nature, finishing off with a gorgeous rainbow.[25]

It was this last act fantasia that drew raves — the *New York Times* called it "so comprehensive a whimsy that everything from French pastry to flowers and thunder may be seen stalking the stage"—but Billie was also congratulated: "Miss Burke proved to be altogether delightful in the leading role.... With the opportunities provided by musical comedy, she was never more lovely to look upon." There was a childlike quality in Billie's stagework that allowed her to play both Annie Leigh and the Little Boy Blue (which was Billie's last "trouser" role for the stage); and it was probably because Flo loved to think of her that way (she signed her letters and telegrams to him, after all, as "Baby") that he crafted the ballet with her in mind.[26]

Bernard Sobel was there on opening night at the Times Square Theatre on November 5, 1924. Of all the men who knew Flo, Sobel knew the best of his best and the worst of his worst — the dreams and the innovations, the womanizing and the gambling. But he also knew, as Billie first walked on stage as Annie Leigh, how much Flo loved her. He remembered that Flo stood in the background, well out of the lights of the stage. He was not aware of Sobel's presence or, if he was, soon forgot as he focused on Billie's entrance. As she came on stage, "I heard a kind of muffled sob," Sobel recalled, "and as I looked up, I saw the tears coursing down his cheeks." What was Flo feeling at that moment of emotion? The thrill of producing a show again for the wife he had neglected both professionally and, occasionally, personally? Remorse over the Marilyn Miller affair? Gratitude at having married such a lovely and talented woman who, though he had given her plenty of reason to walk out, had the grit to stick with him? Maybe none of the above. It was the child in Billie that Flo had adored from the beginning. And if *Annie Dear* emphasized those girlish traits, it may just have been simple sentimentality that caused the tears witnessed by Bernard Sobel. Having given that girl what was the best of himself—a beautiful show that could be enjoyed not just by the audience but by him and her—Flo was giving the best gift he could.[27]

Annie Dear was the last show Flo produced for Billie. She had made her final silent film, *The Education of Elizabeth*, in 1921; movie goers would not see her again until her first talking picture in 1932. And she would not star in another play until 1927. She had entered a period of artistic sterility, where she felt herself a "part-time artist."

"An artist," Billie wrote, "is a person who devotes himself ruthlessly, even selfishly, to his craft or skill." She believed the measure of an artist's integrity was not what critics thought but the greatness of his devotion to his art. She could not spare that devotion, because she had another job to do during those years off stage and screen: "It was simply to hold my husband." And all the sparkling parties at Burkeley Crest, the evenings with composers George Gershwin or Rudolf Friml at the piano, playing just for her, the lavish dinner parties in Palm Beach and the restful pleasures of Camp Patricia, could not take her mind off the one thing that, of all she could command, lay outside her power to possess: Flo Ziegfeld's heart and soul. Her hunger for this man's full devotion haunted her then, as it would haunt her for the rest of her life. If only Billie had looked into the wings that opening night of *Annie Dear*; if only Flo had not been standing so far in shadow.[28]

CHAPTER 14

A Beginning, and an End

If Billie thought the first ten years of her marriage to Flo were a three-ring circus, the next decade was to be far more challenging than anything that had come before, as artist and as woman.

After *Annie Dear*, in 1924, Billie did not work for three years. Not all of this time was spent doing the job she claimed was uppermost, holding on to Flo, unless by that she meant not just keeping him from straying but keeping up with his frenzied pace as he produced each new show, tried to outwit unions and the film industry that was undermining Broadway in general and the *Follies* in particular, kept a foot wedged in the doors of a half dozen high society homes in Palm Beach, where his hard-won friendships meant not just proximity to powerful and attractive rich men's wives but to their husbands' potential investment dollars, and evading his creditors as he hurtled along.

Over the past seven years that he had been managing Billie's career, Flo had tried a variety of ideas on her in a way not unlike Charles Frohman's methods — from drama to high comedy, then farce, and drama again, as if trying to crack the code to a safe. It wasn't that Billie was a complex actress — far from it. In finding the right vehicles, however, she was part of the problem. She was not unusual in having absolutely no idea what was right for her. This was not necessarily because she was deaf to her own talents; but she had been guided and shaped by powerful personalities, including her mother, since the beginning of her career. She had never really had to ponder who she was or what she had to offer. She knew how she wanted to be seen, which is not the same as knowing how she *should* be seen. Heir to her father's comic gifts but dissuaded from developing them by a bent toward high drama instilled in her by Blanche's worship of Ellen Terry and Sir Henry Irving, and by what may have been Blanche's distaste for comedy altogether, Billie found herself approaching middle age, the bloom going off the rose, and with no clear idea where to go next. So for thirty-six months, she went nowhere — except Palm Beach and Camp Patricia and all the other playgrounds the Ziegfelds cavorted in as the Twenties roared on.

Those three years were a time of struggle for Flo, too, characteristically not in terms of his marriage to Billie but his marriage to the *Follies*, but they were also a time of reconfiguration of direction and purpose. Where he and Billie differed was that while she resisted remaking herself to survive as an artist, Flo saw that the era of the *Follies* was coming to an end and that only a new special kind of entertainment could replace it, drawing on the singing, dancing, design and music that made the *Follies* shows great but concentrated within the defined boundaries of a plot and characterization. *Showboat* was to be the result of this transformation of the Ziegfeldian dream and Flo's greatest accomplishment, far outweighing the success of his four big hits of the late 1920s, *Rio Rita*, *Rosalie*, *The Three Musketeers* and *Whoopee!*, the latter a huge success for star Eddie Cantor. These were book musicals, but none of them had the weight or depth of *Showboat*. Edna Ferber's tale of the loves, hates, struggles and pleasures of the staff and passengers of the *Cotton Blossom*, it was to be, in revival, Flo's last expression of the art form he did more than anyone else to create and support, the lavish book musical, the synthesis of words, music, dance and spectacle, just before his death in 1932.

The *New York Times* for these years follows Billie about her routine of being Mrs. Ziegfeld: one article even describes her as Mrs. Florenz Ziegfeld, Jr., "who was Billie Burke"—a telling impression of how she was being seen at this time. In the Palm Beach winter season of 1926, Billie made the news not for her acting but for taking lessons in the "Charleston" from a "negro Charleston exponent" named Lucky Roberts. She was in a car accident, one of her several narrow escapes in automobile crashes: she, James R. Hyde and Louisa Wanamaker Munn (Flo's rumored mistress) were being driven in what was probably Mrs. Munn's limousine when they were broadsided by a speeding touring car and tipped over. Louisa's collarbone was broken and Hyde was also injured enough to need medical assistance, but Billie (in a continued streak of vehicular good luck) got away with a few bruises and some minor scratches to her face. But when the dust cleared and she saw she had survived collision again, did Billie stop to wonder if there was a connection between her cars running off the road and her life running off its rails?[1]

Then it was Patricia's turn to make the papers, in June of that year, when her pink leather jewel case, containing thousands of dollars' worth of keepsakes and gifts from the Ziegfelds' friends, was stolen from Flo's offices. It had been kept in a safe in the office of Sam Kingston, Flo's general manager. Also taken were some of the real jewels Flo had had created for his production of *Louie the Fourteenth*—possibly making him admit for the first time that his demands for authenticity on the stage could be a decided liability. Flo had actually asked for Patricia's jewel case to be taken out of the safe, but as it was being brought down from the ninth floor by Kingston's secretary Emily England, to where Flo's chauffeur was waiting, the man drove off, necessitating the box's return to the safe. It was said that Miss England forgot to lock the safe. Some time after 3 P.M., when Miss England went to Flo's office, the pink box and its contents, worth $10,000, was stolen. Neither were ever found.

This was not the first time stolen jewelry figured in Flo's history. In 1906, during the tryout tour for Anna Held's show *The Parisian Model*, all of her jewelry was stolen while she was on the train was between Harrisburg, Pennsylvania, and Cleveland, Ohio. It was pointed out in one newspaper article that Ziegfeld's passion for realism, which included using real gems, might have unfortunately provided negative advertising for Anna's collection; she herself was quoted as bragging about using real instead of rhinestone. Various theories and leads were explored by police, but the jewels were never found, and the strangeness of the theft—a thief who knew where to find the jewel case on the train, the thief never being caught, the fruitless leads, and Flo's perennial need for money — unsettled Anna, who was already having trouble in her relationship with Flo. Anna's daughter, Liane Carrera, who was no fan of Flo's, insisted in her biography of her mother that Flo engineered the theft to replenish production coffers. There is no proof of this and the dates and circumstances she specifies do not hold up against Flo's known schedule and activities. Had Flo, by some quirk made the more eccentric by the fact that he was a doting father who considered his life's work to make Patricia as happy as possible, somehow been involved in this theft, his daughter's jewel case worth $10,000 would hardly have scratched the surface of his pecuniary needs at the time. He may have needed the money, but if he was going to steal it he needed a lot of it — because his most lavish production was already on its way.

Flo was obsessed with building his own theatre which, aided by his friend and colleague William Randolph Hearst's immense capital, he did, at Sixth Avenue and Fifty-Fourth Street. The Ziegfeld Theatre, as it was called, became every bit the palace of female glorification even Flo Ziegfeld could have dreamed of. Costing $2.5 million and seating over 1600 audience members, the Theatre was a showcase of Flo's entertainment credo: dazzling décor, the very latest in technological gadgetry for the fulfillment of ever more special effects on stage, and rich with dressing rooms and seating in which comfort was no afterthought or accident but the standard upon which the entire house was built. Joseph Urban and Thomas W. Lamb designed the building, and Urban also provided murals, one of which formed the only such artwork in any New York theatre to stretch across an entire ceiling. Urban's frescoed fantasy drew heavily on a mélange of medieval imagery: a "mad medley of knights, ladies, knaves, archers, men-at-arms, charging steeds, antelopes, unicorns, castles in Spain," wrote *New York Times* architecture critic H. I. Brock, erotically crowded together in a style that surviving photographs reveal to have owed something more to Gustav Klimt than to illuminated books of hours. What most impressed Brock was the fact that the façade bore none of the neon jewelry of the conventional Broadway theatre. Where other houses proclaimed their identities on all available surfaces in a gaudy welter of colors and lighting effects, very nearly crowding out the names of stars on the marquee, the Ziegfeld's coolly pilastered, elegantly bowed front, gorgeously washed at night by hidden spotlights, not to mention the building's name and what was offered inside it, served as its own best advertisement.[2]

Castles in Spain indeed — but the wave of success Flo was riding at this point, just before the waterfall crashed over the cliff's edge, seemed to promise even more. The Ziegfeld Theatre, with its splendor and its proclamation that a Ziegfeld show, like a Wagner opera, could only flower in a setting designed by its creator, spoke as much to the spending and heedlessness of the 1920s as to the people who flocked to it and its record-breaking shows. But perhaps even Flo and Billie had some idea of the impermanence of it all, of the need to salvage what they could from the more permanent past. For the laying of the cornerstone on December 9, 1926, at which Will Rogers spoke piously (and not quite truthfully) of the fact that Flo had chosen the corner of Sixth Avenue and Fifty-Fourth Street because of its "absence of saloons," Billie and young Patricia placed a number of items into the bronze box inside the stone. There were some remarkably personal enclosures: photographs of Rosalie, Flo's mother, of Billie and Patricia. There was also a program from *Sally*, that hit that made Marilyn

Miller a household name. There was even a brick from an ancient Greek theatre, the significance of which seemed to be that while the amphitheatres of Aeschylus and Euripides were well and good for their day, they couldn't hold a candle to Flo's new theatre and *Rio Rita*, *Betsy* or *Showboat*, the shows planned for it.

What, though, was the significance of the photograph of Charles Frohman, which Billie reverently placed inside a metal box that was to be sealed and placed forever in the dark, under the weight of tons of masonry? Was she relegating Frohman to the museum of memory, now that he was transmogrified into a Broadway legend? Or was she putting away a part of her past that no longer seemed relevant, or that she no longer wished to contemplate? Did she wonder if it had been worth it to betray and hurt this man who had been the Pygmalion of her theatre career? Or was it Flo's dark joke that the past was the past, and placing Frohman's photograph in a sort of grave was his silver bullet in the heart of Billie's former Svengali, laying him low for good?

Billie, characteristically, says nothing of this ceremony in her memoirs. She, like so many people who were there that day, was blinded by the lights and the glamour that trailed the waning decade of conspicuous excess. And she had a lot on her mind — to get her career back on the rails, though where it was leading her was a place she had tried for years to avoid.[3]

If Billie really did spend her three year hiatus holding on to Flo, she wasn't completely occupied with him. She was also preparing herself for her next big role, one which was a kind of harking back to the elegant drawing room comedies she had played in the early 1900s. In fact Marie Tempest, the actress Charles Frohman seems to have tried to pattern Billie after, had scored one of her biggest London successes in Noël Coward's *The Marquise*, the play Billie was set to perform in. It was also an example of Billie, having been offered a prime part by a producer other than her husband, finally getting her way, this time in a role that worked hand in hand with her age and experience: a woman of the world, in her 40s, and a mother.

An interesting article appeared in the *New York Times* two days before Billie opened in the play. Offering on the surface a story about the genesis of *The Marquise*, the rising career of Noël Coward, and the fact that the play had been written with Marie Tempest specifically in mind, the writer seems to have been privy to the machinations required to sign Billie on with a producer other than her own husband. It is probable that Coward already had Billie in mind for the American premiere, because based on the stipulations he cabled to David Burton, who served as the play's director, Billie was the first actress contacted. Burton had worked for the Frohman Company when Billie had still been on contract there. He sent Billie the script, and cabled Coward asking him his thoughts on the matter of Billie playing the lead role. Coward sent back a one word affirmation: "Splendid."

The producers of *The Marquise* were writer, actor, director, producer and person of interest in Billie's second film career, Kenneth MacGowan, and Sidney Ross (who had only produced one other play, *If*). The article makes an intriguing statement: that as Burton "was stumped for a player not obligated to another management," he approached Billie, evidently believing she was no longer tied to Flo as her manager.

Billie gave something of that impression in her reply to Burton's letter, for after looking the play over she called him and said "she would be delighted to act in 'The Marquise,'" and that she foresaw no problems with Flo. Was Flo just too busy with his several projects of this period to have the time to oversee Billie's return to the stage? Was her career actually under her own control for the first time in years? Had her decision to not divorce him after the Marilyn Miller mess given Billie a certain leverage in choosing her own roles?

The play was certainly the kind she loved: a costume drama set in the mid–eighteenth century, in which she could wear hooped gowns and powdered hair and heart-shaped *mouche* patches on her face (as was seen in a sketch of Billie as the Marquise de Kestournel, appearing in the same issue of the *New York Times* as the above-mentioned article), in which she could stop Time by stepping out of the present back into the past.[4]

Coward, who did not particularly care for Flo (he seems to have considered him something of a sideshow barker), does not mention Billie in his memoirs, and the whole experience of writing *The Marquise* had occurred under circumstances of nervous exhaustion, not likely to have attached fond memories to the play. But he must have been happy with the play's reception at its November 15, 1927, Broadway premiere, and the play itself, which is a frothy bagatelle with a hard, sparkling charm at the center.

This was Billie's first time on the stage playing a character her own age. Described as "a Mother in Frills and Ruffles," Billie swept through the play as the forty-two-year-old Marquise Eloise de Kestournel, a former actress who must confront not just two lovers from her past but the children she bore them, a boy and girl who now want to get married, not knowing they are half-siblings. Besides preventing this incestuous marriage (though only a shade more so than the aristocratic uncle/niece marriages with which the eighteenth and nineteenth centuries abounded), Eloise intends to capture the lover dearest to her memory, the recently widowed Raoul Compte de Vriaac, who has hardened his heart against her. As she had done in saucy *Mrs. Dot*, tailored by Somerset Maugham for Tempest's elegant comic delivery, Billie had fun with this role that was also written with Tempest's voice and presence in mind.

When one character tells her he believes in self-sacrifice Eloise replies with charming drollery, "You're wrong then. It's one of the most sterile forms of self-indulgence in the world." Billie's growing maturity as actress and person was encapsulated in that amusing line, and was not lost on reviewers: Billie was "loveliness itself"—the commentary on her physical appearance that was always to be part of any review of any performance—but it was noted that she presented a sophisticated but feeling portrait of a woman of a certain age. One critic was so impressed he declared that Billie's Marquise should cheer "those who feel middle age creeping on them."

Billie's *savoir faire* was certainly in evidence one night during the eighty performance run. Richard Rodgers was in the front row of the Biltmore Theatre. The play is set entirely in the drawing room of the Compte de Vriaac, with its regulation assortment of side tables and armchairs, tapestries and candlesticks. During one scene in this setting, Rodgers happened to notice that the bell-pull, which Eloise pulls frequently, dissatisfied with the Compte de Vriaac's disorganized household, was on fire. While yanking on the rope Billie must have let it drift too close to one of the several lighted candles on tabletop or mantelpiece. When she caught sight of Rodgers frantically waving his handkerchief at her, she looked at the flaming bell-pull as if it were no more annoying than a fly that had gotten into the house, twitched a cloth off a table, and snuffed out the flames. She then said to her leading man, Arthur Byron, "I've told the butler a dozen times to have that rope repaired."

Billie's quick action was perfectly in character with Eloise, and did not interrupt the play in the least. Rodgers' experience gives a clue to the development of one of the most endearing facets of the persona she was to create as a character actor: a woman so wrapped up in her own fantasy of how life should be, that there is no way a flaming bell-pull (*The Marquise*) or a ruined dinner party (*Dinner at Eight*) or an evil green witch (*The Wizard of Oz*) can move her to do more than register amused dismay at life's often disordered puzzle, and move along, smiling, toward brighter and better things.[5]

Billie's next play, Harrison Owen's bit of tinsel titled *The Happy Husband*, was a throwback to her older roles, where she could skip through the plot, ever the pert Miss Burke, wearing beautiful clothes that earned more applause than her performance, and still emerge a box office draw. Australian-born Owen took stray bits of dialogue and plotline from every playwright who ever penned a drawing room comedy and stitched them into this successful play, which is nothing more than the story of how Dot Rendell (Billie), married for nine years to a husband who takes her for granted, assumes the guilt of Consuelo Pratt, another wife but with a very jealous husband, who has been caught in a compromising situation with the neighborhood rake.

As Brooks Atkinson commented dryly in his review of the May 7, 1928, premiere: "Every charm-

Billie played Dot Rendell, a woman trying her best to earn a bad reputation, in 1928's *The Happy Husband*. This was her last non-character role.

ing woman deserves to be the instrument of scandal." As some in the audience must have been aware, *The Happy Husband* was yet another inadvertently staged piece of Billie's life offstage, perhaps a form of wish-fulfillment for the woman who could not be unfaithful to Flo no matter how many women he bedded and no matter how often she herself must have been tempted; who was far more simpatico with the jealous and outraged Mr. Pratt than her cucumber-cool stage husband, Mr. Rendell. The play would certainly have been fascinating to see from that perspective — no critic, however, dared point it out. But then *The Happy Husband* was a return to the bad old days of lightweight Billie Burke drawing room comedies: perhaps its very lightness glossed over any deeper ironies of its star's role. It is clear that as Dot, Billie's characterization had none of the sweep, charm or pathos of her recent role in *The Marquise*— it was back to Billie's technique of busily rushing about the stage, as if acting as fast as possible achieved the same effect as a magician's prestidigitation, distracting the eye so the wizard can vanish off stage left.

"Miss Burke plays with a girlish rhythm that is often distracting," Atkinson remarked, in the only direct reference to her in a general glowing review that praises the actors for making the most of a poor script. In an article of over a year and a half later, Atkinson was still prodding Billie for resorting to the tricks of her youth. Referring to Billie's abject failure, *Family Affairs*, which followed *The Happy Husband* and ran for only a week, the critic declares that were it in his power to do so, he would close down such "innocuous prattle" as this play and others that season, "merely to rescue such beauties as Jane Cowl and Billie Burke from their current insipidities." Billie was a "beguiling person" who was wasting herself in "fubsy comedy." That this kind of country house comedy was what she had founded her fame on is never mentioned, but anyone with the memory to recollect the Billie Burke of *Mrs. Dot* and *The Amazons* would probably also be able to do the math and see that while Miss Burke was still very beguiling, she was aging, a fact that was becoming more obvious with each season.[6]

It was at this point in Billie's professional experience that she realized the road she was taking had not an end but a fork, and the choice of which side-road to take was now at hand. She was offered a role in Ivor Novello's *The Truth Game*. Matronly Evelyn Brandon was the point at which Billie could not turn back, the stepping over the fine line she had been skirting for years but which pride and fear had prevented her from crossing. She was to play her first character part, and it was, as she recalled years later, "a sad and bewildering moment" for her, when she

Billie Burke beloved stage and screen star, is a miracle of youthful loveliness at 40! "Youth has irresistible attraction," she says. "To keep this charm right through the years you must guard complexion beauty— keep your skin temptingly fresh and smooth. I use Lux Toilet Soap— regularly."

Recent photograph by Nickolas Muray, New York

Throughout her long career, Billie endorsed various beauty products, claiming they helped her retain her youthful beauty. In this ad for Lux Toilet Soap, however, which was run in 1932, she was eight years older than the forty claimed by the ad.

Billie Burke was always careful to quash rumors that she had ever performed in a Ziegfeld *Follies* by pointing out that she was a legitimate stage actress. Here, however, in a still (ca. 1920) from the Burke collection at the University of Southern California's Film and Television Library, she clearly donned *Follies*-like garb on at least one filmed occasion. University of Southern California Cinematic Arts Library collection.

"turned the corner. It was an imposing corner for me, because I have had to try to be funny ever since."[7]

That was hardly the worst corner for her and for Flo to turn that year of 1930. By then, they had lost almost everything they had when the stock market fell. Perhaps, in the way life had with Billie Burke, the trauma of upheaval and the quest to survive it helped ease Billie out of her old and fragile casing of Madame Hayworth gowns, flippant nothings pealed across drawing rooms, beaux swooning at her slippered feet. She had not been that winsome girl for many years. When she and Flo lost their fortune, Billie gained something in return — from the tattered chrysalis stepped a whole new person. And that person stepped into a new career on film, an effort that at first was meant to help her restore her life's equilibrium and security, but which also helped her to become the entertainer she was meant to be: the true daughter of a famous clown. As it happened, Billie did not have to try to be funny at all.

PART II
Silly Woman

She was the good witch with the dimpled voice
Who spoke to Dorothy in the *Wizard of Oz*;
"No place like home," she said, but meant "no choice,"
In terms of going along with nature's laws.

Peter Thorpe
Movie Star Sonnets (2004)

CHAPTER 15

Crash

"Flo's Wall Street speculations, like his show business affairs and like his gambling, were matters I never understood," Billie points out in her memoirs. It is easy to see why. Whereas money, to her, meant the feathering of nest and adorning of person and family, to Flo it was an ingredient which, when properly mixed in the laboratory of Wall Street or a gambling casino with equal parts testosterone and thrill, could sometimes guarantee an explosion of profits. And for Flo, whether profit or loss, it was that explosion (replete with Freudian subtext), what Billie calls his "*coups*," that mattered most.

Flo might have made one of history's more flamboyant military commanders, though whether he would have won any wars is moot. The fact was, everything he did had to astonish onlookers in the flickering colored light of fireworks, or it simply was not worth the trouble; and if the crowds oohed and aahed, he had won the battle.[1]

Yet Flo was clearly worried toward the end of 1929 by rumblings presaging what was to be the earthquake of Wall Street. It was not as simple as many think. One scholar studying the lead up to the Crash has opined that the meltdown was precipitated not just by the usual culprit — a feeding frenzy of speculation that drove the Dow Jones Industrial Average to a dizzying high of 381.2, a record, on September 3, 1929 — but by fear of over-speculation. A comment by Philip Snowden, Chancellor of the Exchequer in London, describing the American stock market as a "speculative orgy;" a decline in stock prices, including those of previously "solid" shares in public utilities; and President Herbert Hoover's campaign to fight speculation: each had a role to play. All of these together, and other factors besides, "triggered the October selling panic and the consequences that followed."[2]

Even at his Canadian getaway, Flo was worried about what was happening on Wall Street. While the Ziegfelds were summering at Camp Patricia, the signs of impending trouble were such that Flo resolved to sell his stocks. He sent the Chris-Craft bearing a telegram addressed to E.F. Hutton, ordering a full sale of his holdings, but a friend talked him out of it, based on advice from *his* portfolio manager. An element of comedy intruded when Flo had to send someone by a faster boat to intercept the Chris-Craft and tear up the telegram. If only Flo had stuck to his guns and allowed the sale, the next few years of his life, not to mention Billie's and Patricia's, might have been completely different.[3]

Far from being a fiddler while Wall Street burned, Flo had a keen enough sense of the pulse of any operation, be it a *Follies* show or the stock market, to know when something was not right. And yet it was for the most mundane of reasons that Flo lost everything in the crash of 1929, a reason peculiarly characteristic of a nature which could spend hand over fist one moment and refuse to pay royalties to his composers the next, which threw money into expensive details few in his audience would recognize or appreciate, and then haggled over small bills that could have been tended to by a lowly accountant. What concerned Flo on October 29, 1929, was a dispute over a mere $1,600 bill, from the Strauss Sign Company, which Flo, unhappy with the work, refused to pay. There was a sad history here that makes it hard to understand why any sign maker, or dress designer or composer, ever had anything to do with an impresario who had the notorious habit of engaging them for work which then had to pass an additional inspection — often the night of an opening — before he would pay them (and sometimes not even then), a habit that extended to royalty payments. Apparently undaunted, Strauss took Flo to court, which raised the Ziegfeld fighting instinct to high pitch. Not only did he appear at court that Tuesday, but brought along his entire staff for support, so certain Strauss could not prevail against such a Ziegfeldian onslaught. This would have left one person at Flo's offices — the telephone operator — but even she was absent the day of the Strauss hearing, having stayed home sick.

The office was, therefore, closed all day, just so Flo could demolish a petty sign maker for having the gall to not take no for an answer. As the market went into meltdown, E.F. Hutton, taking time out of the chaos of his own worst day's trading ever, tried to call Flo but could not find him. (It shows how distant, even nonexistent, Billie was seen to be in relation to Flo's financial affairs that Hutton didn't bother to phone her at Burkeley Crest to alert her, at least, to the unfolding disaster.)

By late afternoon, as Billie later claimed, Flo had lost "something more than a million dollars" in the "Wall Street unpleasantness." Richard Ziegfeld estimates the amount closer to $5 million. Whatever the real figure, except for Burkeley Crest and those bonds Charles Frohman had put away for Billie a lifetime ago, the Ziegfelds were wiped out.[4]

While Flo was spending precious time in a small claims court on the fateful 29th, what were his friends and colleagues doing? Eddie Cantor, who considered Flo his surrogate father and was treated as such by Flo, had just built a mansion in Great Neck, New York, on which he had spent "$65,000 just on shrubbery." Starting from the first days of the Crash, Cantor watched helplessly as he lost sometimes over $100,000 per day, until he realized that the only money he could actually put his hands on was the $60 in his trouser pocket. His heroic wife, Ida, who had seen him through plenty of thin times, was not one to call it quits. She handed Cantor her jewelry to sell, and insisted that letting go of their new home would "do something to your personality." There was a way out of the mess and Ida, Cantor in hand, was going to find it — and they did. Irving Berlin was in Hollywood that October, working on songs for *Puttin' on the Ritz*, when he heard at the studio commissary that the stock market had crashed. Characteristically, despite losing millions (on paper) and having to face the by now unaccustomed shock of having to survive from check to check, the creator of "God Bless America" saw in the Crash an opportunity and the inspiration for what became the

Crash-themed musical comedy with Douglas Fairbanks and Bebe Daniels, *Reaching for the Moon.*

Another member of Flo's circle, W.C. Fields, contented himself with an intact fortune scattered in bank accounts throughout the country — he had never believed in playing the stock market or living on credit. At the opposite end of the spectrum, Flo's publicist, Bernard Sobel, remembered being on the train to Boston when the news broke: men waving telegrams announcing vast losses ran up and down the aisles, the platform in Boston was crowded with people. When Sobel learned what had happened, he hurried to a newspaper, only to find on its front page that the Consolidated Film Plant, in which he held stocks outright, had burned down. Thus he suffered a double financial tragedy. Yet there was a certain solace to be gained even then, because as Sobel soon found out: "Everybody was in the same boat."[5]

To judge from her alarm at Flo's beaten appearance that evening, Billie had apparently been at Burkeley Crest all day, away from radios or visitors from town. When Flo came home late the night of the 29th, he sat on the edge of Billie's bed and looked so terrible Billie took him in her arms and asked what was wrong. Flo told her the bad news and began to sob, "great, struggling sobs." "I'm through," he told her. "Nothing can save me."

The next day, she watched as he walked through his beloved gardens, and again was chilled by the sight of the Great Ziegfeld stumbling along, like a condemned man trying to get in one last look at the world before mounting the scaffold. "I knew then that the next step was up to me," she wrote. She knew she had to go back to work — find a new play. She also knew that she still had some money, because the solid municipal bonds and government securities Charles Frohman and her other managers had put away for her were largely untouched by the crash. She had just had a meeting with her financial advisors earlier in the year, and had been told she had something like a half million dollars clear. It had made her feel so secure then, for Patricia and for Flo — like actress Vera Charles in *Auntie Mame,* who had spent all her money at Tiffany's and at least had something to show for it after the Crash — Billie still had her bonds, but not for long. It cost close to $10,000 per month to run Burkeley Crest, and Flo and Billie no longer had the cash flow to accommodate that expense. So they took out a mortgage on the house Billie had paid cash for in 1911. Knowing she and Flo were living on borrowed time, she sold out her bonds and certificates and gave everything to her husband. And she girded herself to go back to work.[6]

The play Billie opened in New York that December at the Ethel Barrymore Theatre was Ivor

A new maturity glows in this glamour shot of Billie from the late 1920s.

Novello's bright, brittle comedy, *The Truth Game*, the story of a rich young widow, played by Phoebe Foster, who will lose her husband's fortune if she remarries, and a penniless young man who, as it happens, stands to inherit the late husband's fortune if the widow does remarry. The dots are easily connected: Max Clement, played by Novello, falls in love with the woman he is trying to woo, and all ends charmingly.

Phoebe Foster's was a role Billie might well have taken on in her younger years. But her days of playing the love interest were over. Billie played Evelyn Brandon, a fussy, catty, witty and not entirely sincere character ("a young English matron") who "brazenly collects commissions at shops where her personal friends trade." It was Billie's first character role, and she encountered and battled with the frustration, confusion and sadness created when an actor must abandon who she has always been and become someone else.[7]

Billie had known Ivor Novello and Constance Collier for years, back in the days before she even had to think about money. Given the circumstances of Flo's financial failure and the gloom that had descended over New York and spread slowly over the rest of the world, it was a pleasure just to be working again, even if she had to play what she euphemistically termed "a gay little lady" whose effort to turn every friendship into a paying prospect was a far cry from being belle of the drawing room, and was also eerily close to Flo's style of making friends in Palm Beach.

The play's success meant that she was not just able to help her family finances, but that perhaps turning the corner to character acting had not been such a tragedy after all. J. Brooks Atkinson was certainly taken with her performance, as he wrote in *The New York Times*:

> Mr. Novello has conspicuous facility in writing attractive parts for himself and effective parts for actresses. In "The Truth Game" he has been generous not only with himself but with Billie Burke.... Miss Burke is sunny and spirited, bobbing lightly through the minor treacheries of a trade-edition comedy — and very pleasant to see and hear.[8]

Also of interest in Atkinson's review is his comment, among the first to be made by a journalist after the stock market crash, that Novello's romance would ably serve as lovely diversion for the wives of businessmen ruined by the events of October 29th. Soon enough, the entire entertainment industry would find a way of cashing in on diverting housewives and jobless men from their day to day financial distress with plays, films, and musicals, the main theme of which was the fun and romance of which their lives were bereft.

Ironically, Flo was still one of those purveyors of pleasure, despite being far worse off than most of the people who bought tickets to his productions. "The Depression caused Ziegfeld to question the Dream," writes Richard Ziegfeld. The beauty and style, the music and dance, that he had lavished on Broadway in close to eighty productions was disintegrating as if it had all been a mirage. He struggled through 1930 as Billie went on tour with *The Truth Game*, and she was with him their last good summer at Burkeley Crest, but it was a bittersweet respite. Surrounded by "the flowers freshly cut for every room every day, with the birds, the elephants, the little monkey and the porcelain antiques which Flo loved," Billie was glad he still had these, but still knew that despite "the brave show ... it was a travesty."

Flo would produce *Hot-Cha!*, one more *Follies*, and revive *Show Boat*, each turned out at a loss that he could have tossed off before October 1929. Now, each piece of bad news seemed to kill off some part of him. Creditors pressed in, lawsuits were served. Billie noticed that his health was suffering, too. "It was as if the great tree were toppling," Billie remembered, "and I was counting the stray leaves."[9]

The irony of Billie watching the great tree that was Flo slowly topple was that she was unable to be of much use to him, aside from her earnings, because her stage successes required her to tour as extensively as she had done when a young woman. The Ziegfeld bank account needed every cent Billie made, and so when *The Truth Game* went on tour, she packed up Patty and off they went. It was some consolation that the play was doing well — it was listed late in December 1930 as Playchoice's "play of the month," putting it in a league with *Grand Hotel* and Moss Hart's and George S. Kaufman's *Once in a Lifetime*.

Bernard Sobel takes the credit for making *The Truth Game* click with the public. According to his memoirs, he and Flo perceived that the play was weak, and were not happy either with the fact that it was produced by the Shubert brothers, Flo's rivals from years back. Racking his brains to counter the so-so ticket sales, Sobel happened to meet, through a friend, a palmist named Josef Ranald. Sobel's friend swore by Ranald's abilities, noting that he nearly always "hits on the truth." This was the angle Sobel needed. He met with Ranald and convinced him to work the lobby of the Ethel Barrymore Theatre, reading the palms of people arriving to attend the play. Sobel planted shills to overcome people's shyness and skepticism, and soon Ranald was being mobbed, as was the ticket office. The run was extended, says Sobel; and Ranald certainly benefited from the experience, publishing a book in 1932 titled *Masters of Destiny* that included analyses of the Life Lines of celebrated people, replete with images of their palms.[10]

As hard as it was to be away from Flo, Billie enjoyed parts of the *Truth Game* tour. What she calls the bright spot of 1931 was when the company played Philadelphia. Patricia, now fourteen years old, was at the Halstead School in Yonkers, and came down to the city to visit her mother at Easter. While she was there, the young actress playing the part of the maid got sick and had to withdraw. Novello and Billie had the idea that Patricia could play the part. The maid's uniform was fitted for Patricia and she was drilled in her single line, addressed to Evelyn/Billie, which was: "Please, ma'am, may I have the keys to the stable? Sir Joshuah's locked in and he can't get out."

Patricia was a nervous wreck but she braved it till the curtain rose, standing in the wings awaiting her cue. "But my dear lady," said Ivor Novello to Billie, "it is not wicked at all, I assure you..." and the stage manager pushed Patricia toward the stage. Suddenly, she was standing in the disorienting bright lights, her mother gazing at her with increasing concern as beats went by without a word. Finally, Patricia found her voice and said, "Please, Mother, may I have the keys to the stable?" Billie and Ivor Novello sailed through as if the line were delivered exactly as written; and when Patricia got off stage she hurried to the dressing room to cry. But like her mother, she was not one to back down from a challenge. She played the role for five more performances, alternating "ma'am" with "Mother" throughout, and then Flo came down from New York to take her back to school. Now thoroughly finished with the stage, Patricia made her father laugh when she declared that, like the Christmas tree ornament they had discussed outside Marilyn Miller's dressing room, the stage was something she preferred from the front and not the back.[11]

Billie always regarded *The Truth Game* as having led her to her next big character part, the role of Laura Merrick in Paul Osborn's *The Vinegar Tree*, a bittersweet romantic comedy of "smart Long Island." Mary Boland had made Laura her own when the play premiered at The Playhouse in New York in November 1930. J. Brooks Atkinson called it "Mrs. Malaprop, 1930 style," and such is Laura's character in this play: "a twister of lines, a bungler of words, a sore trial for her family." But what Laura Merrick most twists out of line is memory, identity, and the true natures of the people around her. Set entirely at the Merricks' country house, the plot opens with bored Laura awaiting the imminent arrival of her daughter, Leone, home from college and eager to shed her virginity; her boyfriend, Geoffrey, who is not so eager to oblige; Laura's wickedly worldly sister, Winifred; and a man from Laura's bachelorette days, with whom she had a passionate romance — if it really is the same man, that is. The Merricks' guest is actually Max Lawrence, the painter, who is on his way to the house of Laura and her curmudgeonly husband, Augustus, not Lawrence Mack, the pianist she has in mind. Nor is this wrong man there to see Laura but to rendezvous with Winifred. His presence in the Merrick home has the effect of igniting reactions in everyone: amused annoyance in Laura's husband, who suspects all along Max is not the same man with whom Laura had her girlhood flirtation; hopes of learning the ropes from Leone, who then rebounds and runs off with Geoffrey; naughty asides from Winifred; and the undying belief in Laura that her long lost lover has come to rescue her and bear her off, knight-like, from a marriage and life grown too stale for her incontinent imagination.[12]

For Billie, gone were the days when she could insouciantly take on roles made famous by Marie Tempest or Maude Adams, confident that her gift of glamour would make any role her own. But when she was asked by David Belasco and Homer Curran to play Laura in the Los Angeles production, she was in no position to say no. It was far more of a turning point than *The Truth Game* had been, and for far greater stakes. "Do you suppose," she wrote later, "that anybody, even the strongest personality with the firmest intentions and the most logical ambitions, ever controls his destiny?" Something was controlling hers, almost in spite of herself, when she landed the part of Laura Merrick, because with this role Billie began to successfully find her way around a character at total odds with the leading lady type she had so often played. She believed that all the "bird-witted" roles she was offered in film, starting with Millicent Jordan in *Dinner at Eight*, were inspired by forgetful, fantastical Laura, and it is true that she played many roles after this on stage and screen that were variations on this muddled but amusing matron.

Where she was wrong was to continue to pine, even in her memoirs of 1949, for "better parts," believing she could "do better parts better"— the roles she was trained in, "funny but believable." Billie wanted to play parts that were mature versions of Jacqueline from *Love Watches*, or Lily from *The Mind the Paint Girl*. Yet these were not women who would ever really "grow up." Lily and Jacqueline were meant to always remain young and beautiful people, not in some parallel universe but in a fading portrait or theatre program. They did not enjoy life outside those circumscribed limits of their characters. But even so, there is no reason to assume that could they have withstood maturity they would not have become the sort of flighty dowagers, ever on the track of some obsession, while their households or marriages fell apart around them, that Billie herself later played.

Many of Laura's lines from *The Vinegar Tree* are classic examples of the sort of comedy that Billie would come to be admired for. "I love all the old masters," Laura says dreamily, while Augustus glares. "Now take Holstein, for example. I simply worship him. By the way, someone the other day said that I reminded him of a Holstein. Is there anything in it?" Audiences in theatres and cinemas ate this up, but it took Billie a long time before she felt comfortable with their approbation or that the roles she played deserved it.[13]

Edgar McGregor, who had directed Billie in *Mrs. Dot* in 1910, took charge of the Los Angeles production of *The Vinegar Tree*. Billie's costars were Warren William, William Janney, Julie Dillon and William Morris. Her fears that the public's memory of Mary Boland would make things difficult for her were unfounded; the play had a good run in Los Angeles, and was taken to San Francisco for a month's run. Reviews were uniformly positive, but few sparkled like Edwin Schallert's in the *Los Angeles Times*:

> Billie Burke, elfin spirit of gayety, talked her way capriciously into the heart of a brilliant first audience last night at the Belasco Theatre.... [S]he shone as the most deft queen of laughter who has appeared on the stage this season.... One only wonders why she has not brought her rare talent for comedy to the public more often....[14]

Flo had made arrangements for where Billie and Patricia were to live while in Southern California—he'd found a house in Santa Monica that had been designed by MGM's glamorous Cedric Gibbons. Will Rogers, who was with Billie a great deal on this sojourn, worried as she was by Flo's increasingly poor health, tried to cheer her up by joking that the living room was so big you could set it up as a makeshift football field. The house had a pool and tennis court—all the niceties of their Burkeley Crest estate, minus the ménage and the bill collectors. Ill as he was, Billie notes, Flo had found her the best possible home away from home. For himself, however, there was no real home anywhere anymore. Burkeley Crest was mortgaged to the hilt; Billie recalls how before too long creditors came in and took back whatever had not been paid for, which was nearly everything they had. The old fantasy estate of the 1920s, the "Peaceable Kingdom" of Patricia's fairytale childhood, was like a set being struck in slow motion, the flats toppling to reveal raw wires and cement walls, all to a theatre of seats empty of everyone but the Ziegfelds and an army of debt collectors.[15]

When Flo was able to be with Patricia, as when he came out to California in September 1931 to stay with her while Billie toured, it was at the rented house at Santa Monica. But again, this husband and wife whom no manner of marital difficulty had managed to separate, had to live apart, because Billie was now the family breadwinner, and her work was on the road. By November of that year, Flo was back in New York, trying to fend off creditors while preparing *Hot-Cha!* for production—a show that was so under-funded Flo had to borrow capital from star Eddie Cantor and when that was not enough, tap the resources of two notorious gangsters.[16]

Which is possibly one reason why Flo, when he was in New York, did not always come home to the house alone, or so biographer Charles Higham writes: "Now that his potency began to wane, he sought a series of hormone treatments from his doctors, and his desk drawers were stuffed with rainbow-colored pills."

It was during this time of increasing eccentricity that Flo fired off reams of interminable telegrams and letters, rarely to positive effect, ignored even more interminable reams of unpaid bills, and indulged in the occasional act of violence, such as when he smashed a set of jade elephants because they, in direct contradiction to Flo's preferred position, had their trunks pointing down. Uplifted trunks may have been an innocent good luck sign, or they may have symbolized for him a potent erection; either way, what may have seemed small matters to others were adding up to gargantuan failure to the symbolic thinking patterns of the ill and harassed Flo Ziegfeld. Higham claims Flo took his former cupidity to new heights by having carloads of young women driven out to Burkeley Crest for orgies — even in her second, more forthright volume of memoirs Billie does not touch on this, but Higham states there were furious phone calls from Billie in California to Flo in New York, overheard by Alice Poole, the company's switchboard operator, about this very subject. Apparently, Alice would become so disgusted by what Flo was saying to Billie, she would pull the plug, infuriating him as well. Whatever the truth of the matter, Flo was not just a sick man — he was that far worse thing, an impresario at the end of his creative and financial rope.[17]

Billie knew Flo was sick when he saw her off for California and *The Vinegar Tree*. They parted at the Chicago train station, and Billie remembered Flo taking her hands in his and telling her that everything was going to be all right, that he

NOW AT THE **BELASCO**

The Season's Most Distinguished Theatrical Event

BELASCO and CURRAN present
AMERICA'S FORMOST COMEDIENNE

Miss BILLIE BURKE

in New York's Gayest Comedy Hit

"The VINEGAR TREE"

WITH

WARREN WILLIAM

(Courtesy of Warner Bros.)

William Morris ⁄ William Janney

Staged by Edgar MacGregor

The Vinegar Tree (1931), Paul Osborn's domestic comedy of mistaken identity and matronly malapropisms, helped launch Billie's career as the dithery character she played for most of her Hollywood film career.

would do another *Follies*, and this one would be the best of them all. But Billie was not buying it. She who specialized in sunny optimism could not believe that everything would ever be right again. "I believe in premonitions," she wrote later, and that day in Chicago she sensed that the man who had always sprung back upright after being flattened, whose vitality appeared nearly immortal, was sinking. Characteristically, Billie never points out how much of the burden of their joint disaster *she* was shouldering. On the back of this woman, never sure of herself as an actor and now even less so, rested the family's one source of regular income. It was a fate no one could have imagined for her — the fragile, ethereally beautiful Miss Burke, from whose slipper rich men had sipped champagne. "I violated my instinct," she wrote, "overriding my heart with what I argued were practical considerations when I went away from Flo." That is her only lament: not a word about the grueling tours, the lonely hotel rooms, the physical exhaustion. It was being forcibly parted from Flo, just when he most needed her, that pained her most.[18]

Flo's woes continued. Not long after it premiered on Broadway on March 8, 1932, it was clear that *Hot-Cha!* was not a success, certainly not in comparison to *Rio Rita*, which it was hoped the show's resemblance to would help it gain similar success. Before the premiere, during tryouts for the show in Pittsburgh, Flo had already become ill with the flu — the first of several setbacks that would put him in a state of permanently weakened health. He forged ahead: later in March, Flo made his first live radio show, the "Follies of the Air," a weekly program for which he held high hopes. Billie and Patricia were part of the all-star premiere cast, and probably the excitement of trying something new, on what was considered the cutting edge of technology, roused Flo and helped Billie forget both their troubles. There was no lack of evidence that the old Flo was still in control. Despite being ordered by his doctors to slow down, he was issuing orders to Billie in California that spring about percentages and salary guarantees she was to demand from producers; and when Billie herself went on radio, Flo had taken an active part, including coaching as to what he deemed advisable for her to do and say. It was a pace even Sandow would have had trouble keeping up with, and the cracks began to show. In early summer, when Billie, then in California, heard her husband over the airwaves, she was alarmed by the "weariness and sickness" of his voice. Back in New York, she found a sick, aging man who would not rest — could not rest. Besides his several other projects he was taxing his limited physical resources with the *Showboat* revival, which was to be staged at the Casino Theatre. Instead of revivifying him, as Billie could plainly see, these things had sapped him of strength. The endless well was drying up.[19]

By early July Billie, who had signed for another play, begged producer Homer Curran, who had also produced *The Vinegar Tree*, to release her so that she could go back to take care of Flo. Curran, who stood to make as much money from this venture as he had from *The Vinegar Tree*, nonetheless gave her her freedom. It was at this same time that another man entered Billie's professional and personal life, first as a bystander at rehearsals of the Curran play and later with an offer that was to affect the course of her life and career: director George Cukor.

Born in 1899 to a Hungarian Jewish family with the pretensions of the old world and aspirations of the new, Cukor came in with a love of theatre in his veins: when his mother, whom he revered, was not taking him to the theatre his father was taking him to the silent films or "photoplays" being screened as the cinema began edging out the stage in 1900's New York City. But it was theatre that was Cukor's first love. One friend recalled being told that on seeing his mother costumed for a family theatrical, Cukor became hooked on drama, specifically the mannerisms and personalities of compelling actresses and female characters. A list of his leading films and leading ladies underscores this: Greta Garbo in *Camille*, Jean Harlow and Marie Dressler in *Dinner at Eight*, Ingrid Bergman in *Gaslight* and the many films he made with Katharine Hepburn. Cukor had a special understanding of the codes women sent and received about sex, money and power under the guise of being proper ladies, which resonated in his world of half-concealed homosexuality, inconvenient in a time and place — Hollywood from the 1930s on — where gay directors were few, unlike the more accepting world of the stage.

Cukor had long been an admirer of Billie's stage work, remembering her from the days when she had been a leading lady on Broadway and on the touring circuit. He asked Billie if she would be interested in playing the part of the mother in a tense drama called *A Bill of Divorcement*, in which she would perform opposite John Barrymore, as her husband, and ingénue Katharine Hepburn, as her daughter. Cukor's request was the godsend she had asked for. Billie saw this ever after as an answer to all the terrified prayers she had sent up on too many sleepless nights: to get a film again meant leaving touring behind for stationary and steady work, it meant good money, and most of all it meant that she could have Flo with her. With shooting not scheduled to begin till mid-summer, Billie had time to take a train to New York, Patricia and Will Rogers' two daughters in tow, hoping she had not waited too late. (Will himself was performing in Europe.)[20]

To judge from how he looked when he met them, Flo was no better than before: thin and haggard, the proud shoulders slumped. The revival of *Showboat* was a success, but every cent the show made was sucked up by creditors. Burkeley Crest was like an extension of Flo's deterioration — not only was the place in disarray, but as Charles Higham writes, when Billie arrived home butler Sidney told her more than she wanted to know about what sorts of parties and other entertainments had been taking place there. Even had she wanted to, it is hard to imagine the Billie who allegedly screamed at Flo over the phone from California doing so now, when his life lay about their feet in ruins.

Hoping to bring him some pleasure, Billie took Flo out for a night's entertainment, to hear Buddy Rogers' Band at the Hotel Pennsylvania on Seventh Avenue, but he collapsed in the lobby and had to be carried to a room for the night. Billie does not tell us whether a doctor was summoned, but she does recall with what alarm she had touched her husband's wrist, to find not so much a pulse as a wild tremor. The Ziegfelds' old friend from Palm Beach and Camp Patricia days, Dr. Jerome Wagner, tried to reassure Billie by telling her that all Flo needed was rest. That, thought Billie, hardening against the circumstances, was as good as telling him to find a million dollars, something else, besides a restoration of health, Flo could have used.

No one seems to have thought of taking Flo to a specialist or even to get a checkup in a clinic; perhaps Flo, with his fear of sickness and death, refused to go. Next morning, increasingly desperate, Billie bought train tickets for herself, then made arrangements with the railroad to bring Flo along with her. She writes that she had to spirit him out of town, swearing everyone who knew to secrecy. This was a sensible way to avoid reporters finding out what was going on, but the departure has a certain strange edge to it, as if she were absconding with a criminal with a price on his head. Perhaps, given what Flo was worth as a debtor, it was best that none of their creditors know his exact whereabouts.[21]

The trip, made in July, was naturally miserably hot. Katharine Hepburn boarded the train in Chicago when it was switched to the Super Chief, and remembered the Ziegfelds' drawing room being beautifully decorated, "hung with special slipcovers which covered the walls, the chairs — every object in the room." It seemed luxurious to her, but it is possible that Billie, whose sanitation mania led her to put slipcovers over slipcovers, had arranged to have this done in view of Flo's condition. And if slipcovers equaled luxury, the lack of air conditioning did not. Throughout the trip, Billie packed ice in pillowcases to help cool Flo down, but to no avail. Nor does Flo seem to have been wholly conscious. He sounds delirious: Billie describes him making strange gestures, as if writing telegrams, and he murmured to himself.[22]

One curious detail to which Billie does not refer in her memoirs is the stopover in Santa Fe, New Mexico. The *New York Times* mentioned it, on July 15:

From left, Flo, Patricia, and Billie posing for a picture beside their private train carriage. Flo's age and ill health are clearly making inroads on his vitality. Photograph ca. 1929.

Florenz Ziegfeld is gravely ill at a New Mexican sanatorium and constantly under a physician's care, his wife, Billie Burke, who is now playing in a radio studio picture, said here yesterday.[23]

What was this about? Had Flo taken such a turn for the worse en route that it was judged best to leave him at a proper facility, close enough to Los Angeles and Billie so that she could either visit him or fetch him on to California when he had improved? Was she needed so precipitately on the set of *A Bill of Divorcement* that she had to compromise on her plan to bring Flo all the way back to Los Angeles? She does state in her memoirs that filming had already started while she was still en route.

On July 19, another newspaper report was published stating that Billie had hurriedly brought Flo on to Los Angeles, after a doctor had declared him in a "very serious but not critical condition." The seriousness of his condition must have seemed stable enough to keep him out of the hospital, however, because Billie settled him in at the Santa Monica house. This seems to have been a temporary thing: what Flo was waiting for was Will Rogers' return from Europe. Rather pathetically, when offered the use of Joseph Schenk's ranch as a place of rest, Flo refused. Will Rogers' ranch, with its ocean-gazing picture window given as gift from Flo years before, was the only place he could imagine regaining his strength.

It was while all this was happening, including preparations for shooting the film — her first talkie — that Billie had to shoulder more responsibility. She found out that *Showboat* was suffering a dearth of ticket buyers under the summer heat of New York, and the company lacked $12,000 more per week to cover salaries. Billie got on the phone to wealthy Broadway producer A.C. Blumenthal, who had been of assistance to Flo in the past, and got him to guarantee the amount. Not unlike her heroic effort to bring Flo out to sunny California, this last minute monetary transfusion was more quick fix than lasting repair.

"[I]t was a bad summer," Billie wrote, but it was to get much worse as the "great tree" that was Flo began its final fall.[24]

CHAPTER 16

Death, Then Life

Flo was not getting better at the house (where, despite his physical weakness and the family's poor financial state, he was busily running up eighty dollar long distance telephone calls and thousands more worth of telegrams), so Billie arranged for him to be examined by two of the best doctors she could find in Los Angeles. They recommended hospitalization. Thus Flo was checked into Cedars of Lebanon Hospital, located on Fountain Avenue in West Los Angeles, suffering from a severe case of pneumonia. Billie took a room nearby to be constantly at hand, and then plunged into preparations for *A Bill of Divorcement*, which was filming on the RKO lot on Melrose Avenue, several blocks away.

Perhaps, as Dr. Wagner had predicted in New York a few weeks before, the rest that was all Flo needed was in fact helping him improve. "In a few days," Billie remembered, "he seemed refreshed and relaxed." Billie had not yet told him what she — and Blumenthal — had done to shore up *Showboat*, nor had she told him about another piece of bad news, one which she had received just before they had reached Los Angeles: that Dan Curry, Flo's general manager, had died of a heart attack. From that point on, she recalled, "many important affairs were in strange hands." But she hoped there would be time to tell Flo all about these things, when he was well enough to devote his energies to turning the bad news into good, as he had always been able to do.[1]

While Patricia brought her father flowers and read his many telegrams to him, Billie worked twelve hour days on the set. It is no exaggeration to say that she had probably never worked so hard on a film in her life. For starters, she had not made a full-length movie since *The Education of Elizabeth* in 1921. And she had never before made a talking picture. Her voice training was for the stage, in which the way one directed one's voice depended on the acoustic of the theatre and the strength with which one projected it, as shaped and colored by whatever emotions were part of the scene and role one was playing.

In theatre, the most important thing was to communicate with one's audience — and it was that sense of dialogue with a living interlocutor that made the transition to film difficult for many a stage star. One reason why Billie was able to dismiss her silent film work was that it did not seem as real to her as her work in the theatre, not least because her voice, her primary instrument of communication, was never heard. With sound film, Billie was suddenly in a completely different environment, one that was both comfortingly familiar and terrifyingly different. Now Billie had to remember where the microphone was at all times, and while not speaking directly into it, make sure she was not too far away or too close, all the while maintaining the proper proximity to the camera per the director's demands.

The first days on the set of *A Bill of Divorcement*, complicated by the traumas she was undergoing off screen, were a continual struggle for her. She remembered being terrified of moving from place to place, and when we watch the film today we see that there is a frozenness about her, palpable in every scene. George Cukor, "a blessed person," helped her overcome her shyness as best he was able, as did John Barrymore. Not yet the wreck he was to become in a few years, a casualty of alcohol and high-living, Barrymore was the perfect gentleman with Billie: he "crossed over whenever he could so that I would not have to move."

Billie admired Barrymore's still magnificent acting ability, as she had ample opportunity to do in her big scene with him partway through the film. The script was based on a play by Clemence Dane, who had been inspired to write the story by a British law permitting a wife to divorce a husband if he had been declared insane. Billie played Meg, the wife of Hilary Fairfield (Barrymore's role), who had been placed in an asylum fifteen years earlier for what was believed to be war-related mental derangement. In the interim, Meg has been courted by another man, Meredith Gray (played by Paul Cavanagh); after a sufficient time Meg grows to love him and files for divorce from her husband, who it is believed will never recover, so that she and Gray may marry.

A rare sultry glamour still of Billie (by Universal's still photographer Jack Freulich) from after her return to Hollywood in 1932. University of Southern California Cinematic Arts Library collection.

Meg's daughter, Sydney, played by Katharine Hepburn, is also being courted by a man who wants to marry her. While all these plans are being made, Hilary escapes from the hospital and finds his way back to the family home. Sydney has not seen her father since childhood and is first shocked, but then grows fond of him. Billie's reaction is one of abject dismay: how can she divorce Hilary now, when he has returned, claiming to have regained his sanity? In fact, Hilary has not: he is like a child in a middle aged man's body, and to resume life with him would be to condemn herself to a madhouse of her own.

In her strongest scene with Barrymore, Billie is approached by him in what at first seems an attitude of acceptance, but which he twists into a pathetic *scena* of begging and blame, using all his tricks to wear her down into agreeing to let him remain in her home. Meg is on the point of foregoing her plans with Gray when it is revealed by an old family doctor that insanity, once believed caused by shellshock, runs in Hilary's family and was a pre-existing condition in Hilary; and that it is clear that not only will Hilary never get better but that Sydney may also carry the same fatal gene. At the film's end, Sydney sacrifices her suitor, allows her mother to go off with her new husband, and stays with her father to care for him. What started as a modern psychodrama ends on a decidedly dark Gothic note, as if a 1920s flapper had transmogrified into an 1850s Brontë heroine.

As many were, Billie was at first put off by Hepburn — the twiggy young woman with the flashing eyes and flying buttress cheekbones was made the more memorable by a crisp yet drawling upper-crust New England accent and a straight from the shoulder directness that could be decidedly off putting. Her acting did not then have the depth it acquired later, nor were her mannerisms yet sanctified by a long and masterful career. Then, one day, Billie watched Hepburn "really act. Somehow her eyes caught fire and there was a glow," she remembered. "I have seen ever since how beautiful she is." The bond between these actresses of worlds old and new is subtle but strong in all their scenes together, and Billie was to remain a friend and admirer all her life.

All in all, even with the grueling hours and the new equipment to contend with, Billie was making good progress. As, it appeared, was Flo, and his high spirits seemed to support the appearance of improvement. The doctors told Billie that he was making rapid strides toward recovery. The fresh flowers, his favorite foods prepared at home and brought to the hospital, Patricia's and Billie's daily visits, all seemed to be pulling Flo back to his old self. To make things even better, Cukor told Billie he would not need her for a week, effectively handing her a holiday she had not expected (which the kind-hearted Cukor may well have engineered). She planned to spend every moment with Flo.[2]

The morning of July 22 was not unusual. Flo and Billie had breakfast together in his hospital room, as always. Billie was still with him when Patricia came in with lunch, prepared as usual at the house, and they enjoyed a happy family repast. Billie noted how all trace of stress had vanished from her sick husband. She was still hiding from him the increasingly bad news from New York. She had just received a telegram the day before from Flo's business office in New York, urging Flo in no uncertain terms to declare bankruptcy. Western Union had cut off credit to the organization; the Ziegfeld

Theatre's telephones were to be removed shortly. New York State tax officials were ready to attach all of the company's goods at any moment. But Billie was nothing if not a good actress; she swallowed the harsh medicine without a grimace, and told Flo everything was just fine.[3]

Then came an unexpected message from the studio. An apologetic Cukor asked Billie to come in briefly to test with a new actor, Walter Pidgeon, who was being considered for the role of her fiancé. (A part ultimately played by Paul Cavanagh.) Billie asked if she might do an evening test, since that would allow her to see Flo before he went to sleep. Cukor assented. So Billie had dinner with Flo, during which, as she recalled, "we began to plan ... all the things he wanted to do." Then she kissed him goodnight and left for the studio.

Billie got into her costume, a flowing evening gown (possibly the same one worn in the Christmas party scene at the beginning of the film), and full makeup, and was in the middle of filming the test with Pidgeon when a call came. Cukor had taken it and now urgently stopped the camera. He handed the phone to Billie. She found Sidney on the other end of the line. "Come quickly, madam, come quickly," he told her. Rushing to the car, Billie was driven the several blocks to Cedars of Lebanon, a drive of no more than a few minutes' duration. There she found Sidney standing, gray-faced, outside Flo's room. She was too late: Flo was already dead.

Around 10 P.M., Flo had begun to suffer pains in his abdomen. The symptoms got worse, so his physician, Dr. Radwin, sent Sidney to call Billie — obviously, Dr. Radwin knew this was not a case of indigestion (it in fact may have been referred pain from a heart attack). At 10:31 P.M., Flo died. Some accounts claim he was in Sidney's arms at the end, trying to walk across the room — perhaps a last effort to outpace the death and disease he so feared and had always managed to ignore before, but could not escape now.

Patricia arrived around 11 P.M., having been out at a movie, and she was as shocked by the news as her mother, for she had also believed that her father was on the mend. But Flo's apparent improvement had been just the last brilliant sunset, like those he had enjoyed as a boy in the deserts of the Southwest, before nightfall. As Patricia later recalled, what most upset her was that her father had had to die in this sterile hospital room rather than at Burkeley Crest, his little kingdom on the Hudson River, surrounded by his elephants and flowers, his wife and his daughter. Yet she knew that that Burkeley Crest was long gone, struck like the set of a failed Broadway show, and that, "at the end, he was too tired to care more about anything," even the all-important setting of his own death.[4]

Patricia saw that her mother, too, was tired. For over two years, Billie had been working without stop to replenish the family coffers, with few periods of real rest; "[t]he years of trouping, the strange hotel rooms, the long hours of rehearsal," Patricia recalled, and the many disappointments and failures had culminated and peaked the night of Flo's sudden death. The ordinarily resilient Billie was knocked off her feet. Billie wrote later that following Flo's death, she never knew how she had come to be at Will and Betty Rogers' ranch by the sea. The terrifying nothingness of life without Flo had clouded her memory, partly obliterated it — she had allowed him, as she had allowed Blanche and Charles Hawtrey and Charles Frohman, to give shape and direction to her life as actress and woman, and without him she was as lost as if she were suddenly pushed on a stage without script or plot to follow. She had loved Flo, probably never more so than at the end, when the tables turned and she had *him* to care for. Though she made much of how she had been petted and protected since girlhood, Billie Burke was a nurturer who had wanted all along for Flo to depend on her as much as she did on him, to be needed as he seemed to need the many distractions that beset him, chorus girls included. As she related in her memoirs, for a long time after Flo's death Billie was haunted by the sense that "if could only run down the world far enough, somehow I would find Flo alive and waiting for me." That Flo, that materialist par excellence, no longer physically existed was a fact she only accepted years after his death.

Billie and Patricia rested at Will Rogers' ranch for two weeks. Where Billie had become Flo's caregiver, Patricia, who had been mothered and, at times, smothered by Billie's effusive care, traded roles with her mother and took care of her. Along with the Rogers' "love and the quiet of the hills" surrounding the ranch, fifteen-year-old Patricia supported her mother through this hardest of losses. George Cukor, who kept in touch with Billie through Will Rogers, Billie's unofficial mouthpiece to the outside world, heard what a comfort Patricia was for Billie. "She was so understanding and comforting," he wrote later. "In a sense, she mothered Billie in her loss." And Billie recalled, "When our troubles came she was sturdy and comforting beyond her years."[5]

As Cukor observed, almost from the start of her career "Billie was called upon to do things that very few people in their lives are asked to manage," including dealing with the peculiar challenges brought by fame, that dubious gift from the gods; and certainly very few people in her position, with the rug pulled out from under them, could have recovered enough in the few weeks it took her to regain her equilibrium and rejoin the world. But not only did Billie pull herself together. She made two shrewd decisions that few grieving spouses would have had the emotional or physical strength to do.

To begin with, she resisted pressure to stage a huge New York funeral for Flo. New York Mayor Jimmy Walker had called her at the ranch to tell her he was planning a citywide ceremony of remembrance, "to permit [New York] to evince its affection for Mr. Ziegfeld." Billie would have none of it. "She explained," one report ran, "that Mr. Ziegfeld would have been averse to a public funeral," though as we know, he was a past master at planning such spectacles (though never attending them) for Anna Held and Olive Thomas. Perhaps Billie was right, but her rejection of Mayor Walker's offer shows that even in seclusion, she was able to make firm choices and was probably already thinking of Flo's legacy: a huge funeral, with all its concomitant chaos and hypocrisies, would leave a sour taste in the mouth of history.

Instead, Billie and Will gathered a list of no more than one hundred of Flo's and her friends to invite to the small ceremony planned for the chapel of Pierce Brothers' Mortuary in North Hollywood. "My only wish," Billie related through Will Rogers, "is that [the funeral] be quiet, private." And such it was.

As Flo's dull silver coffin lay on the altar, covered in roses and surrounded by a forest of floral tributes, stars of stage and screen knelt in homage: Eddie Cantor, John Barrymore, Bebe Daniels, Katharine Hepburn, Ethel Barrymore, Louella Parsons, as well as big business friends of Flo's like William Randolph Hearst. Eulogies to the deceased were shared with all the quietness and sincerity Billie could have asked for.

Cantor described Flo as "Daring, generous and lovable, he was a master showman of the American theatre," as well as a father figure who had helped make him not just a star but the man he was. Al Jolson said: "To the public the name of Ziegfeld meant the last word in entertainment; to friend it meant the last word in friendship." Will Rogers said: "Good-by, Flo, save a spot for me." John Boles sang "Goin' Home."

But perhaps the words most meaningful for Billie came from the officiating minister, the Rev. Franklin L. Gibson of St. Athanasius Episcopal Church. He acknowledged that death had deprived people of one of the world's greatest impresarios, a theatrical producer without equal. But what the world would most miss was the fact that Flo, for all his peccadilloes, "was, above everything else, a lover of beauty and a true artist." Gibson thus touched precisely on what it was about Flo that, despite the many reasons he had given her for wanting to do so, had made it impossible for Billie to ever leave him. It was that deep, abiding love for beauty that she would miss the most.[6]

More of Billie's strength can be seen in her decision to not take Flo's body back to New York for burial until she had completed her work on *A Bill of Divorcement*—a film in which, ironically, she plays a woman yearning to shed her old life for a new one. No one had a better view on this aspect of Billie's persona than her daughter. Patricia knew her mother had been knocked off her feet, but she also knew she had not been washed out to sea. "She had one lifeline to hang on to—her work," she remembered, "and she clung to it with grim instinct." After the seclusion of the Rogers ranch, Billie could be

A somber Billie buys a ticket to see *A Bill of Divorcement* (1932), the film she was making when Flo died.

forgiven for making little more than tentative steps back out of it; but in fact, she went straight back to the studio and worked. Will Rogers had kept Cukor informed of Billie's progress, so the director had some idea of what to expect. But everyone on the film was amazed. Not long after the funeral, Billie showed up on the set.

"She was a little late," Cukor recalled, "and frightfully apologetic. 'It's so stupid of me,' she said. 'They had a difficult time putting my eye makeup on.' This was all she said about her great loss."[7]

> It almost seems to me now [Billie wrote in 1959] that I went back to work the next day. This is not quite true. There were a few intervening days, during which Will and Betty Rogers took charge of everything, including me and my small daughter, but I did return to the sound stage at once, acting the best I could in a rather difficult character part.
>
> This seemed like a hard and bitter thing to do at the time, a callous thing to do. It was not, though, a matter of "the show must go on," that falsely gallant theatrical legend which is neither true nor necessary.... I was enormously fortunate that I had a job.[8]

She was also dispelling the false legend that the diamonded queen of the Jazz Age, deprived of diamonds, husband, and youth, was a weakling not up to the demands life was making on her. Billie Burke of the Broadway drawing-room comedies proved she was a serious fighter. It helped that the cast and crew showed her "kindness and tactfulness" on her return to the set, particularly Cukor, John Barrymore and Katharine Hepburn. Billie was especially grateful to Ern Westmore, her makeup man, who perhaps more than anyone except for Patricia saw the real situation. Each morning on arriving in her dressing room, her composure dissolved and she gave way to weeping. Then she straightened up and Westmore made her look as if she had not a care in the world. It was not easy, but with Westmore's and everyone's help the picture was completed on schedule.[9]

CHAPTER 17

"A small, bewildered comedienne..."

Flo had once expressed the wish to have his ashes scattered over the Roof—the rooftop restaurant at the New Amsterdam Theatre—but Billie decided to keep to the conservative measures she had adopted thus far. She had his remains placed in a temporary crypt at Forest Lawn, and then stood back to survey her life.

> In 1932 I was a small, bewildered comedienne who for most of her life had been advised and protected, and often pampered. I had enjoyed more than professional advice. I had had, in my mother, in Charles Hawtrey, Charles Frohman, Victor Kiraly, and in Flo himself, of course, not mere guidance but loving guidance. Now for the first time I was on my own.[1]

Before Billie's and Patricia's tears had dried there were six lawsuits against Flo's estate. The newspapers eagerly ventured to guess how much debt Flo had left behind, with figures ranging from $1 to $2 million (in 1932 dollars). The Ziegfeld Theatre's files were seized, and the bills, like some sort of weird confetti, not for celebration but its opposite, continued to rain in. Processes were served, judges heard cases, lawyers met and discussed. In his best years, Flo had made millions, but by 1934 there was little to show for it. Something over $2700 was on deposit in a bank in White Plains, New York; nothing else was in Flo's name, and of course, much of what he and Billie had owned at Burkeley Crest—furniture, artworks, and other assets—had been seized long before his death. Only the house, though heavily mortgaged, remained.

One creditor, the Bank of the United States, tried every method to find Billie's address in Santa Monica, in an effort to collect on a $37,787.84 debt Flo had left. Flo's attorney, Louis Levy, kept one step ahead of them and they never reached Billie. Had they managed to do so, there was very little she could have paid. She had much to worry about in the here and now without having to dig up money for debts from years before. "My immediate need was to make a little money," she recalled, "and look after my daughter." Camp Patricia, which Richard Ziegfeld assumes Flo must have bought in Billie's name, had to be sold at a sheriff's sale for $2500—the original cost to build it had been $80,000—an example not just of the depreciation of Depression values but of the total lack of a market for such luxury properties of a vanished gilded age. Billie and A.C. Blumenthal then did what would have been unthinkable in Flo's lifetime and partnered with the Shubert brothers to bring out a new *Follies*. And she needed to make movies. As much as she disliked making film, Billie would later state, "Motion pictures tided me over the most difficult part of my life. They were a veritable port in the storm, when my life was going overboard in a veritable sea of grief." Her life, and her finances, too, were pulled out of that sea by that most unlikely life saver, Hollywood.[2]

In the end, the debts were paid off, a good percentage of them taken care of directly by Billie's own hard work. Yet as she noted in her memoirs, it always haunted her that she had not been able to do more. This was one of the signal differences between Billie and Flo: where he had always faced debts with insouciance, she went through a hell of worry until they were paid, a legacy of growing up with a mother who knew the value of every penny.[3]

Without Flo's guidance and protection, Billie was certainly alone in one way. But in another, she was as protected as if Flo were still managing her life from the great beyond. Will Rogers had been and would continue to be, until his own tragic early death, Billie's greatest champion in time of need. But she could also count on George Cukor and producer Sam Goldwyn to fill the void left by Flo's death. Both accomplished that not only with emotional but with financial support. Goldwyn asked Billie if he might serve as her agent, with the unusual clause that he would pay her a "retainer" of $300 per week regardless of whether or not she was working. This money came as a great boon amid the disaster of Flo's finances.

Cukor was also of great assistance in the matter of how Billie was to find work, understanding both her need to work and what kind of work best suited her. There must have been many a conversation about this between the two that Billie does not record, but it is clear she was wrestling again with her old demon, her belief that if she announced her return to the New York stage, the offers and financial rewards would rain down.

"I think I can say that I had a name in New York," she writes in her memoirs, "I know that I could have found good plays and good producers, and I am reasonably sure that I could again have been a star on the New York stage."[4] Without any detailed rationale from Billie, it is difficult to fathom what she could have intended by hanging on to this last of her undaunted ideals. Her most recent performance on a New York stage had been in a subsidiary character part that had won her good notices. While it would appear to have signaled that her days as a leading lady were over, it was clear that she had a whole new career as a character actress opening before her.

Had she returned to New York—fighting through the ghosts of the past which, in fact, she confessed kept her from returning to Broadway for years to come—would it have been to try to play leading roles again, somehow and some way? Would she have discovered the hard way that those days were as much a thing of the past as Maude Adams and Mrs. Patrick Campbell, Charles Frohman and dinner parties at Sherry's? Computing all her other losses, could she have withstood this additional defeat? One respected critic who had the advantage of tracing the entire arc of Billie's career was of the belief that Billie had never been anything but what we know of as a character actor.

Years later, George Jean Nathan would write that anyone who thought Billie Burke was capable of playing anything other than Billie Burke was sorely mistaken, especially if he had not had the benefit, as had Nathan, of seeing her on the stage since her earliest days in London. Writing of her final Broadway performance in 1944's *Mrs. January and Mr. Ex*, Nathan noted that he had first seen Billie with Charles Hawtrey in *Mr George* in 1907. "Although the plays and roles in which she has since offered herself have intermittently varied," he wrote, "she is still giving almost exactly the same performances in them that she gave shortly after her emergence from musical comedy.... For, regardless of her parts, she has always played Billie Burke In Person And In The Flesh with a vengeance."

It was always as if, Nathan believed, Billie's roles were never more than temporary assumptions of characteristics, as for a movie role, in which Billie was not just playing a part designated in the script but putting in a sort of cameo appearance for her fans. She had virtually founded a "Billie Burke School," in which young women relentlessly "gurgled like soda fountains," behaved like coy parakeets, and threw themselves about the stage "like excited schoolgirls under the misapprehension that they were simply too darling for words."

He was willing to give her this: since her first appearance as an actress and for every moment of theatre or film since, Billie had the virtue of having offered herself not in bits and pieces or as a deluded Duse but as "Billie on all cylinders." Her energy and her verve, Nathan believed, as well as her audacious exuberance as "Billie Burke ... In The Flesh," no matter the vehicle, were her chief gifts. What he also makes quite clear is that from the very beginning, not just when she was forced to it as a character actor, her greatest gift of all was her knack for comedy.

The Billie Burke of George Jean Nathan's experience and the Billie Burke of Billie's own self-conception were clearly at odds — which was the real Billie Burke? But Nathan touched on both the problem and the opportunity of what it meant to be Billie. What had worked for her since the beginning of her career, though she does not seem to have grasped this, was just being herself. And that self was a comedy specialist, not a tragedienne; and this comedy was, as she aged, a natural progression, not a detour from the dramatic heights where she felt she belonged but was, in fact, completely wrong for her. So might Eddie Cantor, who had had early aspirations toward drama, have attempted *Rosmersholm* or *The Cherry Orchard*, or Sophie Tucker, who had dreamed of being a serious singer, offered herself in the songs of Debussy. The mind boggles, though we can be sure that these efforts would have brought both right back to where they belonged: comedy.

Just as perspicacious as Nathan, though far more dazzled by the aura surrounding a former leading lady of the stage, George Cukor also knew all this about Billie. And obviously he did talk sense into her where her Broadway aspirations were concerned, because instead of a return to the stage he found for her a role in one of the greatest comedies ever filmed: as Millicent Jordan in the George S. Kaufman's and Edna Ferber's wicked tale of a supper party saved from disaster — *Dinner at Eight*. Billie's daffy Millicent was to prove the solid bedrock of her new career — that second act that F. Scott Fitzgerald, fallen prophet of the Jazz Age, had declared impossible in America. Billie's career would have a third act, too.[5]

In later years, George Cukor confessed his conviction that he had irrevocably type-cast Billie when he cast her in *Dinner at Eight*. As he said at Billie's memorial service, "I have one great regret in my relationship with Billie. That was the great disservice I did her. I cast her in *Dinner at Eight*. This was the first time she played a feather-brained flibbertigibbet. She did it so well that unfortunately she was cast in similar roles for the rest of her career."[6]

But Cukor was indulging in a bit of dramatic hyperbole. Billie had already started down the road of flibbertigibbets when she accepted the role of Evelyn Brandon in *The Truth Game*. It was this role that led Homer Curran to cast her as the queen of daffiness, Laura Merrick, in *The Vinegar Tree*. And it was Laura, according to Billie, that led Cukor to consider her for Millicent Jordan. What Cukor did her in *Dinner at Eight* was not a disservice at all but a form of rescue that not every aging stage beauty with immense debts to pay could hope to rejoice in. And with this one role, Billie was able to set a standard of quality for herself for all her future film work: rarely did it get this good for her, in terms of her fellow cast, her director, everything.

But more importantly, she set a standard for herself as a comic actress. As her first two sound films, serious dramas that painfully stretched the limits of her dramatic abilities, bear out with a vengeance, tragedy was not where Billy Burke's daughter shone brightest.

Prior to Billie's casting in *Dinner at Eight*, producer David Selznick clearly felt she had done well enough in one intense melodrama to try her in another. This was 1933's *Christopher Strong*, a film that should have been titled *Cynthia Darrington*, since it is this character around which the plot turns, and it is as this character that Katharine Hepburn is at her most radiantly elegant. It is as if Hepburn inspired director Dorothy Arzner, one of Hollywood's great female directors, to turn out a film to match, full of beautiful angles, rich lighting and adroit glimpses into each character's soul.

Set in London in the 1920s, *Christopher Strong* is the story of illicit romance between Conservative MP Sir Christopher Strong, played by Colin Clive, and Lady Cynthia Darrington (Hepburn), an aristocratic aviatrix whose whole life is a series of dares. Sir Christopher is married to Elaine, Lady Strong, played by Billie, and they have a daughter, Monica (Helen Chandler), a debutante turned flapper who is involved with Harry Rawlinson (Ralph Forbes), an unhappily married man. Despite the fact Sir Christopher is old enough to be Lady Cynthia's father, he and she are drawn to each other, becoming so heedless in their affair that Lady Strong and then most of their friends soon discover the truth.

When Lady Cynthia finds out she is pregnant, rather than destroy Sir Christopher's career she sets off in her plane to set an altitude record, deliberately dying in the attempt: the sort of suicide by heroism Hollywood tended to give to male actors rather than female, saved here from being a piece of sexist moral rant by the fact that Lady Cynthia, victim of no man, chooses her own fate.

Billie's part at first seems a throwaway role—the gracious, devoted wife, wafting in and out of rooms in gorgeous clothes, gazing after her absent husband, weeping when she discovers his unfaithfulness, being magnanimous to the "other woman." It is notable that in this film, as in *A Bill of Divorcement*, Billie's actual speaking voice is much lower, less musical, than in any of the comedies that followed. When she performed dramatic roles, did she feel she had to darken it? Had Cukor guided her in this, or was this her real voice, sans the alleged artificial brightness that characterized her work as comedienne? If so, the irony is that this dramatic darkening of timbre seems more artificial than any of her trilling "silly women."

There is a sense in this film, as in Billie's other serious movie roles, that she is perilously close to overplaying. The labored effort here to semaphore every dramatic emotion is almost completely absent from her comedy performances. As in *A Bill of Divorcement*, in *Christopher Strong* Billie performs as if playing to the galleries, every motion and emotion recognizable from a block way. But even in the face of this effort, Arzner plausibly dovetails Billie's uneasy histrionics into the character's own personality.

In her marriage to Flo, Billie had certainly known all about the whispering that goes on at parties and in theatres, at dinner and in the street, when a wife is no longer the sole source of comfort for her husband. Arzner mines this pain, still at the surface, throughout the film. Arzner, who became a good friend, may have also worked into the role Billie's experience as a deceived wife who pluckily determines to make a success of her marriage, however many other women there are.

In one scene, when Lady Strong accidentally sees her husband passionately kiss the young Lady Cynthia, she falls on her bed and sobs, not like an actress emoting — as she has done through most of the film — but like a woman genuinely mourning the loss of the man she loves. This was not the first time Billie would portray this depth of despair on screen, but it is close enough to the years when Flo was alive and making merry with mistresses to hint at the kind of pain Billie suffered during her marriage. That pain is underscored in another scene, in which Lady Strong comes to her husband after a quarrel over their daughter's intention to marry the divorced Harry Rawlinson. Half turned toward the camera, Billie seems to be thinking of other such intimate talks with another man (Flo), when she had raged and broken things and still never made him change or understand. Yet she says: "Of course, I'll do just what you wish about Monica's marriage, or ... or *anything*." In that weighted "anything" is eighteen years of marriage to an unfaithful man, a union which, through the battles to preserve it, had taught Billie not resignation but something more meaningful: a mature approach to love.

This maturity is seen again in a scene where Lady Strong speaks to Lady Cynthia at a party, long after it is clear that Cynthia and Sir Christopher are romantically involved. As Lady Strong expresses her joy that daughter Monica and husband are to have a baby, in a long closeup Arzner exploits a tangle of emotions in Billie's eyes: a sense of surprise that she has matured to such degree she is actually speaking to her husband's lover, and is able to thank her for helping both Sir Christopher and herself realize that Monica's happiness with Harry matters more than societal censure; and a touch of tenderness toward this sporting young woman who, for all her beauty and fame, has not known what was then considered the acme of womanly joy: motherhood.

This scene is what has been called the quintessential Dorothy Arzner face off, in which the ultra-feminine, man-pleasing female is set against her "other," the cocky, self-sufficient, "butch" female who needs no man to define her life. Arzner could have found few other actresses besides Burke and Hepburn to make this irony function as powerfully as it does here.

The ultimate irony, of course, is that even while Lady Strong is making amends, she is wounding Lady Cynthia, who is indeed pregnant with Sir Christopher's child but for obvious reasons cannot reveal this, because that which was fulfillment for Monica was a curse to the unmarried Lady Cynthia. There is courage and bravado and desperation in Hepburn's huge tearful eyes. It might be said that she has made her decision, right then, to not allow Sir Christopher to proceed with divorce, and to live by her last words written to him before she sets off in her plane: "Courage can conquer even love."

It was a credo that Billie the woman and the actress could easily have changed: "Love can conquer even courage." That was a lesson, perhaps the most important one, she had learned from Flo Ziegfeld.

"*Dinner at Eight* was the plum that George [Cukor] next dropped in my lap," recalled Billie. And that is all she does say about it: in her memoirs, she goes into more detail about a run of *The Marquise* she did in Los Angeles shortly before casting and filming of Cukor's classic comedy. Yet her role in *Dinner at Eight* would become at least as immortal as the part of Glinda, The Good Witch of the North in *The Wizard of Oz* six years later. And far more than Glinda, Millicent Jordan would reveal what Billie could do when she gave herself permission to be an all-out comedienne, when she stopped struggling with fate and relaxed into the rightness of a comedic role.

Sometimes a work of creative genius — a painting, book, play, symphony or opera or ballet — comes to birth right at the time that it is not only most needed, to satisfy some collective thirst for what it represents, but seems created not just by one man or woman but by those same collective human desires. It is as if the *Zeitgeist* of an age made palpable something sensed but not seen.

So it was when Edna Ferber's and George S. Kaufman's play *Dinner at Eight* came to Broadway, in October 1932. Not that its cast of characters was a precise mirror image of the society of its time. The straitened circumstances of most of the formerly wealthy permitted no more than a brief backward glance to times when dinner parties even mattered. For every ruined shipping executive like Oliver Jordan, concealing his bad finances as well as his failing health, there were men who had lost it all in 1929 who were working at whatever jobs they could find and trying to rebuild their lives; for every silly society matron like Millicent Jordan, troubled by nothing more than the plotting and fretting over a dinner party, there were strong women facing the facts of real life without complaint.

Nor were Broadway or Hollywood crawling with the likes of aging former stage beauty Carlotta Vance or decrepit screen idol Larry Renault; high flying crooks like Dan Packard were not growing on trees, nor social-climbing bimbos like his wife, Kitty Packard, who will "be a lady if it kills me." Yet during these first years of disarray, after the explosion of 1929 faded into the cold, quiet Depression of the 1930s, there was something morbidly entertaining and even comforting in the spectacle of Millicent's manic effort to collect just the right guests for her dinner for jumped-up aristocrats Lord and

Billie seized the opportunity to reprise her Broadway performance in Noël Coward's brilliant bagatelle of a comedy, *The Marquise*, in Los Angeles (and touring therefrom) in 1932. She poses here with co-star Alan Mowbray. University of Southern California Cinematic Arts Library collection.

Lady Ferncliff. The crisis comes when the Ferncliffs skip off to Florida without warning. Millicent has to scrounge for whomever she can find to fill up her elegant table, one of which last minute guests happens to be the same Dan Packard who plans to buy out Oliver Jordan's failing business, while another, the burnt out Larry Renault, who is having an affair with Millicent's daughter, throws another wrench into Millicent's plans by committing suicide. All that matters to Millicent is that her dinner, eventually pulled from the brink of disaster, should go on without fail for eight o'clock, the chairs filled with enough guests of alternating sexes and the wine ready to pour. It is an empty victory, as audiences of the time would be sure to acknowledge. If the movers and shakers of this world were so miserable, surely life was not so bad for your average Joe, who knew better than to let a dinner party absorb all his attention. As a film critic observed after the movie's premiere, *Dinner at Eight* "caused one to forget about the deluge outside." It also helped put the deluge in perspective. It did so in a way that permitted those observing it to laugh as well as groan.[7]

In this light, the characters in *Dinner at Eight* are symbols of all that had gone awry with the world after the decade of the Roaring Twenties came to pieces. But they were also characters who proved in various ways that they had a right to some modicum of sympathy. That people cared about them as much as laughed at them was borne out by the six months' run of the play, followed by George Cukor's perfect timing in bringing the play to the screen. As a movie, *Dinner at Eight* would reach its most welcoming audience: the real John Q. Public, who could not afford theatre tickets but could always find the cash for a movie ticket and the soothing diversion from everyday life that movies provided. *Dinner at Eight* thus captured an even bigger audience, even as it captured a dozen actors each as perfectly set in his or her role as a Tiffany diamond.

Spare, sad Lionel Barrymore was chosen to play ailing Oliver Jordan, Billie to play anxious, obsessive Millicent and Madge Evans their petulant daughter, Paula. Marie Dressler sailed grandly through the part of Carlotta Vance, a former flame of Oliver's, trailing outmoded perfumes of the 1890s and tiny dogs on leashes. John Barrymore enacted the alcoholic has-been Larry Renault, in a weird foreshadowing of exactly how he himself was to end up in a few years' time. Wallace Beery glowered and gloated as Dan Packard opposite the white satin and mischief of Jean Harlow's Kitty. Never was a film more spectacularly staffed by artists at the top of their game, who did more than play the roles assigned to them — they gave their characters life outside the confines of the movie theatre, fully in harmony with plot, sets, and the time in which the film was set and created.

Much of this harmony can be chalked up to Cukor, a great synthesizer among directors, for whom every detail of mood and setting mattered as much as the general whole. If he did later regret offering a part to Billie that would forever type her as a scatterbrained rich woman, obsessed with the minutiae of her own life, it cannot have escaped him that in all his actors, not just Billie, he had found exactly what each of them did best. This was the plum Billie so appreciated, however much she dismissed the roles that her success as Millicent Jordan led producers and directors to offer her during the next twenty-eight years of her career.

Strange as it may seem to us now, George Cukor was not much more impressed by *Dinner at Eight* than Billie. Having just signed with MGM, the most elegant of Hollywood studios, Cukor seems to have felt he had bigger fish to fry, and wanted to get the job over with. *Dinner at Eight* has become a classic, but Cukor thought it paltry in content, finding fault with everything from writer George S. Kaufman's lack of profundity to what he considered the miscasting of Marie Dressler as former stage beauty Carlotta Vance.

It is laughable to question Dressler's rightness for this film — without her Carlotta it is certain *Dinner at Eight* would enjoy considerably less popularity; and in considering her wrong for the role Cukor, who sometimes couldn't see the trees for the forest, completely missed the irony and pathos of casting Dressler as a beauty at all. As a worshipper of the leading ladies of a former age, Cukor surely knew that even the greatest of them were no match for the onslaught of age. Dressler's great gallantry in this role makes the issue of physical attractiveness irrelevant. Like Billie Burke, once a

The cast of George Cukor's 1933 comedy par excellence, ***Dinner at Eight***, live it up on Coca-Cola. Billie (third from left) sips with the best of them, including Marie Dressler (fifth from right), Lionel Barrymore, and Jean Harlow (both standing behind Dressler), with Cukor smiling paternally at the hearth, script in hand. University of Southern California Cinematic Arts Library collection.

famous stage beauty herself, Carlotta Vance is a survivor; like Billie, too, she does what she has to do to survive, never letting the loss of past greatness embitter her.[8]

For all her dismissal of her work on this film, Billie turned in a performance at least as exuberant as that of her one Oscar nominated role, as Emily Kilbourne in *Merrily We Live* from 1938. Almost everyone in the film is playing a caricature of him or herself, using elements of their own lives to enrich their performances: Marie Dressler and John Barrymore both knew too well the tragedy of the actor who outlives his fame; Wallace Beery could not have been better cast as Dan Packard, who it is easy to imagine slapping women around, as Beery was infamous for doing; and Billie, who with Flo had lived a life of conspicuous consumption, has no trouble convincing as the thriftless Millicent, even as the outmoded histrionics of her comedic acting style, full of the broad double takes and despairing hand-to-brow gestures of Victorian melodrama, perfectly meshes with all we would expect of Millicent Jordan.

But this role signals the maturity of the comedic character acting that Billie, according to her daughter, worked so hard to develop. Millicent at first glance is a flighty, thoughtless woman, flitting from thought to thought like a sparrow from twig to twig, in aimless pursuit of some desideratum important only to her. That is one side of what Billie called her "silly women." At second glance, you see that there is more to these silly women than breathless flutter. It is not that Billie's characters have never known grief, have been so protected by the cotton batting of wealth and privilege they have no concept of pain. It is that these characters know pain and grief all too well, and in their manic activity are staving off confronting it. There is as much fearful sob in Millicent's or Emily's bubbling laughter as mindless mirth.

Dinner at Eight was shot in an amazing twenty-eight days, which accounts for the sense while watching it of having ridden an especially vertiginous roller-coaster. The presence of so many top talents, crashing along through the plot like hyperkinetic bowling balls, keeps the viewer on edge, challenges him to appreciate the clever, bitchy phrases and double entendres lobbed by the actors at each other and from them to the audience, dares him to feel sorry for or make fun of any of these troubled people. The *New York Times'* Mordaunt Hall was impressed: "It is one of those rare pictures which keeps you in your seat until the final fade-out," he wrote, "because nobody wants to miss one of the scintillating lines."

Certainly anyone disposed to leaving the cinema before the film's final line would have missed a great one indeed: As the guests file into Millicent's dining room, Kitty Packard, having struck up a conversation with Carlotta Vance, idly observes that she has been reading a book, which causes Carlotta to stop so suddenly in the hall her swinging ropes of pearls threaten to throw her off balance. Yes, says Kitty, she had read a "nutty kind of a book" about how modern machinery will eventually take the place of every human profession. Eyeing Kitty's lovely figure from head to toe, Carlotta resumes her composure and as they continue to walk toward dinner, says: "Oh, my dear, that's something *you* need never worry about."[9]

If Billie was not so sure about her part in this classic film, another actress who had had to remake herself all over again knew exactly what had been accomplished. When interviewed in October 1933, a little less than two months after the premiere of *Dinner at Eight*, Marie Dressler was asked what it was like working with such a stellar cast, ranging from veterans like Billie and John Barrymore and a newcomer like Jean Harlow. Refreshed and glowing, as if having returned safely from a dangerous expedition, "She insisted Miss Harlow had walked, if not run, away with the honors."

> In rapid succession, then, she awarded second prize to Billie Burke, third to Lionel Barrymore and fourth to Wallace Beery.
> "But how about yourself? Where do you come in?" came the chorus.
> "Oh, me? I guess I might come in after the rest," she replied placidly.[10]

It is a measure of Dressler's greatness that she knew from the start just who she was and what she did best, and never looked back or regretted her choice (or demanded to be put first)—a lesson that Billie, with her snobbery toward film and comedy, still had to learn.

Addendum

During my research into Billie Burke's work and friendship with Dorothy Arzner, I encountered a few sources hinting that Billie and Arzner had had something more than a platonic friendship.

As I looked more deeply into the subject and asked questions of the most plausible of the sources, film historian Anthony Slide, I assembled and reviewed the data, sifting chaff from corn (and corniness). The rumors offered as fact by Darwin Porter in his 2004 book on Katharine Hepburn (published by Blood Moon Productions) can be dismissed as such. When deconstructed, the chain of hearsay for Porter's claim, in one risible instance, of Billie's attempt to seduce Katharine Hepburn on the train out from Chicago in 1932 (ignoring the fact that the dying Flo and young Patricia were also on the train, and that Billie was completely focused on caring for them), is that Hepburn told her "lover," Laura Harding, who told Hepburn's husband, Ludlow Ogden, who told his "lover" Jack Clark, and that the news somehow got back to George Cukor, who in a characterization quite unlike the friend who is known for having looked out for his friends, allegedly enjoyed tattling the story to all and sundry behind Billie's back (which incidentally stereotypes Cukor as gossiping, back-stabbing homosexual). Not only does Hepburn state in her memoir, *Me*, that she only met Billie once they both reached Los Angeles (p. 132), but using Laura Harding as a source does little to ensure that the story is more truth than mere gossip. It should go without saying that relying on a story that made its way through Harding and down to the man Hepburn later divorced, stating it and other rumors as if they were factual events that the author witnessed, has no place in rigorous scholarship.

I know and respect Anthony Slide's work, and felt that if he believed something to be true, there must be some validity to it. I should clarify at this point that as a gay person myself, while reviewing the evidence I knew I needed to be completely objective. Any gay man who grew up loving Billie Burke in *The Wizard of Oz* will know what I mean when I say how validating it would be to discover that the fairy who taught Dorothy how to know herself was one of our tribe. On the other hand, the job of a serious biographer is to interpret the facts at hand, leaving his or her subjective reading of them to one side. And I can say I found nothing in the known primary sources to indicate that such a relationship existed, or that Billie was anything other than a heterosexual female.

First, the rumor. Slide believes that there was a relationship between Arzner and Billie based on two factors, one a story told to him by a Hollywood director, the other his subjective reading of newsreel footage of Billie and Arzner attending a premiere. Slide was told in 1995 by director Andrew Stone, a Hollywood veteran since the late 1920s, that Arzner "was the only lesbian he knew back then," and that he was "aware, like many, of her affair with Billie Burke." He also cites a *Hollywood Reporter* item from November 20, 1936, that Arzner and Billie were living together, and in an interview with me in September 2007 indicated the information was to be found in gossip columns and was "common knowledge." With regard to the newsreel footage, Slide described to me seeing a clip of Arzner and Billie, some time in the mid–1930s, approaching a theatre for a premiere, only to separate conspicuously as they glimpsed the camera rolling, as if unwilling for the camera to capture their private moment.[1]

If Billie and Arzner *were* romantically involved in the early to mid–1930s, the question is begged: where was Arzner's long-time companion, dancer and choreographer Marion Morgan, with whom Arzner began living openly in 1930 and with whom she stayed till the end of their lives? (They were photographed together by Arnold Genthe as early as 1927.)[2]

The story goes that Billie lived with Arzner (and Morgan?) in Hollywood, and Slide recalls hearing from a source that Billie stayed with Arzner while she was between houses. After Flo's death in 1932, Billie left the leased Santa Monica house and moved to a two story Spanish-style bungalow in Beverly Hills, a house which was so associated with her that photos of it, of her and Patricia in and outside it, and of its interiors were circulated to the press. In 1939, Billie purchased the South Woodburn house in Brentwood. It is certainly possible that Billie, a lifelong friend of Arzner, who was well known to Billie's grandchildren later on, moved in with Arzner and Morgan between the Beverly Hills and the Brentwood houses. What I find difficult to accept is what those who believe there was a relationship fail to take into account: the devastation of Flo's death and the debts he left behind, Billie's consuming efforts to get work in Hollywood to make money to live on, and the presence of young Patricia, who was her primary concern above all.

There is another issue to consider. One does not suddenly become homosexual. There should be signs (and I looked for them) earlier in Billie's life and in her surviving correspondence, as there are for Eva Le Gallienne, for example, of at least bisexuality, of intensely close relationships with other women. In the theatre and in Hollywood, especially, there were and are absolutely no secrets, but there is also a huge amount of sensationalist speculation, as Billie herself knew too well: "Hollywood gossip is cruel and cynical." (As is, she might have added, much of Hollywood media.)[3] I have found nothing to indicate that Billie was anything other than heterosexual (and she hints throughout her candid final memoir, *With Powder On My Nose*, that she appreciated men physically very much indeed). Ironically, in contrast to his suggestions that Billie was a lesbian, Slide is the source for another popular rumor about her sex life involving a man: that she had had an affair with Thomas Ince during the filming of *Peggy* in

Following Flo's death, this Beverly Hills house was home to Billie and Patricia prior to Billie's 1939 purchase of her beloved cottage in Brentwood.

1916.[4] When I asked another respected source, film and feminism historian Judith Mayne (author of *Framed: Lesbian, Feminists and Media Culture* [University of Minnesota Press, 2000], and *Directed By Dorothy Arzner* [Indiana University Press, 1994]), what she had ever encountered in her research into Arzner's life and work in Hollywood regarding a possible romantic attachment to Billie, she indicated to me she had never found anything to support allegations that Billie Burke had a relationship with Arzner or any other woman.[5]

Billie's notes, whether to lesbian Nancy Hamilton or to the gruff director of Westerns, straight John Ford, are uniformly gushy, breathless as love letters, and cannot be taken (as some have done with the Hamilton letters) as evidence prima facie of the writer's sexuality or her deeper feelings toward the recipient. Nor have I been able to locate any letters from or to Arzner or Billie that would point to anything more than the long-time friendship of two women brought together, as they were, in a time important to both: Arzner's stunning rise to prominence as a director, Billie's loss of Flo and her need to reinvent herself as a film actor.

It has to be understood that Billie was a person who needed people, and not just because she desired the comfort of friends — she believed her career was dependent on keeping up relationships (hence her overflowing notebook of addresses). Having been bred from earliest girlhood to believe that the way to get ahead in show business was to please and flatter her audience, Billie developed an interlocutory style that at worst is unctuous, at best is disarmingly charming in its honest expression of affection, which for her was one way of holding on to friends and developing an intimacy of communication that smoothed the way for approaching these same people for work in theatre, film, television or radio. Billie confesses in her last memoir that she bombarded her publisher, Coward-McCann, with endless telegrams throughout the process of writing and printing *With Powder on My Nose*; she probably did the same with her first book, too. A review of the Hamilton letters provides all the evidence of this that anyone could require.

Billie never really stopped being an Edwardian beauty, with all the exaggerated characteristics of behavior and address that this implies. Her effusions strike a note either false or sensual to the modern ear. But they were neither — they were simply the way Billie Burke knew best how to express herself and further her interests at the same time.

CHAPTER 18

The Great Ziegfeld

In her memoirs, Billie lists eighteen films she made over the fifteen years from 1932 to 1949, which she seems to have considered among her best efforts: *She Couldn't Take It, Girl Trouble, Doubting Thomas, My American Wife, The Bride Wore Red, Merrily We Live, Eternally Yours, Irene,* the *Topper* series, *Becky Sharp, Everybody Sing, Forsaking All Others, The Man Who Came to Dinner, In This Our Life, They All Kissed the Bride, Hi Diddle Diddle, Breakfast in Hollywood* and *The Cheaters.*

In this list are only two of the thirteen dramas (silent and sound) she had made up to 1949 (the year her list was published in the first volume of her memoirs), yet seventeen of the forty comedies she had made by that year—obviously, playing a "silly woman" was not entirely the workaday job Billie implies. Only one of the comedy roles she liked, that of the poised, acid-tongued Contessa di Meina in *The Bride Wore Red*, is less comedy than drama; in only one of the total films cited, the scenery-chewing Bette Davis vehicle *In This Our Life*, is comedy completely absent.

The others on the list are the daffy society matrons associated with Billie, from Emily Kilbourne in *Merrily We Live*, Billie's one Oscar nominated role, dizzily disrupting the lives of everyone around her in pursuit of a personal obsession, to Daisy Stanley, the wife in *The Man Who Came to Dinner*, whose orderly life and family are changed for ever by the impishly impudent radio lecturer Sheridan Whiteside, and Mrs. Pigeon in the dark Christmas comedy, *The Cheaters*, in which she shows how amenable a society wife can be to the idea of bilking a needy woman out of her rightful inheritance, but how even she and her family can be redeemed, like Scrooge, by Christmas cheer.

Billie made many films in rapid succession over the nearly three decades of her second career, and played in them characters that we do not need George Jean Nathan to tell us are almost all the same person in marginally different settings and plots. Some of these are such caricatures of what was already a caricature of Billie, they stand out for reasons other than what Billie or her director may have hoped. A prime example is her role in the 1946 comedy *Breakfast in Hollywood*, about how Tom Brenneman's live radio show broadcast from Hollywood Boulevard impacts the lives of several of the show's female fans. Billie played the part of plain, downtrodden but devoted wife Mrs. Cartwright, whose husband skips out on her constantly (shades of Flo).

Mrs. Cartwright suffers Mr. Cartwright's indifference until she wins a makeover prize on Brenneman's show, overhears her husband bragging to his barber about his latest conquest, and decides to tempt him back into the home by luring him to a night-club, where he finds her at the bar in sequins and satin, rouge and mascara. Billie, whose advice to married women boiled down to almost exactly this formula (even when the husband is unfaithful, his wife should be able to seduce him back using beauty tips superior to those of his secretary), comes off less clever than deluded in this film, and certainly older than is plausible for the character, which should have been played by an actress like Anne Sheridan or Rosalind Russell. In a few significant instances Billie offered either superior interpretations of the patented "silly woman" or performed in films that made their mark in cinematic history or in her own personal experience, but most of her roles are small, the character parts that flutter into the plot only to flutter out again, leaving no more durable trace in the memory than if a small bird had suddenly swooped into the theatre only to swoop out again.

By the end of the 1930s, the role Billie loved best — that of Glinda the Good Witch in MGM's monumental fairy tale *The Wizard of Oz*— was fast approaching. But between *Dinner at Eight* and the yellow brick road, Billie needed to deal first with the drama of her life off the movie set — with the last remnants of her old life with Flo; and while laying the ghosts that had kept her away from New York for several years, she gave the *Follies* a new chance for continued life and herself a new challenge in resurrecting them.

The making of *The Great Ziegfeld* in 1936 was part of the process that helped ease Billie back into her role as Florenz Ziegfeld's wife and widow, safeguarding his legacy and dealing with the reality not just of his death but allowing her to look back over the eighteen years of their lives together.

Billie was settling into life in Los Angeles. Patricia was enrolled in school, making friends, becoming interested in boys. Billie had found them a small Spanish-style house in Beverly Hills to call home, the starkly furnished rooms of which set an almost deliberate contrast to the excesses of Burkeley Crest. She had become part of George Cukor's social circle, sitting to dinner with Katharine Hepburn and Dorothy Arzner, Joan Crawford and William Haines, Ethel Barrymore and Elsa Lanchester and laughing it up in Cukor's leather-lined drawing room. Back in summer 1932, just after Flo's funeral, Billie had stated to the press her intention of finishing her work on *A Bill of Divorcement* before taking Flo's body back to New York for burial. Yet more work and, likely, her fear of the wasteland New York had become for her, scattered with the remains of both their failed dreams, kept her in California.

With each year after Flo's death, the landscape of the entertainment world, and the one he had known and created in particular, was changing as fast as that of the economic one. In mid–April of 1933, the Ziegfeld Theatre, Flo's pride and joy, reopened — as a movie house. The irony of this transformation, which amounted to a final victory for film over live theatre spectacle, was not lost on anyone who attended the tribute held in the theatre shortly afterward. "Old stars and new stars of the stage whom the late Florenz Ziegfeld helped to make famous," reported the *New York Times*, "show-girls from former 'Follies' and first-nighters who had never missed a Ziegfeld premiere in fifteen years" joined hundreds of others who came together at the theatre in Flo's memory. The sadness of so many losses gave the event more the tone of funeral than grand re-opening: Eddie Cantor barely smiled, Charles Winninger asked everyone to stand in silence, and when Lillian Lorraine, now a wreck of her former self, tried to sing "By the Light of the Silvery Moon" to Gus Edwards' orchestra, she collapsed in tears and could not go on. Billie, tied to Hollywood, could not attend and listened in via radio. She was presented in absentia with a memorial scroll, which was described as destined later for a "Ziegfeld Museum" to open on the theatre's mezzanine — as sure a sign as could be found that Ziegfeld was truly a thing of the past. But as with Billie's decision to join Flo's foes the Shuberts to keep the *Follies* afloat, she and others who held a stake in the theatre had the satisfaction of knowing that the makeover ensured that the Ziegfeld Theatre would at least survive in situ and that they, too, would make some profit out of it after all.[1]

The Shuberts were very much a part of Billie's life for the next several years, as battles raged in courtrooms and legal offices over who had the right to the *Follies* name. The Schuberts and representatives from the Ziegfeld Company sealed a license agreement that same year for a "Ziegfeld Follies of 1933," 3 percent of the proceeds of which were to go to Billie and the estate of Abe Erlanger. But when the show made real money — $60,000 per week — Flo's creditors swooped down for a slice of the pie. This scramble led to an argument over who really had the rights to the *Follies*' name. Billie ignored a court order to prove why she should fork over what was considered her per-

Speaking the famous line "There's no place like home" was no stretch for Billie Burke — and she made a warm, loving home for daughter Patricia. Photograph ca. 1937.

centage of ownership in the name (amounting to $5,000), because she wanted to wait for her claim to be proven. She quite simply did not have that much money to give, but she also did not feel she should have to prove her ownership to what was hers by right of marriage to Ziegfeld.

She had also sunk large amounts of money in his shows when cash flow ran thin. In June 1934, Flo and Billie's former secretary, Catherine Dix, testified in White Plains that in the days before Billie took Flo to California in summer 1932, she was at Burkeley Crest with the pair when she overheard Flo say to Billie: "You have loaned me a lot of money, but don't worry, Bill, the paper I gave you covers you and Patricia," giving them right and title to his businesses. Miss Dix had been in touch with Billie since Flo's death, and had been told by Billie that the paper Flo referred to was still extant, though Miss Dix was unable to find it in Billie's safe deposit box in New York. The very least Billie could hope for was a modest return on her investment, but such was not the case. At this 1934 hearing, Flo's debts were finally determined to amount to something in excess of half a million dollars. Every creditor who was part of that army of unpaid debt wanted his cut. Ultimately, Billie was not to receive anything. In 1935, the Surrogate Court handed down the ruling that after deductions for legal expenses, everything that remained was earmarked for the IRS. Like Flo's other bogeyman, death, the taxman had caught up with him. The tragedy was that Billie and Patricia were left holding the empty cash bag.[2]

In May 1935, Billie headed back to New York for the first time since Flo's death almost three years before, and it was not an easy trip to contemplate. "She could not bear to return and face the old associations," wrote Harrison Carroll of the *Los Angeles Evening Herald & Express*. She had buried herself in film work, Carroll explained, so that she could stave off the inevitable return, though he was too polite to point out what must have been common knowledge by that point: after the Surrogate Court ruling, she also needed the money.[3]

"Billie Burke," declares an interviewer for the *New York Times*, "has a trick of meeting questions and questioners with a contemplative, detached stare," reminding him of "a kitten's apparent indifference toward the ball of yarn that has not yet begun rolling."[4] She was definitely on the defensive during this trip back into old territory — a photograph taken of her and Patricia on the train, Patricia now an elegant young woman with a guarded stare, Billie flushed in her crisp tailored suit, as she fielded questions from a half dozen reporters and photographers, says a great deal about how both mother and daughter felt about their return "home." No more than she had a place in a Broadway theatre did Billie have a place now to call home anywhere in New York. Blanche was gone; Flo was gone; Cherry Watson had married and left show business. The stars Flo had launched in the *Follies* were now shimmering in their own firmaments, occasionally dropping in when the Shuberts and Billie revived their ghost version of the *Follies*. Charles Dillingham, Flo's old friend and business partner, had died in summer 1934, outstripping Flo to the last: he owed several million dollars and left assets of only a little over $100,000, a spectacular financial disaster that may have consoled her by putting Flo's losses in perspective, had it not been that Dillingham's many heavy investments in Flo's productions had played a part in the devastation.

Billie was more frank about her situation with Leo Mishkin of the *Morning Telegraph*. She and Patricia had attended the New York premiere of *Becky Sharp*, the first three-strip Technicolor film in which Billie played the part of Lady Bareacres, whose once great wealth has been seized by creditors: "...Lady Bareacres splendid then, and radiant in wealth, rank and beauty — a toothless, bald, old woman now [wearing] a mere rag of a former robe of state."[5]

She had not seen Burkeley Crest since her last time in the city, in 1932, when she had scooped up Flo and brought him out to California; she was not interested in seeing it now, shuttered and empty, a reminder of not only the glory days of Flo's successes but of her own success, before Flo had ever entered her life, as a young leading lady. She told Mishkin that as she sat watching herself play Lady Bareacres, the quintessential impoverished aristocrat and aging ex-society beauty of Thackeray's novel, she felt that "the part I played ... is quite appropriate, I think. I could never live [at Burkeley Crest] again. The place is too full of memories. I want to stay in California." Yet unlike Lady Bareacres, Billie had not withdrawn to her shabby mansion to pretend that all was well with the world — she had tackled her fate in Hollywood and was making lemonade out of lemons. It is characteristic of her reluctance to cede her film work any value that she could compare herself to a woman who did not know the first thing about pulling yourself up by your bootstraps. Thanks to Hollywood, Billie had become much more Becky Sharp than Lady Bareacres, had she only been able to recognize it.[6]

It was Flo's past, and his legacy, that occupied Billie most, and was the theme of her recorded commentary during her New York sojourn. News had reached New York that Metro-Goldwyn-Mayer was planning a massive film tracing the arc and fall of Flo's career, to a script written by William Anthony McGuire. In later years, Billie confessed she did not care for *The Great Ziegfeld*. "I could not bear to see it [in 1936]," she wrote later. "No movie, and not anything I can write now, can recapture the gentle moments which were our real life together." Only one scene which still moved her years later, when she caught it on a television rerun, was the depiction of Christmas Eve at Burkeley Crest, the drawing room filled with the outlandishly expensive and outlandishly creative presents the Ziegfelds' gave each other and their daughter, in those days when money seemed to fall like rain.

This happy memory certainly posed a contrast to the other side of the marriage — Flo's philandering — which was depicted with as much fidelity to truth as Louis B. Mayer's strait-laced standards and the censorship office allowed. Billie had no significant control over the film (and was not a performer in it, despite rumors to the contrary — Patricia helped with research, and Billie occasionally advised, but that was all), and no direct interest in it, aside from a clause in the contract with McGuire assuring her a percentage of receipts. So there was not much she could do about the way she or Flo or their marriage were depicted except muse to reporters how happy she was that motion pictures were being subjected to "clean up" — the Breen Office's censorship that began in 1934 — and to state how happy she was that William Powell had been selected to play Flo. She also stated she hoped that Miriam Hopkins, with whose Becky Sharp she had had a few scenes, would be selected to play herself. "Perhaps I am flattering myself,"

Billie, center, and daughter Patricia, at her left, talk to reporters in their train carriage on Billie's first return to New York since Flo's death in July 1932.

Billie said, "but I have always felt that Miss Hopkins is much as I was years ago." She had the same "spirit, fire, optimism, love of life" that Billie believed had characterized her, and there was certainly the same impression in Hopkins that, like Billie, she would set up a magnificent tantrum if given half a chance. But Myrna Loy, who had the requisite beauty and elegant poise, was selected instead. (She did not have Billie's unreserved approval: Billie told Barbara Rush in later years that "I thought [Loy] was lovely, but she doesn't much look like me, does she?" Loy herself, in an interview in the *Los Angeles Times*, April 5, 1935, admitted that impersonating Billie was "embarrassing" for her: "Billie was on my conscience throughout the making of that picture," she confessed. Billie also told Barbara Rush that while she admired William Powell's acting, he was "nothing, absolutely nothing" like Flo.)[7]

The Great Ziegfeld is ironically not quite the fast-paced entertainment that its inspiration was so famed for demanding from his cast and crew. One of the most expensive films ever made by MGM, *The Great Ziegfeld* followed Flo's career from his Sandow days at the Chicago World's Fair to the *Follies*; through Anna Held (played by Oscar-winning actress Luise Rainer), Lillian Lorraine (renamed Audrey Dane and played by Virginia Bruce), Billie, and the other women in Flo's life; the lavish lifestyle and spending; the debts and altercations with designers, performers, artists and composers; the stock market crash and, finally, Flo's death with Sidney Boggis (played by Ernest Cossart) by his side. Artistic license is rife: Flo is shown working as a common sideshow barker at the World's Fair; Billie arrives at the famous New Year's party at the Sixty Club not with Somerset Maugham but with Billings, a friendly rival and investor of Flo's who may have been inspired by Charles Dillingham (played by Frank Morgan). Flo died not in an apartment across the street from the Ziegfeld Theatre but in a hospital in Los Angeles. There was only so much time for exploring any deeper conflicts in his character or his marriage to Billie in a script that called for several re-enactments of *Follies* shows, the most gargantuan of these being the giant twirling wedding cake stacked with singers, dancers, musicians and *Follies* girls, performing the number "A Pretty Girl is Like a Melody."

Ironically, the movie lacks the powerful sense of momentum said to have characterized every production Flo oversaw, and there is something a little macabre about a film that overtly displays the philandering of a famous impresario a mere few years after his death *and* with his widow and ruined mistress looking on from the audience — a widow, as we have seen, who during their marriage had made a point of denying to the press that her husband was any kind of philanderer. And the film, and by extension Billie, was a victim of its own success. When it, despite its high costs, did well at the box office, garnering Oscar nominations and two wins — Best Picture and Best Actress (Luise Rainer) — creditors came out of the woodwork again and demanded their share.

It would be fascinating to know exactly how it felt for Billie when she stepped off the train with Patricia in Grand Central Station that spring of 1935 and found herself back in the thick of New York — the setting of her and Flo's triumphs and abject failures. Perhaps it comes as a surprise to those who know Billie Burke only through her character roles in film, in which her swift oscillations between tears and laughter appear to peg her as fragile and weak, that she was never a complainer. While she could wax rueful about her stage career and what she thought it should be, she was not one to dwell on her miseries or expound on them, either to the press or to the pages of her memoirs. Only later, and in private letters to a friend she loved and trusted, would Billie confide the darker parts of her soul, which New York seemed to call forth every time she set foot in the city. (This is why we don't hear a whimper from her about another tragedy that befell her after Flo's death: the death of Will Rogers in an Alaskan plane crash in August 1935.)[8]

Burkely Crest may have been unendurable to Billie, who when she referred to it at all in interviews she gave at this time does so as if speaking of some cursed place instead of what was once a house of joy. We do not know if she visited the house on this trip, and it is unlikely she would have mentioned it in her memoirs had she done so — it was not her way to record what was to her unspeakable. Perhaps, too, her habit of sweeping things under the rug played its role. But as sad as Burkeley Crest was to her, she held on to it until she could not do so any longer. The estate was finally sold in 1940. "Billie Burke Sells Her Estate," blared the newspapers. Mortgaged more than once, Burkeley Crest and whatever was left in it of Billie's and Flo's household goods were sold for pennies on the dollar for a total of $42,000.

Even with the success of *The Great Ziegfeld* four years before, there is no indication that anything auctioned off from Burkeley Crest was sold at better than garage sale prices. Given this discount, it is more likely those who snapped up the grand piano, once played by Gershwin and Friml, Romberg and Berlin, for $135, or Flo's special walnut bed, constructed to permit him to conduct business over the phone without ever leaving his bedroom, which sold for $31, or the dozens of other items that could just as easily have been left on a roadside table with a "Free Stuff" sign on them, were more attracted by the bargains rather than the items' contact with the famous. The estate itself, on which there was a past due mortgage of over $20,000, sold for an appalling $36,000, which even in 1940 values amounted to a little over $500,000. Billie had paid

Billie Burke seated at her desk in the study off her bedroom at Burkeley Crest, the Civil War-era mansion she bought at the height of her Broadway fame in 1911, and lost to bankruptcy thirty years later. Photograph ca. 1915.

In the "fine days," before the stock market crash and Flo's death ended the enchanted world of the *Follies*, composer Sigmund Romberg had often played just for Billie at Burkeley Crest. Here they are pictured years later in Hollywood (ca. 1938).

the 2007 equivalent of $1.5 million for the estate in 1911. (As a sad footnote, a bust of Billie went for a mere $7.)[9]

In one of her few references to the liquidation of Burkeley Crest, Billie is clear about what it all meant to her. She had felt long ago, that last summer Flo was alive, that "Burkeley Crest had lost its charm. It was still and sad, like a house long neglected, like a home where there is no more love." It had become a "mock home," a vacation spot for creditors instead of friends, a flashpoint for anxiety instead of pleasure. And yet without this house, how much worse off would the Ziegfelds have been? The first manifestation of Billie's success, it is fitting that Burkeley Crest was the last of her tangible assets to hold firm till the end. Yet she was to retain from it certain special exceptions to the rule of making a clean slate of a complicated mess: many of the elephant figurines with which Flo had filled the home were transferred to Billie's little house in Brentwood, where she was photographed years later surrounded by them. Various costumes from famous Ziegfeld shows were also saved. And the great bronze name plates that had adorned the stone pillars at Burkeley Crest's entrance were given to Billie by the estate's buyer (the house was later razed by a developer), and are displayed by the Ziegfeld descendants to this day.

Billie had not given up on the New York stage, which she would remain convinced was where she belonged, long after it was clear that Broadway had left her behind. At first she had jumped at the chance to be part of Zoë Akins' 1935 play, *The Old Maid*, an adaptation from an Edith Wharton novella about two cousins, Charlotte and Delia, who look out for each other through a variety of romantic and rather more shocking vicissitudes. Billie was particularly happy that the premiere was scheduled for a Los Angeles theatre. She was not the only actress with a Broadway past to find L.A.'s serious but far less traumatizing theatre world a better place to open a play than among the knives of New York's feared drama critics (Billie had already felt the sharp edges of a Woollcott review). Adding to everything else, George Cukor had impressed upon Billie that the play was perfect for her, and she already loved the story, which had "the kind of beauty and character in it that I had always hoped to bring to the theater." With her mannerisms, many of them learned from moving among twittering grandee dames of London and New York, Billie was well-suited to play a Wharton character.

At the last minute, however, the production of *The Old Maid* was shifted from a Los Angeles to a New York premiere, and not just to any old Broadway theater but to the Empire, where Billie had had her first success with John Drew in *My Wife* nearly thirty years earlier. In her memoirs, Billie explained how risky it was to leave secure employment — her film work in Hollywood — to venture out in a new play, and to prepare oneself for the exhausting weeks of rehearsal and the run, and then the reviews and interviews and assorted other draining activities: an admission, in a way, that her age was catching up with her.

There is something more, however, behind what amounts to a paper and ink version of one of her own "silly women," proffering a prolix explanation of something that could be clarified in a few words. Perhaps her most telling comment is: "my courage failed me." In the eternal wrangle between reality and dreams, Billie had come to the point where, as she put it, if given a choice between tin and gold, she who would have seized on the gold without a thought now realized it was more practical in the end to choose the tin. "And so I turned down the play," she finishes, "and went back to trying to balance a feather on my nose." She had discovered something about herself, and it was not without despair: the film work, the roles she had assumed, the necessary evil of Hollywood, was not just a temporary annoyance that she could leave once a production wrapped, returning to the beautiful temple of live theatre, where her true happiness could bloom. It was her life now — the ship she had chosen to sail in.[10]

But it took two more sallies at the harsh fortress of the theatre before Billie came to accept — or, more likely, to sublimate the fact — that Broadway had no use for her special abilities any more. Billie was not to walk a New York stage again until 1943, when she appeared in *This Rock* at the Longacre Theatre. Playing a role that should have ensured success — that of the breezy lady of a manor who is bequeathed a houseful of children evacuated from the bombed East End of London during World War II — Billie did not get good reviews nor did the play, which ran for only thirty-seven performances. As critic Lewis Nichols pointed out, while Billie "still has the vague, flighty gestures of old," these mannerisms, as he terms them, would have been put to better use in a script that "did not so bother her." This was one of the ways in which reviewers had been soft-pedaling their criticisms of her for years: it was the play that was at fault, though reading between the lines we can see that in fact Billie's mishandling of her part had something to do with the play falling flat. (And, too, perhaps her growing trouble remembering her lines.)[11]

Billie's next venture the following year was another Akins play, *Mrs. January and Mr. Ex* (an effort to make up for missing out on Akins' *The Old Maid?*), in which she played a wealthy woman gone Communist who wants to see what it is like living the proletariat life, and ends up renting a house from a former Republican president of the United States whose views, naturally, do not at all jibe with hers. Billie played her by now patented scatterbrained upper class matron role opposite Frank Craven's terse realism in what, like *This Rock*, should have been a successful pairing, whatever the critics thought of the play itself. But despite fair reviews for the actors the production was not well received. The *New York Times'* Nichols thought it "talkative and long and [getting] nowhere in particular." Billie, wrote Nichols, "seemed to be trying a little too much, as though she realized the limitations of the script and hoped to help it along by sheer exertion and goodwill," an opinion shared by the reviewer of *Time*: "In terms of plot, [Akins] has little more to offer than that Karl Marx is no match for Dan Cupid." Billie would have tried hard, because Billie was a fighter — not just for her friend Zoë Akins' play, but for her own survival as a stage actress. But it wasn't enough.

For the first and last time, Billie was caricatured by Al Hirschfeld of *The New York Times*. He depicted her in the diadem and flowing society matron's evening gown of Mrs. January, curving toward the cowering Frank Craven like a chiffon scimitar (much as Hirschfeld famously caricatured Charlotte Greenwood, also for the first and last time, in the role of Juno in Cole Porter's *Out of This World*, a show her performance, like Billie's in *Mrs. January*, was believed to have kept running long past its natural life). But what seem to have been the considerable charms of the Craven/Burke partnership and Billie's efforts to do her best were not enough to ensure continued life. The play closed after a short run of a month, what Billie aptly calls a "quick failure." It should have been a success, she pointed out in her memoirs. "It had all the ingredients, but it hadn't the spark," she added, "so let us leave it in peace." Clearly, Hollywood, radio and nascent television were the places for Billie to be, even if her work there also made it necessary for her to sell gas refrigerators and toothpaste. At least radio work allowed her to perform again with faces from her and Flo's past — John Barrymore, Eddie Cantor, and others, and to host her own show. But all this came after the film role that would define Billie Burke for all time.[12]

CHAPTER 19

Good Witch

When Hollywood approaches a blockbuster book and considers how to turn it into a blockbuster movie, it acts upon the material less like a literary editor and more like a mutant virus, the sole unchanging characteristic of which is to gain the most nourishment from its host.

Not all filmed novels survive this process, but a few were born to give an inspiring literary work a second cinematic birth. Margaret Mitchell's *Gone with the Wind* is one larger than life example. The plot endured changes, reconfigurations, outright elisions, and inauthentic exaggerations to become as much classic film as it is classic novel. Where L. Frank Baum's *The Wizard of Oz* is in a class all its own is in the fact that MGM's film version, through the scattered efforts of an army of hired and fired writers, became something bigger and, in the some ways, better than the original conception. No matter what decisions, for good or ill, were made about the script or the cinematography or the casting, no matter the blunders or inspirations of judgment or taste, *Oz* seemed to have a personality of its own that willed itself to become what we know today: one of the greatest movies ever made, and a classic cinematic parable on the human condition.

The story of how L. Frank Baum and, later, Louis B. Mayer, made *Oz* a permanent fixture of Western popular culture, has been told many times: how Baum, one evening in May 1898 at his home in Chicago, was entertaining the neighborhood children, as well as his own, by telling them the adventures of a cast of make-believe characters. One of the children asked Baum where the Tin Woodman and Scarecrow and Dorothy lived — quick thinking Baum happened to notice the alphabetical label on a file cabinet and told the kids his stories took place in the Land of "OZ." By 1899 Baum, who had tried and failed acting, playwriting, traveling sales, and a variety of other jobs that would have spun the head of a Figaro, before finding success with children's stories, had published the book called *The Emerald City*, which became known as *The Wizard of Oz*.

Oz is the story of a little girl named Dorothy, who lives in a one-room Kansas farmhouse with her Aunt Em and Uncle Henry. With them lives Dorothy's dog, Toto, sketched by illustrator William Wallace Denslow as a cairn terrier. "Not a tree nor a house broke the broad sweep of flat country that reached to the edge of the sky in all directions," described Baum. "The sun had baked the plowed land into a gray mass, with little cracks running through it." It is never explained what happened to Dorothy's parents, but she was brought to the farm as a very young child, where her laughter startled Aunt Em so much she would "scream and press her heart." Surrounded by this grayness and the two older people, mute in their day's endless chores, Dorothy has only Toto to make her laugh.

One day a tornado overtakes the farm. Before she can join Aunt Em and Uncle Henry in the storm cellar, Dorothy and Toto and the house are swept away to a strange land, where "[b]anks of gorgeous flowers were on every hand, and birds with rare and brilliant plumage sang and fluttered in the trees and bushes." Small people, known as Munchkins, emerge from this lush landscape to greet her and to pay her homage, for the house has fallen on the Wicked Witch of the East, ending her reign of terror over the Munchkins. All that remains of her are her magical silver shoes, which a sweet little old lady, who announces herself as the Witch of the North, urges Dorothy to put on. Because Dorothy is afraid and wants to get back to Kansas as soon as possible, the Witch of the North advises her to follow the yellow brick road to the City of Emeralds, where there is a wizard who can help her. From this point the reader encounters Dorothy's meetings with the Scarecrow, Tin Woodman and Cowardly Lion, all of whom, like herself, hope to get something from the wizard.

The wizard, who takes on various shapes, including a great head, a ball of fire and a beautiful lady, tells the four seekers that if they bring him proof that the Wicked Witch of the West is dead, he will grant their wishes. This Wicked Witch, who has one piercing eye, already has her sight on Dorothy and her friends, ambushes and captures them and brings them to her castle, and tries to get the silver shoes for herself. She eventually gets one of them, but before she can take the other Dorothy tosses a bucket of water at her, melting her. She and her trio return to the Emerald City, where as they explain to the wizard that they have killed the Wicked Witch, Toto knocks over a screen, revealing that "Oz, the Terrible" is actually not so much wizard as wizened, an old man who trembles at being discovered to be just an ordinary man. After the initial disappointment, however, "Oz" does give the Scarecrow, Tin Man and Lion the attributes they sought (via a kind of auto-suggestion, appropriate for a sideshow magician), and tells Dorothy that he will take her back to Kansas with him in a balloon. But on the day of the ascent, Toto goes missing and "Oz" flies away by himself. It is suggested that Dorothy go in search of Glinda, the Witch of the South, who lives in a palace of rubies, and after several adventures, including traversing a country made entirely of china, Dorothy reaches Glinda's ruby castle.

Glinda is indeed as beautiful as described: she "knows how to keep young in spite of the many years she has lived," says one character — this and another passage could stand as a description of Billie herself: "Her hair was a rich red in color and fell in flowing ringlets over her shoulders. Her dress was pure white but her eyes were blue, and they looked kindly upon the little girl." Glinda tells Dorothy all she needs to do to get back to Kansas is click the heels of the silver shoes together three times, and tell them where she wants to go. No sooner has she done so than she wakes up in a field just beside where her aunt and uncle's farmhouse once stood. The first clue she has that she is back home is the image of Uncle Henry milking a cow.[1]

It did not take long for this story to make it to the stage and even to a few early

Billie would jokingly describe herself in an interview as looking "like a fugitive from German opera ... but, in a way, I'm supposed to. Glinda's a heroic figure. She has only to wave her wand, and the world is changed...." Clarence Sinclair Bull shot this image of Billie's one immortal role in an immortal film: as Glinda the Good Witch of the North in MGM's *The Wizard of Oz*. **University of Southern California Cinematic Arts Library collection.**

silent films, but it was not until February 18, 1938, when MGM vice president Eddie Mannix purchased the screen rights to *The Wizard of Oz* from Sam Goldwyn, Billie's old benefactor, who had been approached by several studios hoping to capitalize on the success of *Snow White and the Seven Dwarfs*. The hardest character to cast was that of Toto—played by a female cairn terrier named Terry—but with a few hitches the rest of the cast was placed with what can only be described as genius: Judy Garland as Dorothy (winning out over what would have been the miscasting of Shirley

Billie's role as Glinda the Good was a brilliant amalgamation of L. Frank Baum's elderly sprite of a Good Witch of the North and his elegant young queen of a Glinda, Witch of the South. Illustrations by W. W. Denslow from 1900 first edition of *The Wizard of Oz*. Bekah and Fern Galindo collection.

Temple); Ray Bolger as the Scarecrow (he had originally been set for the Tin Man but fought his way to the role more appropriate to his talents); Jack Haley as the Tin Man (replacing Buddy Ebsen, for whom the aluminum-based makeup had almost cost him his life); Frank Morgan as the Wizard, as well as Dr. Marvell and a coachman, doorman and guard in the Emerald City (a feat Ed Wynn, originally tapped for the role, could never have pulled off as well), and the adorable but troubled Bert Lahr as the Cowardly Lion, pulling out all the vaudeville stops. Circus impresario Leo Singer managed to gather an army of one hundred twenty-four little people to populate the thatched cottages of Munchkinland.[2]

For the two witches in the script, none more evil of visage or more convincing of character could have been found than the actually sweet and charming Margaret Hamilton, whose green talons, knife-like nose and screeching voice have haunted many a child's nights since 1939. In typical *Oz* fashion, in which production looked at all the wrong people before finding the person born to play the part, actresses as varied as Edna Mae Oliver and Gale Sondergaard were considered — the latter was actually tested in costumes that varied from sultry "fallen woman" to plain sourpuss.

It's sometimes said that Billie was the first actress the studio thought of to play Glinda, but such is not the case. To complicate matters, the script amalgamated the Witches of the North and South: the giggly elderly Northern witch was subsumed into the beautiful red-haired Southern Glinda. The personality of the Northern witch first made it seem a comedienne would be the best choice, which is why performers such as Fanny Brice and Beatrice Lillie were at the top of the list. But what the studio wanted was at least one glamorous witch, and when it was clear Margaret Hamilton would create a witch wicked to the core, it was obvious Glinda would have to be her opposite number. Thus emphasis was placed on the girlish appearance and coolly elegant manner of Baum's Glinda, and Glinda the Good Witch of the North was born. And Billie Burke, with her red hair, blue eyes and unique grace, was selected to play her.

It took a while before the world of this film, with its myriad of details, coalesced and formed a harmonic whole. Uncredited early director Richard Thorpe had Judy Garland got up in blonde hair and ribbons; her magic slippers were restyled many times, ranging from a kind of Ali Baba pointed toe shoe, more appropriate for a Munchkin, to the pumps we know of today (and changing from silver to ruby to take better advantage of Technicolor's possibilities). The Tin Man and Scarecrow and Lion went through phases of development before their "look" looked right. George Cukor's appearance as temporary stand-in, after Richard Thorpe was fired by producer Mervyn LeRoy and before Victor Fleming took over, had a great deal to do with making the film look the way we know it today. It was originally assumed that Cukor would fill in where needed, but he did more than that: strongly disliking Thorpe's work, he reshot numerous scenes after stripping costumes, sets and actors of what he considered extraneous and irrelevant details. The simplicity he gave Judy Garland is as important as his efforts to emphasize the sharp features of Margaret Hamilton. Each character's individuality emerged and bloomed from this brief but potent Cukorian reorganization.[3]

Shooting began in October 1938, under Richard Thorpe; by the time it wrapped in March 1939, Thorpe had been replaced by Cukor, who then made way for Victor Fleming, whose work on *Gone with the Wind* required him to drop out toward the end of filming; the last few scenes were directed by King Vidor. The musical chairs aspect of direction was of a piece with the generally accident-prone atmosphere on the set. There were a few near tragedies in this happiest of film fairy tales. Buddy Ebsen, the first Tin Man, ended up with a life-threatening reaction to the aluminum-based makeup worn for his role, putting him in a hospital for weeks and out of the cast of the film.

Margaret Hamilton's accident, during her exit from her first scene, as she departs in flames from Munchkinland, is well known: as Hamilton descended through a trap door, jets of fire burst too soon and burned her face and hands, which were covered in toxic copper oxide makeup to make her skin look green. Immediately after the accident, her burned flesh had to be rubbed to get the makeup off before salve could be applied — an excruciating necessity. She could not return to the set for six weeks, during which the studio, which did not even send her home in a studio car, called again and again to find out when she was returning to the set. In our litigious age, Hamilton could have sued MGM for all it was worth, but "I wanted to work again," she explained. Had she sued, she knew she would forfeit ever getting a job with another film studio.[4]

The two witches did not have much in common in or out of costume, and were often not even on the set at the same time (there is only one scene, when Dorothy first arrives in Munchkinland, when both women are actually together), so that sometimes Hamilton was able to eat her lunch in Billie's splendid dressing-room (standing up, she was careful to point out). She later described the room by contrasting it with the canvas cubicle allotted to her — she may have been playing a part that would make her immortal, but Margaret Hamilton was still a small contract player, not a star character actress like Billie. The dressing room sounds like a throwback to Billie's bedroom at Burkeley Crest: it had, according to Hamilton, walls of pink satin, with matching furniture, including a chaise lounge. All its appointments were done in pink and blue (including bowls of pink and blue mints).

As if to imply that queenly settings beget queenly behavior, Hamilton remembered Billie leaving the set one day while she was waiting for a costume photo test, and not returning in time for the appointment. Staff were sent looking for her, and when she did arrive, in a studio limousine, an assistant director had the temerity to anxiously ask where she had been, pointing out how expensive the delay was and how it had thrown off the schedule. Hamilton watched as Billie began to cry. "You're browbeating me!" Hamilton heard her sob. Or so author Aljean Harmetz recalled.

Harmetz' interviews with Hamilton give the overall impression that Hamilton was critical of Billie, drawing amused attention to the décor of her dressing room, referring to her as "the fairy lady," and expressing astonishment that when Billie injured her ankle on the set (she tripped over some wires, much as one of her ditzy "silly women" would do), the studio made a big deal out of the small incident by sending for an ambulance. No such attention had been accorded Hamilton when she had nearly burned to death. But one *Oz* expert, John Fricke, criticizes not Hamilton but Harmetz, claiming her interview skews what were very likely harmless anecdotes taken out of context and recorded without the reader knowing with what warm and kindly humor they were shared.

"Part of it is," says Fricke, "when you read Maggie saying those things, they don't come off with the charm with which she would say them in person. I knew her well here in New York, and we had mutual friends. She was as down to earth and sweet and funny about that sort of thing as she could be." In any case, knowing how important it was to Louis B. Mayer to be seen as the Great Father of his stable of stars, it is as plausible that Billie, with all her past baggage of a life of great luxury, should be typecast even in an ankle cast as the studio whisked her away in a shiny limousine/ambulance. "Do we know how to take care of our stars," L.B. might have said, with a leonine grin, "or *don't* we?" Hamilton was not a star, so sending her home with a friend and then badgering her about when she planned to return to filming was part of how a contract player was treated in the studio hierarchy, something Hamilton well understood.[5]

Munchkinland Coroner Meinhardt Raabe remembered Billie not being all that involved with the others on the set — she was only in a handful of scenes, actually, and would not have even been on the set much of the time — but did recall seeing her sitting outside her dressing room, almost as if hoping for company (and perhaps to escape her dressing room's unrelieved pink and blue color scheme). "She didn't mingle with the little people like the rest of the cast," he wrote, but she always chatted with people who stopped to say hello. (It must be remembered that she was not on the set as much as the principal players; nor, for that matter, were the little people.) He also recalled hearing about an extraordinary on-set performance she put on for director

Billie posing at the Los Angeles premiere of *The Wizard of Oz* with Munchkinland Mayor Charlie Becker and other cast members. She loved what she called the "wonderful little people," and the feeling was mutual.

Fleming — not a man who was, one might say, all that receptive to actresses pulling a fast one on him. (Many were physically afraid of him.)

Karl Slover, the first Munchkin trumpeter, told Raabe that Billie walked on the set the first day wearing nothing but black. She was wearing not just a black dress — she also wore a black hat, black gloves, and carried a black cane, with which she stumped her way across the set like a bent old crone. She crept across to where Fleming stood, no doubt frowning as he said, "What's the matter, coming in here like that, all hunched over? Stand up straight." "At which," reported Slover, "Billie Burke stood fully upright," tossed off the hat and gloves and cane, and announced to Fleming, "If I am going to work with all these wonderful little people, then they should know what I really look like in real life[!]" Fleming grunted, but the little people who met and got to know Billie adored her for this comic side — it was the sort of comedy routine many of them knew from their work in vaudeville and the circus. (Raabe knew that Billie's father had been a famous circus clown; perhaps the others did, too.) Slover couldn't believe she was in her fifties — to him, especially in her Glinda costume, Billie looked like she could not have been much past thirty. This, too, to little people who had labored all their lives under the burden of being treated like children, would have made her feel one of them, and perhaps more so: Billie didn't mind at all being treated like a child — it was one of the best ways to gain control of a situation (it had worked with Flo).[6]

The creation of what became Glinda the Good started, as noted above, with a blending of both the witches of North and South: the elderly but jocular old granny and the ever youthful, red-haired Glinda. It is one of the many happy coincidences in the casting and conceptualizing of *Oz* that Billie should be hired to play a character who is both old and young — at 53, she was not so far from the age when many women were dandling grandchildren on their laps. Yet her seemingly unchanging youthfulness and beauty were as much her hallmark as they were the singular characteristic of Baum's Southern sorceress.

Like Glinda, Billie wore a gown covered in stars, though designer Gilbert Adrian had the happy idea of tinting the gauze skirts the palest shade of rose-pink, which echoed Billie's red hair, set off her Glinda-like blue eyes and put her in tune with the imagery associated with all such pink gauze females: ball-gowned debutantes, pliéing ballerinas, and queens (soon to include the drag variety). Billie would jokingly describe herself in an interview about the role as looking "like a fugitive from German opera ... but, in a way, I'm supposed to. Glinda's a heroic figure. She has only to wave her wand, and the world is changed...." But this was her favorite film role of all — not just because she was so smashingly gowned, but also and especially because of that combination of beauty and heroism that she never got to enjoy in most of the film roles over her then thirty-six-year career.

With its puffed sleeves and corseted waist and acres of flowing skirts, Billie's gown was similar to costumes she had worn before — as the Comtesse de Candale in *A Marriage of Convenience*, as Eloise de Kestournel *The Marquise*. Victor Fleming wanted her to appear to actually float; and as can be seen, anyone watching Billie levitate through *Oz*, with the gliding gait of a high-born lady at the French court, can appreciate why this was the one film role of the forty-five she had made by the time she was cast in *Oz* that she singled out for especial approbation. Glinda not only reminded Billie, as she stated in her memoirs, of "the kind of parts I did in the theater." The beautiful fairy who could change the world with a wave of her silver wand was that ideal self Billie wanted to be — which, for a time, she had had a taste of as the wife of Flo Ziegfeld. In so many ways, Glinda was both Billie's ideal role and her ideal woman.[7]

Of all the Hollywood musicals made by MGM or any other studio, *Oz* seems richest in the possibilities of subtext and symbolism. Various commentators have ascribed different meanings to the characters in *Oz*, including socio-political symbolism: the Scarecrow as American farmer ignorant of his own power, the Tin Man as heartless industry needing to wake up to its compassion for mankind, the Lion as a judicial system that needs to find the guts to do its job, all of them led by Dorothy, a daughter of the people, down the yellow brick road (as in gold, or money), to depose an unqualified potentate ruling by fear a city of deluded happy people and install her three members of the grass-roots proletariat in his place. The witches are especially ripe for expository theories. In her valuable study of the genesis and making of *Oz*, Aljean Harmetz offers the idea that in the film the Wicked Witch of the West and Aunt Em are two sides of the same coin, the Bad Mother/Good Mother opposites, joined by the shared attribute of absolute power over Dorothy. Harmetz points out as proof the scene in the Wicked Witch's castle, where Dorothy is given a glimpse in a crystal ball of Aunt Em calling for her, only for the familiar face to dissolve into the hateful visage of the Witch.

Sir Salman Rushie comes to a different conclusion: "Glinda and the Witch of the West," he writes, "are the only two symbols of power in a film which is largely about the powerless." He sees the film's power center as a triangle of Glinda, Dorothy, and the Wicked Witch; the Wizard, imagined to be another powerful figure, is actually not, underscoring the relative powerlessness of men in this female-driven story.[8]

The Wicked Witch, as with all villains, has tended to draw the most attention over the years, with various authors speculating about who she really was, what she stands for, what made her so wicked, and so forth. Rushdie even questions what the Wicked Witch of the East had done to share the sobriquet of "wicked" with her western sister — after all, Munchkinland has clean streets, and seems too ideally innocent a setting to have been only recently overrun by a sorceress whose death has the Munchkins singing (which is a bit like wondering how, if the streets of Moscow or Beijing looked so tidy and their citizens so content, how could Stalin or Mao be quite so bad?). As late as 2003, the musical theatre success *Wicked* offered a rehabilitation of the Wicked Witch at the expense of the ambitious, social-climbing Glinda (typecast not unlike many a character part played by Billie Burke). Rushdie would concur with this characterization, though he seems to be more critical of Billie than of Glinda; he dubs Billie's Glinda "a trilling pain in the neck." But when considering how crucial Glinda is to the momentum and resolution of the plot, what can we discover by looking past comparisons with the Wicked Witch, literal readings of the film and viewers out of tune with Billie's "silly women," facing that vision in pink tulle head on? [9]

As we know, it's easy to love a character we love to hate. It is as easy as it is to take for granted the surface sparkle of a role, like Glinda, that can be mistaken for a cardboard cutout: the cookie cutter good fairy who descends in a dash of glitter to make everything right again, then disappears from thought. The Wicked Witch has some redoubtable lines and she throws out some zingers: "I'll catch you, my pretty, and your little dog, too!" is one of several statements that Margaret Hamilton made classic (and camp). But it is Glinda, not the Wicked Witch, whose lines are most crucial to the development of Dorothy's adventure, not to mention adding several idiomatic sayings to the English language. Lines like "Come out, come out, wherever you are," "Are you a good witch or a bad witch?," "Just follow the yellow brick road," and "There's no place like home" have passed into immortality, in everything from children's books to Castro Street lingo (much as Billie Burke remains fixed in the cultural firmaments of both children and gay men). Above all, Glinda is just as vital in sending Dorothy on her journey to Oz as she is to awakening her to what she needs to do to get back to Kansas: that home is where the real Oz is, if she can only train her eyes and heart to realize it.

That Glinda's importance was understood at all levels of the production of *The Wizard of Oz* can only be described as obvious. Can it be a coincidence that the first and last notes we hear of the score, a repeated, urgent descending passage in a minor key, both joyfully annunciatory and darkly ominous, is that which heralds Glinda's first appearance when Dorothy arrives in Munchkinland? Or that when Glinda appears and disappears she does so in a rainbow-colored sphere, linking her to the rainbow over which Dorothy, clutching Toto in Aunt Em's farmyard, longs to fly?

Just who is Glinda? The Scarecrow, Tin Man and Lion have their *Doppelgängers* among Aunt Em's Kansas farmhands; screeching old maid school teacher Miss Gulch becomes the Wicked Witch; humbug magician Professor Marvell becomes the humbug Wizard of Oz. Glinda does not have an opposite number, unless we consider an important presence missing from Dorothy's life, in Baum's book and in the film: her mother. When Dorothy comes to live with her aunt and uncle, she is an orphan. Aunt Em becomes the surrogate maternal figure, but with her brusque farmwoman's ways she is no substitute. It is when Dorothy has survived her descent in the wind-whipped farmhouse, killing someone in the process, into a world stranger than anything she could have dreamed on a Kansas farm, that she is met by a good fairy who is every child's ideal mother, in her beautiful appearance, her caring concern and in her resolve to teach her child that life's lessons are not learned the easy way. Glinda represents that maternal presence absent in Dorothy's hardscrabble life on the farm. She can also be seen as the personification of Dorothy's highest self—Dorothy thinks her the most beautiful person she has ever seen, but is not even aware of the purity of her own heart.

In Glinda's worldview, only good can be taken seriously. In her serenity, so unruffled there is plenty of opportunity for detached amusement at the inexplicable wickedness of the Witch of the West, Billie glows with an inner beauty and calm that is everything worried, frantic and lost Dorothy might aspire to. Using equal parts "silly woman" and stage beauty, her Glinda is too good to conceive of evil as being anything more than a brief annoyance which can, in any event, be ignored because it cannot be taken seriously. Evil is treated like a temporary imbalance in a world of otherwise constant fairness, order and, above all, goodness—a goodness that is the essence of that undamaged purity seen nowhere but in a child, a saint, or a flower.

There were artists and philosophers who, after the horrors of the Nazi death camps were known, declared that a newer, harsher world had unfolded, where belief in fantasy and in a God were severely challenged by the realization of what people could do to torture and degrade their own kind—philosopher, musician, critic, and all-round Renaissance man Theodor Adorno even declared (though he later retracted) that "to still write poetry after Auschwitz is barbaric." But the poetry of believing in good continued to live after the world's convulsions of 1939–1945. Glinda descended into Dorothy's fantasy and that of moviegoers a little over a week before the start of World War II, and outlived the carnage. Sparkling, floating, evanescent, here one moment and gone the next, a sort of human butterfly perpetually hatching from her iridescent chrysalis, Glinda is all of those lovely un-nameable, indefinable ideals in the human soul that cannot be pinned down or quantified, but which are no less substantial and real.

One *Oz* controversy, not raised till years later, still continues to live around the role of Glinda — namely, whether or not Billie sang the lyric to "Come Out, Come Out, Wherever You Are."

In John Fricke's book, *The Wizard of Oz: The Official 50th Anniversary Pictorial History,* the author himself states that "Lorraine Bridges was later called in to redo the singing for Burke's Glinda," and this is the party line held to by several *Oz* writers. But a lot has been added to *Oz* scholarship since 1989. Fricke says it is now accepted by most historians that Billie did her own singing, and there is proof to back it up.

"There are scores of 5 × 7 cards from the MGM files that cite, movie by movie, who was brought in to do vocal double work or extra work or pre-recording work," Fricke says. "The card for *The Wizard of Oz* cites Lorraine Bridges working on *Oz* and as being paid $25 extra to dub for Billie. Once a few writers and historians got hold of this, it was trumpeted around the world. One author even comments on this remarkable vocal sound-alike, Lorraine Bridges. Well, when we did the first deluxe laser disc, in 1993, of *Oz,* to include all the surviving pre-recordings from the sound track, underscoring and alternate audio tracks, we went back to the documentation, and it's not just the tracks — you hear the technicians say 'OK, production 1060, take twenty,' something like that. And there's Billie, and Judy singing, at the beginning of the Munchkinland sequence. It's obviously the track that was included in the film. From the paperwork we know that Lorraine Bridges did later tracks, but they did not use these. Her tracks were not even kept, which is more proof positive."

"There's no question that it's Billie Burke," Fricke adds. "The paperwork proves it. Period." As we know, Billie had had formal vocal training as a young woman, and indeed got her start in musical comedy. She had sung on the stage, and while those examples are lost she did sing in several of her films before and after *Oz,* as well as on her radio show of the mid–1940s. And Billie's own granddaughters, to whom she taught several of the songs she had made famous since her London musical comedy days, would not be likely to mistake the voice of a dubbing artist for that of their grandmother.[10]

One other area where Aljean Harmetz may have given a skewed impression in her book is in her account of the film's critical reception. "It is tempting to imagine," she writes, "that the film was embraced by the critics. In fact, most of the serious critics thought it dreadful."[11] John Fricke demurs: "The reviews for this movie are like love letters, for the most part," he says. "In fact, those few who didn't like it are taken to task by the others: 'Who are these dummies who are saying bad things about this wonderful entertainment!'"[12] Aside from a few naysayers at the beginning, starting from the film's advance screening for international press on August 9, 1939, reviews were very much the love letters Fricke describes. The *Hollywood Reporter* wrote that "*Oz* will, beyond question, be accorded recognition as a milestone in motion picture history," adding that the movie "scintillates with artistry." The *Los Angeles Illustrated Daily News* described the film as "a lush and lovable production, told with laughter, song and pathos," while the *New York Mirror* adjured its adult readers to hie themselves to the cinema to experience a masterpiece: "Borrow a child and see it." And of course, the soulful performance of Judy Garland, the dastardly witch of Margaret Hamilton, and the adroit antics of the trio of Ray Bolger, Jack Haley, Bert Lahr, and Frank Morgan were extolled in column after column across the country. But Billie drew notice, mostly, as Fricke explains, because nobody could believe their eyes.

"One of the points that several of the critics make is how Billie Burke looks like she stepped out of the pictures in the book," Fricke says, "and you can't believe how lovely she is. I think that's a compliment to the people who saw Billie socially around Hollywood and knew she looked like a 54-year-old woman. Then you factor in the concept that 54 then was like 70 now. But they did everything they could do for her makeup and tricks with the hair and wig—and it's stunning."[13]

The *Los Angeles Times'* Edwin Schallert, whose sometimes flinty ink and paper persona belied a sentimental heart, wrote that Billie looked as if she had stepped out of one of Denslow's illustrations. "She appears almost like a being eternally young," he observed. Louella Parsons thought the same thing, writing on August 10th in the *Los Angeles Examiner* that "Burke looks like a twenty-year-old ... she is a delight to the eye." Burns Mantle of the *Chicago Sunday Tribune* was more fascinated by the iridescent bubble from which Billie appears: "Of course, you expected Sally Rand," he quipped, "but Billie is better for the children." The *Dallas Morning Star*, whose critic may well have seen Billie on one of her many provincial tours back in her glory days, was unreserved in its opinion: "Billie Burke is as dainty and lovely as anybody has ever remembered her."[14]

For all that she may not have mingled much with the little people on the set, Billie clearly enjoyed their company. One of the happiest photos taken of Billie at any of her premieres (and certainly an improvement on her sad, black-clad person waiting for her ticket at the premiere of *A Bill of Divorcement* seven years earlier), is one of her kneeling in her evening gown outside Grauman's Chinese Theatre on Hollywood Boulevard (August 15, 1939). With the Munchkin Mayor (Charles Becker) to her right and a Munchkin maiden and Soldier on her left, Billie grins with them as if sharing some wickedly comic secret that will never be known to the photographer, let alone those of us looking at the photo today. What does come through is a sense of the camaraderie Billie shared with the little people of *Oz*—that canny twinkle of a circus clown's daughter enjoying a joke among her own kind of people.

Chapter 20

"Oma"

After *The Wizard of Oz*, Billie settled back into the routine, increasingly unsatisfactory to her, of the average Hollywood character actor. For the next ten years, she played two dozen roles that were, in essence, the one role she was most famous for, that of the daffy wife or spinster, all in comedies; compare this to the two serious parts in all that time, in 1940's *And One Was Beautiful* and 1942's *In This Our Life*, and it is easy to see why she was anxious about the direction of her career. She took her two Broadway comeback failures not as lessons learned but as fodder for future dreams of doing it all over again and coming out a success, a desideratum she was never to attain. Billie could not let go of that fantasy of returning to Broadway, in a play worthy of the boards and of herself. Billie suffered greatly when it became increasingly clear that her dream was no more attainable than it had been in the 1920s, when she had been in her theatrical prime. Billie's constant search for this ideal was sharpened by the fact that, having been forever shocked into awareness of the importance of money by Flo's posthumous debts, she worried over cash flow almost as much as she worried about her career, and seemed to believe that if she could land a success on the stage, she would answer two needs at once.

It is hard to determine just what Billie's financial fears of these years were based on. She was far from destitute, never being without work until age slowed her down in the 1950s; and much was made, in 1958, of Billie picking up her first Social Security check in Santa Monica. The occasional glimpse of her begging George Cukor for roles, cited by one Hollywood historian,[1] was less a symptom of her financial state than an indication of how deeply she believed in Cukor's ability to understand her as an actor and place her in appropriate roles.[2]

Neither her daughter nor her grandchildren recall a state of poverty, and her very address in these years tends to discount the notion. After renting a small Spanish bungalow in Beverly Hills, the rather spare rooms of which were photographed and distributed to the media, in 1939 Billie bought the home where she lived the rest of her life, a cottage-like two story house in Brentwood that more than recalled her similar cottages in London's St John's Wood and in Yonkers. She described 205 South Woodburn Drive as a "small, comfortable, compact house jam-packed with mementos," and it certainly was, including fans she had used as props in *The School Girl* and *My Wife*. Not everything in Burkeley Crest had been lost: there were herds of Flo's elephants — quartz, metal, porcelain — pictures of various stars of stage and screen, framed programs, props and costumes from *Follies* productions, many books and many images of Billie herself, including portraits and magazine covers and stage and screen stills. To add to the pieces saved from Burkeley Crest, Billie's friend Gilbert Adrian designed furniture for the house: the dining room table with its faux marble top and chairs of silver leaf were among his contributions.[3]

There was even a touch, and a big one, of Billie's fabled ingénue days on the Broadway of the early 1900s. George Cukor had found at auction a larger than life poster of Billie as Jacqueline in *Love Watches*, bought it, and gave it to her. It, too, hung in the Woodburn house, with Eddie Cantor's sombrero, the entrance plaques from Burkeley Crest and the solemn bronze head of Flo Ziegfeld.[4]

Billie's desk, a photo of which is reproduced in Patricia's memoir, *The Ziegfelds' Girl*, was a kind of archeological trench sunk into the side of one actress's life, with its piles of letters (fan mail and, no doubt, those bills that Flo had so hated), pinned up photos and programs from as far back as Charles Hawtrey in London, snapshots of family, a tiny picture of Billie and one of the Munchkin Soldiers at the premiere of *Oz*, sheet music from *The Mind the Paint Girl*, and Patricia and husband William Stephenson emerging from the church where they had been married. "It is a good life," Billie wrote of South Woodburn, "a generous, happy life," and her own generosity had gone toward creating that happiness. Shortly after her daughter's marriage, Billie deeded half her enormous garden to the Stephensons, and William (who would become renowned for designing the first all-electric home, for Ronald and Nancy Reagan, in 1956), designed for it a house where, until his death in late 2007, he and his wife lived and brought up their four children, three girls and one boy. It was probably her way of making amends for having stood between the couple just because they had met in what Billie regarded as a most unconventional way.

Patricia and Bill, as she called her husband, first met through a dance class the future architect was teaching in Los Angeles. Billie had always fussed over Patricia's health and would transfer this concern to her grandchildren. There was always a new diet or vitamin, a new exercise, a new way of breathing or stretching, that Billie was convinced one only had to follow rigorously to reap the benefits of lasting good health. "She took what was convenient for her from religions or health fads," remembered Bill Stephenson. Always concerned about her own weight, Billie oversaw Patricia's with an eagle eye, and when she felt it would do the most good she enrolled her in a dance class to slim her down. She was a doting mother, watching with pleasure as Patricia went through high school and college, that cavalcade of "new dresses and new crushes." But when Patricia met Bill Stephenson, she recalled, "I knew that my last crush was over. I had met the man I wanted to marry."[5]

"I had been squiring debutantes about in New York," recalled Bill Stephenson, "and one of them, Jennie Jones, came out to California. I came out, too, and started a studio. And here was Patricia joining my class. I took her to dinner and dancing, and that's how it all began." Their courtship was all right by Billie so long as it remained thus, but when things started getting serious Billie did all the things a mother did in another era to separate a daughter from an unwanted potential fiancé, including sending Patricia to Europe to cool off. Her reasons for disapproving of Bill's intentions always made Patricia laugh.

"What a way to meet — at a dance!" Billie had exclaimed.

"It's exactly the way you met Daddy," responded Patricia. "But that was in *New York*," reminded Billie, though unconvincingly.

As it turned out, nothing, not even a summer in Europe and winter in New York, damped the flames. It took an accident on the set of *The Wizard of Oz* and Billie's being laid up in recovery to seal the engagement. Having been called back by MGM for retakes, Billie was crossing the set when her foot caught in some wires and she fell — the Stephensons insist she did not sprain, as often reported, but actually broke her ankle. The flurry this caused, and the necessity for Billie to remain in stationary convalescence, brought Patricia and Bill back together. Bill seized the day and asked Patricia to marry him. When her daughter told her she had accepted, Billie looked at Patricia for a long time, much as she might have gazed at Flo, who would have his way come hell or high water, and heaven help the dissenter. Then, with "a graceful gesture of defeat," Billie asked, "How many bridesmaids shall we have?"

There were many bridesmaids, and lots of special touches. The Stephensons' wedding was a fairytale affair, with orange blossom and lace and white satin and bubbling champagne — all the old fashioned elements of a wedding from Patricia's grandparents' day, so different from the hurried and confused ceremony Billie and Flo had had in Hoboken. "Daddy would have absolutely loved it," Patricia recalled later.[6]

As remembered by her grandchildren, Billie could be a strict grandmother, but she was a loving one, and in most respects as unlike the grandmothers of their peers as could be imagined. She was quite proud of how rapidly she was able to learn the lingo of the young people of the late 1940s. "I learned 'square,' 'hep,' and 'dig,'" she wrote, "just as those terms — I think — went out of style." But she kept up with the latest equivalents as fast as her grandchildren and their friends started using them. No old-fashioned granny was Billie, and her granddaughters' friends caught on: one of them "thinks, because I am an actress, that I know all about Sin and Wickedness and may tell her some perfumed secret. I sponsor this delusion to keep her respect."[7]

With this modern adaptability came an old-fashioned discipline that required certain standards of behavior even as it accepted a bending of them where syntax was concerned. Second granddaughter Cecilia Duncan remembers how she and her elder sister Florenz were required to behave as proper young ladies — the way one sat, lifted a tea cup, made conversation, all those elements of elegance that Blanche Burke and a half dozen elocution and dance instructors had inculcated in Billie since her girlhood. She was also still the same "clean freak" she had been in Patricia's childhood. She scrubbed down every hotel room she stayed in, recalls a granddaughter who went on tour with Billie. "And we were always having to wash our hands!"

But Billie was also a source of fun. The children called her "Oma," the German familiar term for Grandma, because Florenz had had a German nurse who referred to Billie by that name. The short, elfin nickname stuck. Billie seems to have regarded herself as belonging not so much to the adult world as to the same tribe as her grandchildren — her inherent sense of playfulness, so evident in her film work, resonated to the impromptu amusements of kids. The grandchildren still recall with pleasure how when

Billie returned from the studio, she would let them peel off her false eyelashes, the children screaming with laughter as they did so. Billie jokingly described the Stephensons' house, which was separated from her garden by a wall with a gate (which Richard Lamparski described as looking "like the picture perfect gate in a sitcom"), as her "playhouse," and would often call over the gate to her grandchildren. Her "Yoo hoo!" became as much a part of South Woodburn Drive's language as "Oma"; the children would call it out when they came over to visit their grandmother, yoo-hooing up the white staircase that led to her bedroom.[8]

If "Oma" spelled fun for the Stephenson children, for her they were something even more significant than just companions to her own inner child. They, and their promise of all things future, their rooting the family tree a little deeper into the soil, meant something quite serious to the doting grandmother. Whenever she returned from filming or from touring, Billie would hug the children to her and tell them, "You keep my feet on the ground!"

So much a part of their lives was this grandmother who to many other children was a fairy in pink named Glinda, that Cecilia Duncan still remembers the strangeness of hiding from Billie during the 1949 "This Is Your Life" segment that featured her grandmother. Many old friends came out of the woodwork, including Goldie, Flo's Girl Friday, and the Stephenson grandchildren were concealed for a surprise appearance. It seemed odd, "the way they hid us," Cecilia recalls. She had traveled, and would do so in future, with her grandmother in various touring performances, and visited her on film sets, but Billie had still seemed to be the same "Oma" who sang "Yoo hoo!"

With the birth of Florenz Stephenson in 1940, Billie became a grandmother, though she looks young enough here to be daughter Patricia's sister.

and delighted in the children's playing about the back garden. As many children and grandchildren of prominent people come to see, their parent or grandparent belongs not just to them but to the world at large — a sobering, strange realization. It was odd, indeed, to stand at the cusp of a life that had brought Billie to "This Is Your Life" in the first place, the uneven juncture between her warm, loving, comparatively normal domestic existence and the lights, camera and action of her career.

In her 1959 memoir, *With Powder on My Nose*, Billie was able to be more herself — the straight-shooting, straight-talking woman of the world, the absolute opposite of the ditzy typecast. "Oma felt she could say what she wanted to say in that book," says her grand-daughter Cecilia Duncan. One of Billie's more practical concerns of the 1930s, which she forbore from sharing with her readers in her first memoir, was whether or not to marry again after Flo's death. Those who started or heard the story about Billie wearing her widowhood with a morbid vengeance, like a Cosima Wagner of the Broadway theatre world, were mistaken — Billie actually believed, after the dust had truly settled, that she should have married again. Not that she could bring herself to even think of this in 1932 and for some years after. "Marrying again was for a long time an incredible and disloyal thought," Billie wrote, "and I am still lonely." But she who rarely flinched from the truth when it came up to look at her knew in her heart "that it would have been better if I had married again."[9]

She had, per her account in *With Powder on My Nose*, three chances not just to marry men who cared for her but who had the financial wherewithal to ease all her fears of shortage of money. As with her "Irish beau," Captain Francis Cary of Follaton House, Billie played the game of not revealing the identities of these three men — even her grandchildren do not remember who they were. Perhaps certain characteristics that she does dwell on at some length will coalesce in the memory or knowledge of someone reading this and the names will come: a social butterfly, and widower, of New York and Palm Beach, whom Billie had known while married to Flo, whom she "saw a lot" of after Flo's death and who asked her to marry him (she turned him down cold: "If he approached every pretty woman while his wife was alive, he'll keep doing it if he married again"— the last thing the widow of Flo Ziegfeld needed); the millionaire cattleman from out west who wanted to rapt Billie away to his ranch ("I may not be the only woman who let a herd come between herself and a man"); and finally, and most tantalizingly, a man she calls "a famous comedian," who knew the same people Billie did, read the same books and thought the same jokes funny, who had "a funny face to go along with his talent." It was the idea of waking up to that face that kept Billie at arm's length.

And so, she who claimed that "the most expensive cold creams, clothes, furs, jewels and furniture are no substitute for a man" had to make do without one. Perhaps, in the end, it was because of something even she could not confess to herself any more than she could do to the page: at the end of his life, Flo had belonged entirely to her. Had she married again, that chrism, unbroken by Flo's death, might have vanished. And no man on earth could have made up for the loss this would have caused Billie Burke.[10]

When Billie, who hated television but could not be happy without work, signed on for a local television program with KCTV, she did so knowing she would be playing the self that so many viewers expected of her — the elegantly dressed lady of a certain age, chattering and laughing with guests but never getting too serious, much as she could be seen doing in any of the comedies she acted in. The program, called "At Home With Billie Burke," even had a set that replicated many features of Billie's own living room at South Woodburn Drive, with chairs set before a small fireplace. On seeing the program, it was Patricia's turn to echo her daughter's discomfort with hiding behind the sets of "This Is Your Life."

"I never understood why Mother did that show," Patricia said in an interview in

2007. "She sat there and interviewed people. I didn't like her doing it. She had to talk and laugh like a woman much younger than she actually was. They made her up to look younger. I couldn't bear to see her doing her face that way."[11]

In an interview with Walter Ames in June 1951, Billie put on a brave, even feisty front when asked about her television work. "I've conquered the stage, the screen and radio," she told Ames, "and now it looks as if I'll have to bear down to whip television." As can be seen from publicity stills from the program, one of which features Billie doing something she likely never did at home — stirring a mixing bowl held under one arm, while dressed in chiffon and made up within an inch of her life — the fit was not a perfect one. (A great irony of her career is that this medium she disliked was, through yearly reruns of *The Wizard of Oz*, to ensure her immortality for future generations far more than anything else she did on screen, and certainly more than anything she ever did on the stage.) But even with the much-needed work, and her happy home life as "Oma" to the rambunctious Stephenson children, Billie continued to wander in the dark wood of doubts about her professional future.[12]

These wanderings are nowhere more apparent than in a series of superficially bubbly letters she wrote over a period of some fifteen years to her friend Nancy Hamilton, the writer and lyricist who won an Oscar in 1955 for directing and producing a documentary on Helen Keller. For the daughter of a clown, who proverbially masked tears beneath a painted smile, these letters are the bright sequins covering a darker reality: Billie coming to terms with who and what she was as an actor, and just in time for the final two roles that would show the world not just the youthful energy of this aging woman, but the realization that she had finally found a way to use her diverse gifts.[13]

Writer, lyricist, director and actress Nancy Hamilton was born in Pennsylvania in 1908, the year of Billie's fabulously successful hit *Love Watches*. She was educated at the Sorbonne and at Smith College, where she first met actress Katharine Cornell, who was to become her partner, professionally and personally, until Cornell's death in 1960. It isn't known just when Billie met Hamilton. The earliest of the letters from Billie to her, preserved at Boston University, dates from July 1944, one year into Billie's eponymously named half hour radio program, "The Billie Burke Show."

While she is not credited as such, according to various hints dropped in this letter and succeeding ones, Hamilton wrote — officially or not — lines for Billie to use in her show, and Billie considered them the best she'd had. That is hard to imagine now, listening to the show with our age's more jaded ears, because they all sound very much a part of that species of entertainment rushed to the airwaves during World War II to gladden grass widows and their mothers of a Saturday morning's chores, loaded with one liners that would not draw the laughs now that they did then (or would, but for different reasons). "The Billie Burke Show" sponsored by Listerine toothpaste (that "delightful beauty aid"), was a showcase for the blithery character Billie now personified on the screen. To make her more palatable to a wider audience she was reconfigured from ditzy society matron to ditzy small town spinster "in the little white house on Sunnyview Drive." She was that "bright morning star," forever trying to help those in need and always managing to do so, regardless of implausible plot tangles, her character's hilarious habit of malapropism, and her tendency to drive her snarly brother Julius (played by Earle Ross) out of his mind.

In a characteristic plot, from a show called "The Tramp" (broadcast April 27, 1946, five months before the program ended), Billie takes in a street person who has asked the housekeeper for something to eat. When told that a transient has appeared on the doorstep, Billie is at first alarmed: "A transient! Goodness, chase it away! Those big spiders are poisonous!" The tramp, who calls himself Willy, tells Billie that "I'm what you might call a knight of the road." "Oh yes," Billie coos, missing the sarcasm, "English nobility!"

At first furious that Billie has brought a bum into the household, Julius remembers having heard the story that a local millionaire is masquerading as a tramp

Billie's radio show, titled "Fashions in Rations" during its first year, ran from 1943 to 1946. Here Billie gives kitchen hints in full makeup and a diamond brooch.

to find out for himself who among his fellow men has true humanity, with the intention of giving the winning Good Samaritan half his fortune. Believing him the disguised Croesus, Julius brings Willy into the house, giving him free reign over his clothes closet and everything else that might curry the covert millionaire's favor. Eventually Billie discovers that the story is actually a dozen years old, and that the alleged millionaire in their midst is just the down and out guy he first appeared to be. But like all such improving radio shows of the period, crabby misanthrope Julius learns a lesson in generosity from the experience, giving Willy not just his clothes but a room in the house and a job, all to the approval of sister Billie, who at the program's end, as she did after each program, appropriately sings a verse of "Look for the Silver Lining."[14]

This show was broadcast long after Nancy Hamilton flew the coop. Because of this defection, Billie's July 14, 1944, letter to Hamilton is written with a "heart ... almost too full of things I want to say." Hamilton had not only played a significant role in Billie's professional life, with her "grand work on our program," but was also "such a grand person to be associated with," who had made life "really quite wonderful." Yet even in the middle of all the loving gush, ever practical Billie drew attention to the fact that while she was happy about what Hamilton was going to do, she was concerned that the level of writing for the show would suffer; and if that happened, she had more to worry about than just the absence of a friend: "naturally, it is my means of livelihood and I am greatly concerned having it successful."[15] What Hamilton was actually going off to do was to serve as production assistant and understudy in a touring company of *The Barretts of Wimpole Street*, performing for battle units stationed in parts of the wartorn Continent (1944–1945).

The production starred Brian Aherne as Robert Browning and Hamilton's closest friend, Katharine "Kit" Cornell, as Elizabeth Barrett, with Kit's husband, director, writer and actor Guthrie McClintic as Doctor Chambers. This was plenty enough reason to want to be part of the show, not to mention the excitement of performing this most intimate of family dramas in a theater of war. Hamilton may have also just wanted to be close to Kit, but they were certainly all motivated by the need to contribute something of substance to the American troops fighting in Europe. Without question it was an effort worth leaving the dotty "Billie Burke Show" for, though Billie could not seem to bring herself to see this. Hamilton and, by extension, Kit, who was just the kind of larger than life actress Billie had always hoped to become herself, had obviously become a kind of extended family to Billie, one of them a writer she believed could help her make the most of her ability, the other a theatrical ideal to aspire to, to worship from afar, through whom to enjoy a vicarious thrill for following a career trajectory she herself had aspired to but never achieved.[16]

Billie didn't hear from Hamilton for some time, perhaps a year, and was in any case unable to meet with her when she went to New York a few years later. "The Billie Burke Show" had ended in September 1946; in the middle of its run, for six months in 1945, Billie had played the lead in another radio comedy, "The Gay Mrs. Featherstone," another dizzy woman of a certain age who got too involved in her daughter's and son-in-law's lives (incidentally the opposite of how things were on South Woodburn Drive). By the time she checked into her room at Essex House, an elegant hostelry on Central Park South, Billie was without work and was dismayed by the troubles cropping up in a play she was working on which she does not name, and which she did not ultimately perform in.

"I have no work in sight," she wrote Hamilton. "So I'm a little droopy about it. I wonder how I ever faced a New York audience — youth I guess or just a happy fool — I doubt if I would have the courage now." The letter leaves a poignant image of bright Billie Burke, sitting alone in her hotel room, watching the sun rise one morning over the towers of New York, which suddenly seemed transformed from the gloomy place it had been since Flo's death, only to have it all darken again as she pondered her unemployed state and her once-exuberant acceptance of Broadway's challenges, or worried about what kind of world her grandchildren would live in now that the uneasy entente between the U.S. and Russia was breaking apart into open enmity, further endangering world peace.[17]

Hamilton made up for lost time with a letter subsequent to this one, "a nice newsy letter" full of the theatre gossip Billie loved and hungered for the longer she herself was away from the milieu. This is also one of the first letters in which Billie asks Hamilton for advice and help on an idea, one of many she would continue to bounce off her friend. "I want to do some recording for children," Billie writes. She was enjoying being a grandmother, and had an affinity for children that went beyond parental enjoyment to a connection on the same level as a child — she who had been petted and adored since her childhood days in London pantomime and musical theatre had never stopped needing that pampering, even as she grew into a woman of assertive personality. Billie would later produce a small 45 rpm record of herself reciting nursery rhymes and singing "Twinkle Twinkle Little Star," to the accompaniment of a music box — an effort both sad and charming, in that her film persona clings to her every word and makes the listener envision not a kindly grandmother entertaining children with nursery rhymes but a somewhat eccentric old dame with a fugitive sparkle in her eye, a child trapped in an aging body. It is not known whether Hamilton was able to help her with this project; the record in question actually came out several years later.

On a personal note, this 1947 letter is even more confessional than the one before: "I can't get a picture," Billie laments, "and radio doesn't seem to want to bother with me any more." She was, she said, "a little in a daze to put it mildly." She also confesses her disgust with Zoë Akins' *Mrs. January and Mr. Ex*, calling it "that dreadful play" which had depressed her considerably. She should have known, she says, that the play was worthless because Guthrie McClintic had all but told her so: "he saw no hope in it." Frank Craven, she says, "just shriveled up and went on to the Happy Hunting Grounds" after appearing in Akins' disaster. (Craven actually died a year and four months after the closing of *Mrs. January*, having made three films in the meantime: his heart, not Akins' play, was the culprit.) In Billie's bitterness can be detected a sense of betrayal — this play had been, after all, her second bid for a comeback on Broadway, and while it had run longer than *This Rock*, it had not had the desired revitalizing effect on Billie's theatre career.[18]

The next letter in the series is from this same period. Billie tells Hamilton that she has been "buried" for weeks in the making of a movie for Hal Roach Studios, and as if having emerged from a cave she notes her astonishment at hearing that Hamilton had been in town with her new show, *Three to Make Ready*, a follow-up to her Broadway hit *One for the Money* (1939). (It is not clear what film this was. Billie's last film for Roach was *Topper Returns* in 1941, five or six years earlier.) Billie's gushing praises for Hamilton, which must have become somewhat of a challenge for the hard-headed writer-producer-director to read without a wry smile, start mounting toward the heavens from this point in Billie's correspondence, and after reading through all the "darlings" and "terribly happys" and "thrills" and "geniuses," among many other superlatives, it is possible for us even at remove of over sixty years to detect an underlying wistfulness, even desperation. "There is no thrill like hav[ing] a success, a real live breathing thing," she says, speaking from long ago experience as well as from longing.

She recalls working on *The Wizard of Oz* with Ray Bolger, star of *Three to Make Ready*, for whom she "had such great admiration," and tells Hamilton she had seen a beautiful photograph of Kit Cornell "in some weekly," as if the tabloid had just happened to fall at her feet. Did Billie scan these magazines for pictures of her New York

Billie played Cecily Stanley, an upper-crust British matron saddled with refugee East End children during the London blitz in Walter L. Faust's 1943 play *This Rock*. It ran on Broadway for less than a month.

friends and colleagues, from whom she felt as separate as if living in Los Angeles was actually life in a distant foreign country? With a sad smile, she ends the letter with: "Long may your banner wave my darling."[19]

Whatever her expressed fears that her prospects were dim, Billie was not without work during this letter writing period — far from it. In 1945 she was cast in the still unsung marvel of a Christmas film, *The Cheaters*; in 1946 she was in the strange but moving Golden Pictures production, *Breakfast in Hollywood*, playing the sort of forlorn but brave older lady that she seems to be in the Hamilton letters; and in 1948 she made two short films where she was cast as herself (deliberately this time) in all sorts of improbable situations. And between these shorts and *The Boy from Indiana*, the film she was making when she wrote her next extant Hamilton letter, there were two other films, one of them, *The Barkleys of Broadway*, reuniting Fred Astaire and Ginger Rodgers for the last time.

The Boy from Indiana was something of a rehash of the 1941 drama *Home in Indiana*, a story starring the handsome young Lon McAllister as the boy who makes good with a racehorse that nobody else believed in (and co-starring Billie's friend, comedienne Charlotte Greenwood, in her first serious film role). Billie does not seem to have much liked *The Boy from Indiana*; in her letter to Nancy Hamilton she describes it as "a horse opera." The only good thing she can say is that the deserts around Phoenix, where the location footage was shot, were beautiful — but then her main focus, vicarious as always, is on Kit's recent opening at the Martin Beck Theater in *That Lady*, a play set in the Spain of King Phillip II (written by Kate O'Brien). The reviews were not uniformly good — *Time Magazine*'s critic summed up the general opinion by pointing out that "*That Lady* accelerates now and then from the speed of a glacier to that of glue."[20] Billie adjured Hamilton to ignore the "gastly [sic] critics," as nothing they could possibly say would have the slightest effect on Kit's success. (Though they probably did; the play had a shorter run than most of Kit's others.) Again pleading poverty in her roundabout way, Billie tells Hamilton that she would have sent flowers if she could have afforded them — but the message she asked Hamilton to send Kit was certainly worth more than a dozen roses: "just to think of her is a prayer."

Exuberant about Kit's prospects, Billie bemoans her own. She wishes that the show Hamilton is working on had a role in it like the old Countess in Irving Berlin's *Miss Liberty* (1949–50), referring to the genteel poor grandmother of Monique, model for the Statue of Liberty. It was getting harder and harder for her to find good films, and "the things they bring me to do in t.v. I just can't believe my eyes when I read them." (In another Hamilton letter, Billie has more of a sense of humor about the new medium: "I've got to find a little place in t.v., if only selling pots and pans — but with a manner!!")[21]

Zoë Akins was after her again to take *Mrs. January* on tour, but she had no faith that Akins had solved the play's many problems. She takes comfort in knowing that if Hamilton may happen to catch Billie in some less than optimum role in some less than optimum film or television program, "you will always love me and that big beautiful heart of yours will have my little place tagged." Billie claimed not marrying again had left her lonely, but this was not loneliness to be helped by a man or a woman at her side: she needed the professional assurances and magnanimous advice from someone like Nancy Hamilton to truly feel that she was not disappearing, bit by inexorable bit.[22]

Billie's letter of February 11, 1952, is frostier than all the foregoing, in part perhaps because she was now working five shows a week on television, "which gives me very little time to write." She informs Hamilton that she had a man on the show the day before, a writer named Paul Crabtree who had taken over the scripts of "The Billie Burke Show" "when you went out of my life, so to speak," though she adds, curtly, "thank heavens, I never lost you completely." She touches on Kit's current play, a revival of Somerset Maugham's *The Constant Wife*—she would "give all the teeth I have left" to see it. But then she's back to her dreaded television work, with a touch of resentment. She again brings up what seems to have been a touchy subject: who can grant Billie the rights to make a record of three of Hamilton's songs. There is a sense of urgency to her request that overlays the business-like sheen of the language — she wants to know "how we can go about making the arrangements;" and even in sending Hamilton a "world of love," she reminds her at the letter's end that she needs to know where things stand with the songs, "when you can spare a moment."[23]

But by autumn 1953, Billie was back in full gush — over the summer, she had spent a few days with Nancy and Kit at the latter's house on Martha's Vineyard:

> That day was one of the loveliest I have ever had — all radiance with a blue sea, smiling faces, fun and laughter, wonderful things to eat that my Nancy seemed to accomplish by just waving things in the air over something. It was a lovely, lovely day in my life.

And though she does not say, this day probably recalled many such she had experienced with Flo, in the days of the yachts and Camp Patricia and Palm Beach, which may partly account for the huge let down on her return to California. Later on in the letter she refers to coming back home to Woodburn Drive and not quite collapsing but experiencing "a kind of battle fatigue." Not just her few days with Nancy and Kit but the summer stock she had been doing in Palm Beach, "the exhilaration of acting every night" had lifted her temporarily above "all of the obstacles" that were plaguing her that season.[24]

Paul Crabtree, who had been one of the writers for "The Billie Burke Show" and had been interviewed by Billie on her television program, managed the Palm Beach Playhouse, where he had coaxed Billie to take on some summer stock. A graduate of Sawyer Falke's drama classes at Syracuse University, Crabtree was a multitalent, perfectly suited to the entertainment needs of the day: he could act (he had played Will Parker as first replacement in the original *Oklahoma!*), had been stage manager for the first *Carousel*, had been involved in running Westport Country Playhouse (founded by director Lawrence Langner, whose assistant Crabtree had once been), as well as writing one liners for Billie's radio show and working on film scripts in Hollywood.

"Palm Beach Playhouse produced one-week star-package stock," says Jim Crabtree, Paul's son, "drawing heavily on Dad's Theatre Guild contacts." Crabtree ran the theater from 1950 to 1956, when it was converted. Paul's actress wife, Mary, loved the Playhouse, which she thought "charming," and the charm it had was partly due to the fact that it had not been built as a theatre at all but was converted from the greenhouse of the old Royal Poinciana Hotel, a vast place built in the 1890s with a dining room seating over 1500 people, its yellow and white Georgian walls stretching almost 2000 feet along the shores of Lake Worth. Functioning as an entertainment venue in one guise or another since the 1930s, under Crabtree's management the theatre had even attracted the First Lady of the American Theatre, Helen Hayes, who performed there in *Mrs. McThing*.

Now Producing Director of the Cumberland County Playhouse, Yale School of Drama graduate Jim Crabtree started early on the stage. "I made my stage debut at age eight," he says, "with Billie Burke in *Life with Mother*. I played the role of Harlan, the youngest of the Day family sons, and had my hair dyed red for the role." Best known for his 1935 novel *Life with Father*, Clarence Shepard Day, Jr. did not live to see publication of its sequel, *Life with Mother*, which served as the basis for the play by Howard Lindsay and Russell Crouse (1939) and the later film with Irene Dunne in the starring role.

Mary Crabtree was enchanted to have Billie at the theatre, not just because she admired her as a performer but because Billie and Flo had been such ornaments of old Palm Beach, in the days when the Royal Poinciana Hotel had been the ultimate in glamour. She perhaps was not prepared for the reality of an aging actress, whose memory was not what it once was, who was worried about getting work and then worried, once she got it, about carrying it through to her own exacting standards. She reminded Mary, says her son, of a line spoken by faded southern belle Amanda Wingfield in *The Glass Menagerie*, describing what to her was the worst possible fate — to become like the "little birdlike women without any nest — eating the crust of humility all their life."[25]

Billie had received a glowing tribute for her performance in the Los Angeles production from crusty critic Edwin Schallert: Billie was "radiant" in the play, which her presence ensured "[had] never been more effectively exploited than in this production with Miss Burke." But as any actor knows, even those who had been trouping for years, being radiant on command is not easy, especially after decades of doing so on a nightly basis in a half dozen cities of a given week. "Evidently one week stock was tough on Miss Burke at that time," remembers Jim Crabtree, "with its rapid memorization, and I evidently added to the company's (and my parents') anxiety by being pretty lackluster during rehearsal." Sixty-two years older than Jim, Billie was not on much firmer ground: Mary Crabtree remembered her fragility in rehearsal, her fluffing of lines, the sense of deep uncertainty, even fear, in this actress whom everyone thought of as endearingly daffy Clara Topper or serene Glinda the Good.[26]

But on opening night, something happened to both the little boy and the elderly woman he was to share the stage with. As Mary drove Jim to the theatre, nervously coaching him on his role (part of which required him to recite a lengthy poem during a dinner scene), and "fearing the worst from her son's apparent lack of theatrical aptitude," Jim turned to her and said quietly, "I think I'll surprise them tonight."

When Billie went into her dressing room that evening, as much the little birdlike woman as during rehearsal, the Crabtrees had concerns more far-reaching than whether young Jim would be able to carry his part successfully. It was when she opened the door to come out that everyone was amazed — though stunned would be a fair word to use. "Magic had occurred behind the closed door," recalls Jim Crabtree. "Miss Burke emerged, bewigged and beautifully made up, with assurance and command, as the great star and personality that she was, transformed somehow via tape, paint, smoke and mirrors into the beautiful and charming Mother of us all, and the audience took her to its heart." It also took young Jim: "Apparently, I was transformed by the audience and the occasion nearly as much as Miss Burke herself, and nearly stole the show from everyone but the great lady herself." Perhaps the situation required a child to do what Billie's own grandchildren were able to do for her and which she was increasingly unable to do for herself: put her feet back solidly on the ground.[27] (Billie also performed at the theatre, renamed the Royal Poinciana Playhouse in 1956, in *Lady of the House* and *The Solid Gold Cadillac*.)

The adrenaline rush of summer stock was an increasingly distant memory by the time Billie wrote her November 1953 letter to Nancy Hamilton, and she was already worried about future work. Like one of the little birdwomen pecking for a crust of bread, Billie asked Nancy if she had time to consider writing something that Billie could do for television, that hated medium that she now seemed resigned to. She was sure, she told Hamilton, that were she to write something (for Billie), any number of producers would rise to take it on. That said, Billie retires with her imaginary crust, saying pathetically, "Please don't worry about me asking you this. It is just one of those dreams."[28]

Her dreams were still pushing her onward. In 1957 and 1958, Billie bravely made her final bid for Broadway. Paul Crabtree and his partner in the Royal Poinciana, Frank Hale, got Billie to agree to play the senator's wife in *Bette Bibb*, Crabtree's own play. All the action occurred in the Senate Office Building in Washington, D.C.—perhaps not the most scintillating of settings even in uproarious political times, but Billie was game: "It is the humorous, warm and touching play I had hoped for," she told the *New York Times*. "And it's as fresh and controversial as anything one might read in this very day's newspaper." The play had already been tested on television in a previous iteration, starring Lillian Gish. But if Crabtree and Hale were hoping for a repeat performance of *Mid-Summer*, the play in which they had introduced Geraldine Page in 1953, they were mistaken. There is no record of *Bette Bibb* going any farther than the pages of its own script.[29]

The saddest of the two would-be Broadway comebacks was that of Edward Chodorov's murder mystery, *Listen to the Mocking Bird*. Chodorov had had plays on Broadway since the late 1920s, but his last hit, *Oh Men! Oh Women!*, which ran for almost 400 performances in 1953–54, was not followed by another, and he had been blacklisted by Senator Joseph McCarthy (Jerome Robbins had named him as a member of the Communist party).

Billie was to perform with Una Merkel and, in an irony both women may have appreciated, Eva Le Gallienne, who had played the role of Princess Alexandra in Molnár's *The Swan* that Billie had wanted for herself in 1923. The play was to open on Broadway in mid–January 1959, rehearsing and holding out of town tryouts in December. By early January, it was clear the play was in trouble. Billie was having such trouble remembering lines, according to Dorothy Kilgallen, a kind of walkie talkie had to be devised for her, "with a chap in the wings feeding her lines and guiding her movements." According to Kilgallen, one of the other actresses, name not given, was threatening to leave the play before it made it to New York because Billie's memory lapses were causing frustration and chaos on the stage. And there was more. "The Playwrights Company is mulling over the possibility of closing its touring company of *Listen to the Mocking Bird*," reported the *New York Times*. The play was set for Boston the first week in January, and it was in Boston, after a meeting between Roger L. Stevens of the Playwrights Company and Chodorov that it was decided to close the production down. There had already been one very bad sign, when the Shubert Theatre in Washington, D.C., burned to the ground after the last act—no doubt neither Chodorov nor theatre owners wanted to risk further disaster by prolonging the play's guttering existence.[30]

The play's quality or lack thereof aside, this would have been Billie's best opportunity to perform with one of Broadway's great actresses, who had attained so much in her career that Billie had dreamed of for herself. In the irony which seemed to attend all of Billie's efforts to get back to Broadway, even a cast of this quality, in a play by a successful playwright, could not make the impossible happen. The best thing of all was what was most characteristic of this survivor of many a cataclysm on stage, screen and life. Besides the grand ladies of the cast, there was another cast member that Billie especially adored — an amber cat named Tommy, whom the plot had die of poisoning. Every time she took her curtain calls, Billie would bring Tommy out with her and wave his paw at the audience, smiling widely.

It must have seemed that the gods were punishing her with especial vengeance when the show closed, because the producers also talked of closing down, or putting down, Tommy. Horrified, Billie would have none of this. She abruptly took the cat with her and boarded her plane for California, where on arrival she ensconced Tommy on a bed in her silver-leaf Adrian dining room, an amiable young companion to three elder feline peers of the Burke household. It was like the last scene of a goofy Billie Burke comedy, and in any event, was the best possible ending to her last attempt to shine again on Broadway.[31]

CHAPTER 21

Final Curtain

If film, which had become so big and baffling to Billie, and television, which was so small and petty, continued to frustrate her, and Broadway did not want her, she found an outlet for memories and emotions in ink and paper, in the form of her two memoirs, *With a Feather on My Nose* and *With Powder on My Nose*, published in 1949 and 1959, respectively.

Flo's former publicist, Bernard Sobel, was disappointed in Billie's first memoir, annoyed by her inability to recall details of famous productions she had been in and famous playwrights she had worked with. Though Billie had worked with Booth Tarkington, Noël Coward, and Somerset Maugham, "she never seemed to remember anything in particular about these notables and how they acted at rehearsals or what they did to their scripts." He was also bothered that the real Billie Burke that he knew—the woman whose beauty belied the clear-eyed realist, whose a personality was every bit as big and colorful as Flo Ziegfeld's—had concealed her light under a bushel. Because they were as concealed in her memoirs as they were in her frothy film performances, the world never had "the opportunity to judge her wisdom and depth of feeling."[1]

Broadway press agent and critic Richard Maney found the book "gallant" in Billie's depiction of herself as loyal to Flo throughout their many troubles extramarital and financial, but felt it was clear that Flo's advent in Billie's pre–1914 life as an admired stage beauty of Broadway had thrown a monkey wrench into her "dreamy existence." While Billie's memoir chronicled a lost age of "fabulous parties, dinners at Sherry's, Bustanoby's and Rector's, special trains, parades of the notables," and other fanciful symbols of an utterly lost gilded age, Maney would have agreed with Sobel: a "surface salute to the theatre, frequently naïve and sugary." The book does read as if captured from the cushions of a satin chaise lounge, and in fact it partly was. *With a Feather on My Nose* is one of the last of the old-fashioned theatre star memoirs, written with the assistance of Cameron Shipp, a ghost-writer and magazine journalist who had worked with Lionel Barrymore on *We Barrymores* and Mack Sennett on *King of Comedy*; he also played a role in Fred Astaire's memoir, *Steps in Time*. According to Billie's family, Shipp's role in the writing of Billie's memoirs was to take dictation from the books' subject. Shipp himself said their work consisted of interviews, telephone conversations, her many notes, and a tape recorder, which she could talk into for hours.

We know from some of her early articles and from her letters that Billie Burke was a fluid, witty writer, and we also know that anyone as headstrong as she would not have brooked having her life ghosted by anyone. Perhaps the elisions noted by Bernard Sobel are a result of a number of dictation sessions stitched together into a biographical narrative. Or perhaps like her friend Charlotte Greenwood, whose memoirs, never published, are close-lipped about matters that the author felt uncomfortable sharing even with the blank page, Billie held certain parts of her past close, unwilling to share them. She unwittingly mirrored the very stage manner that had made critics like Alexander Woollcott accuse her of superficiality for her performances on the stage, of never sharing all the richness she had inside her heart.[2]

She had some amusing times promoting the book, as she described later on in her second memoir:

> As an Author — an exciting new role for me and I played it to the hilt — I made the usual number of talks to literary club ladies in which we looked over each other's hats and they wondered how old I was. I went to stores in New York, Chicago, Detroit, Brooklyn, San Francisco, and a number of other cities. I autographed flyleaves with deep gratitude, counting the profits. And I overheard something ... when one woman said to another: "I saw her in a play in nineteen-seven — and she was no child then — but right now she doesn't look a day over forty!" Dear overheard lady, may the saints keep you![3]

Ten years later, when she came to write *With Powder on My Nose*, Billie was a different person, whether through age or experience or both. "She felt she could be more herself in that book," says granddaughter Cecilia Duncan. "That she could really show her personality."[4] And show it she does. *Powder* is not quite a memoir, because interspersed with recollections of her past, Billie delves into topics she evidently felt were of interest to women not only "of a certain age" but those who were younger and might be seduced by the feminist movement into losing their femininity.

Her chapter headings tell the story: "The Trouble with Women," "Kitchen, Bedroom, and Bath," "Why I Never Married Again," and "When to Tell Your Age." These sound like the fluffy topics they are, but the tone is anything but. This is possibly the closest we come to the way Billie really talked when with friends. Not at all the breathy, wide-eyed ingénue of her first memoir, this Billie Burke is wise, witty and says it like it is, making no apologies for her unfashionably dated opinions on feminism:

> Up to the time I began reading and clipping from newspapers and magazines, I thought there was nothing wrong with women that Slenderella couldn't fix.
> Now when I pick up an article about women I don't know whether I'm reading science fiction or a horror story.... [S]omething's wrong or all these article writers and researchers wouldn't be so vehement about women. Even a lady anthropologist takes off agin us. Dr. Margaret Mead comes up with the statement that more than a quarter of a million women in the United States are "articulately and definitely disturbed about their lot as women."

"I gather," Billie writes further on, "that the main trouble with being a woman is not alcoholism [or] office work ... but a revolt among women themselves *against being women.*" Her solution was that women get back to being not just women but feminine women, no doubt earning plenty of irritated sighs from the nascent bra-burners of the late 1950s and early 1960s. Even as Billie's voice is more authentically hers — sturdy, no-

nonsense, practical, opinionated — it still reflects the mentality of the days when women worked all day not at desks or on corporate boards but to be beautiful for their husbands on their return from work in the evening. There's even an illustration in this chapter, by Mircea Vasiliu, showing a businessman smitten with a sexy half-clothed statue of Venus, dropping his paper in awe to the floor, while ignoring a sour-faced businesswoman striding by, glaring through cat-eye glasses under the straight bangs of her severe dutch bob. Only the pretty girls get the guy, Billie seems to be saying, though she acknowledges she had enough trouble holding on to the man who meant the most to her, Flo Ziegfeld. Even then, she has a theory to share: Men will be men. It behooves woman to be ever more womanly to counteract this minor complication of hormones and gender.[5]

These and some of Billie's other pronouncements would have ruffled feathers elsewhere (although there is some truth in her flip maxims):

> It's no surprise to me that Communism has produced no heroines or female saints or prophets. Women are much too practical to believe in Communism. When some woman claims to be a Communist, she is following some man.[6]
>
> Marriage is still woman's chief aim and business in life. This is easy to prove. Look at the many excellent mass-circulation magazines edited specifically to teach women marriage. There are no such magazines for men.[7]

And a sample of her racy sense of humor: "Women may think sex is fun, but only men ever think it is funny."[8]

At the end of *Feather* Shipp shares an amusing and fascinating account of what it was like working with Billie Burke on this most sensitive of jobs, the writing of a life, the immortalizing of a personality in paper and ink. Billie had been working on her memoirs for ten years, says Shipp, "writing notes in pencil on yellow scratchpads and essays in green ink on embossed letterheads." She stuffed these under cushions and among the detritus on her desk, and lost plenty of them in the process, consulting a leather notebook filled with the names of a thousand friends, filled with clippings and poems (some of them in French, which Shipp claimed she read fluently), distressed to lose it but always finding it (or having it found for her) again.

Shipp recalled how one of these finders, a woman, called Billie from Los Angeles to say she had located the famous notebook, clippings intact, but wanted Billie to come to her to get it. Billie found herself in a downtown bar, where "she spent four hours ... happily discussing poetry. She was surprised, later, when her family scolded her and told her she might have been in danger and that, at any rate, a bar was not her style. 'Why, it was delightful,' Miss Burke said, 'and besides, I could have handled the situation if necessary.'" Remembering her performance as the revamped vamp in *Breakfast in Hollywood*, knocking one back at the bar before sweeping off in sequined tulle, it is just possible she could have "handled the situation" just fine. (Just how the notebook had got from Beverly Hills to downtown remained a mystery.)[9]

Shipp discovered that Billie was nothing like the character she played in films, though she tended to revert to typecast type without warning. People sometimes wondered whether she did this on purpose or by accident or when possessed by the devil of daffy in the roles of Clara Topper or Emily Kilbourne. But make no mistake, Shipp warns: "The lady knows what she is doing at all times."

She knows what *non sequiturs* are and thoroughly enjoys dropping them for other people to trip over. She looks on her own work with a clear professional eye. She is forthright, astute, and precise when she wants to be. But she is capable of saying, "It doesn't make any difference what I mean, you know what I say," and of leaving the matter there if you don't get the point. [10]

"I imagine some of this will be a funny book," she told Shipp. "It will almost have to be because I want to say some things that are true, and to say them all of a sudden. If you do that, you usually create an effect of shock, the truth being such a rare thing."

She had not always had the best relationship with truth, any more than Flo had had, or her mother. But now, when she had nothing to lose, the truth that was the basis of her relationship with her father, that allowed him to step out from behind his clown costume and sing his heartfelt songs, blending comedy and pathos in a way his daughter yearned to do on the stage, finally came into its own for Billie Burke. She discovered it through her two last roles for

Co-star Barbara Rush recalls how much she and Paul Newman enjoyed working with Billie Burke in their 1959 film, *The Young Philadelphians.*

the big screen: as Philadelphia millionairess Mrs. J. A. Allen in *The Young Philadelphians* and as Cordelia Fosgate in the ground-breaking drama of race relations in the wild West, *Sergeant Rutledge*. That she was indeed that smiling clown with a tear in her eye.[11]

The role of Mrs. J. A. Allen was offered to Billie almost as soon as she returned to California from the aborted *Listen to the Mocking Bird* venture. Warner Bros. wanted her for *The Young Philadelphians*, a drama starring Paul Newman and Barbara Rush that has been described as Main Line Philadelphia's answer to *Peyton Place*. Cameron Shipp recalled with what enthusiasm Billie took on the part. As she told him, she liked Mrs. Allen "because this woman ... gets down to brass tacks. She's smart. I used some people I know in creating her"—herself primary among them, though she coyly leaves us to guess at that.[12]

Newman plays Tony Lawrence, of the Rittenhouse Square Lawrences, whose mother, Kate Judson (Diane Brewster) marries William Lawrence (a brief glimpse of Adam West), son of a draconian matriarch, rather than her lowly boyfriend, Mike Flannigan (a handsome and burly Brian Keith). Things go sour on the wedding night when

One of Billie's greatest performances, and her next to last film appearance, occurred in John Ford's 1960 Western, *Sergeant Rutledge*. Here Billie, as the judge's wife Cordelia Fosgate (with Carleton Young, as Rutledge's racist prosecutor, at her left, and an uncredited actor at her right), is puzzled as to why she has to take oath on a Bible.

Lawrence admits, drunk, that he is impotent. Off he goes (to die in an accident); Kate seeks solace with Mike, who fathers a child that is then passed off, once William's death is known, as a Lawrence. Kate then spends every waking hour over the next several years working to get Tony into the right schools, in with the right friends, constantly having to prove herself to her impossible to please mother-in-law (played by Isobel Elsom).

Tony goes to law school and emerges a cut-throat lawyer; he also falls in love with Joan Dickinson, played by the lushly beautiful Barbara Rush, whose father, a prominent attorney, could be a step higher up the Main Line ladder. But Daddy throws a wrench in Tony's plans: if Tony keeps away from Joan, he will give him a place in the firm. Tony doesn't hesitate to break with Joan, who rebounds into marriage with a man who then dies in the Korean War, by which time Tony is having an affair with bored aging beauty Carol Wharton (Alexis Smith), younger wife of a big shot attorney in whose home Tony lives as assistant. Then Tony goes to Korea and comes back a hero. With him comes an old friend, party boy Chet Gwyn (Robert Vaughn), who has lost an arm and gained a greater thirst for alcohol. While Tony is earning the good graces of millionairess Mrs. J. A. Allen (Billie), taking her away from her former attorney and advisor in the process, Chet is hauled in by the police on suspicion of murdering his wealthy uncle. Tony gets involved in the case, but an old friend of the Lawrence family, Dr. Shippen Stearnes, closes the Rittenhouse Square ranks against him and threatens to expose Tony's illegitimacy. Tony by this time has discovered the truth himself, and realizes he still loves Joan, and that the right thing is to defend his friend whether or not his and his mother's past is revealed. In this game of courtroom chicken with Dr. Stearnes, Tony wins Chet's case and Joan's affections. He also has Mrs. Allen clapping for him in the wings, or as much as her omnipresent lap dog, a Chihuahua, allows.

Critic A. H. Weiler of the *New York Times* was not too impressed by "this sudsy Warner Brothers drama," in which Paul Newman "personifies most of the challenge in an all-too-frequently pallid drama." Billie is dismissed as a "slightly addlepated multi-millionaire" who "lends a cute touch to the somber goings on."[13] *Newsweek* Magazine, on the other hand, declared of Billie: "The Dowager Is a Thief," pointing out, truthfully, that she does manage to upstage nearly everyone in every scene in which she appears — even her little dog, a feat any actor will affirm is nearly impossible to accomplish in the movie studio or in the theatre. Newman was the outstanding cast member, Newsweek's critic opined, but even he could not stand up to her by the latter part of the film: "the picture is stolen from him by none other than Billie Burke, the 72-year-old flutterer, in her first film appearance in six years. Miss Burke's caricature of a dowager who owns controlling stock in a corporation the size of Standard Oil ... is a special delight."[14]

Cameron Shipp noted that "Prophets in Hollywood quickly forecast that she would be nominated for an Academy Award," and while this did not happen, the performance deserved at least that. As Barbara Rush points out, when recalling her work with Billie, while the older actress was "very birdlike, kind of fragile, with that wonderful fluttery voice, and a certain sense that she would go right up into the air if you didn't tie her to the ground," she had grown less fluttery with age and seemed more centered in her acting.

"She was such a legend, you know," Rush remembered. "And her manner was very much like that of Mrs. Allen in the film. She had lived a charmed life, really, because everybody had adored her. We did — Paul Newman certainly did. After all, she got to play the good fairy in *The Wizard of Oz!*"

But Billie was also a thoroughgoing professional, who knew her lines cold and was utterly unfluttery in the workaday world of shooting scenes as well as in the interminable waits between them. She warmed to Barbara Rush from the start, enjoying the role of actress dowager dispensing wisdom to a beautiful and sympathetic young acolyte.

"I asked her all sorts of questions," Rush says. "I asked her about *Dinner at eight*, and what it was like being married to Flo Ziegfeld, whom she called Mr. Ziegfeld. 'My goodness,' I said, 'Mr. Ziegfeld was surrounded by beautiful women, but he singled you out to marry you. And she said, in that inimitable voice, 'Yes, he *loved* me.'"

Always fascinated by character actors, whom she describes as the elements "that give depth and texture to a picture — the Kathleen Nesbits and Edna Mae Olivers and

Billie Burkes of the business," Rush was also keen to talk shop with another actor who had had such a long and varied career. "When you lived in the age of Ziegfeld," she says, "and had made so many films from an early period, you naturally worked with many wonderful people. Billie had worked with the Barrymores, with Katharine Hepburn, so many of the greats. As she told me, it was a wonderful experience for her, but only in looking back at it all. She said she hadn't really thought about it at the time because she was so busy working on one film and learning the script for the next. She only saw all this, as we all do, after it was over and she could look back from a distance." The young actress and the aging one also agreed on how important it was to have a strong script to work with, something that had made Billie lean on Nancy Hamilton and other writers of her acquaintance whose work she trusted and admired.

"And she had great technique," Rush adds. "I love the scene where Paul Newman tells her that she could be saving a huge amount of money with the right tax shelter. She doesn't talk so much as stutter in absolute surprise. And that wonderful line she tosses off when she leaves Paul's office, after he has agreed to become her advisor. 'Talking about money always makes me so hungry!'"

"There should be a home for people like her, when they grow old," Rush says. "You just want to take the Gladys Coopers and Kathleen Nesbits and the Billie Burkes and house them in some wonderful place on a lake, to keep them all safe and together. These were wonderful women, elegant women, who aged so gracefully. There was something about Billie," she adds, "that is hard to describe. But it was like lace. Fragile, beautiful lace."[15]

That laciness was brought to the fore, and not as a fragile decoration but as a symbol of bourgeois hypocrisy, in Billie's penultimate film, *Sergeant Rutledge*, John Ford's cowboys-and-Indians flick with a twist — a rare Western in which the plot turned on the issue of racism in a garrison town of the late nineteenth century American west.

As film scholar Frank Manchel pointed out in an article on Ford's *Sergeant Rutledge*, "Nothing is more unpredictable in the movie business than a message movie." From the beginnings of the genre, when D.W. Griffith made a statement about the Civil War in *The Birth of a Nation,* to the message films of Oliver Stone, "filmmakers never know whether their morality will be rewarded or ridiculed."[16]

Set in a garrison town in the Arizona of the early 1880s, *Sergeant Rutledge* tells the story of the murder trial of 1st Sergeant Braxton "Brax" Rutledge, C Troop, Ninth United States Cavalry, a black soldier of spotless reputation who has been accused of killing his superior officer, Major Dabney, and of raping and murdering his young daughter, Lucy. The assumption on the part of everyone in town is that Rutledge is guilty as charged, the color of his skin being prima facie evidence of his culpability. Only his fellow black soldiers, his defense attorney, Lieutenant Tom Cantrell (played passionately by Jeffrey Hunter), and the educated daughter of a local landowner, Mary Beecher (Constance Towers), know otherwise — the soldiers because they know Brax and how easy it is to convict a black man for a crime he did not commit; Cantrell, because as an educated Easterner he is a stranger to the entrenched racism of the frontier settlement, and is a man of intense honor and principle; and Mary Beecher because

Rutledge saved her from an Apache raid which had killed her father and guarded her overnight until she could get help.

These three elements battle against an army of ignorance in form of Judge Otis Fosgate (Willis Bouchey), a disillusioned military operative the high point of whose career was the sack of the south at the side of General Sherman; his wife, Cordelia, played with vicious naiveté by Billie, her silks and laces as incongruous in the Arizona outback as her bigotry is perfectly placed within the settlement's enclave of insular white merchants and their wives; and Captain Shattuck (Carleton Young), the racist army prosecutor who has pegged Rutledge guilty by reason of skin pigment alone. Between sips of "water" (whiskey proffered by an aide who barely knows how to read the law books of which he is in charge), Fosgate is less intent on railroading Rutledge than on fending off his heckling wife, who presents herself in the courtroom with a gaggle of bonneted ladies like her (including Estelle Winwood in an uncredited part). Whenever possible he calls recess to escape her and the serious business of Rutledge's fate to play a round of poker in the backroom.

Captain Shattuck believes he has the case sewn up, and it is easy to see why, since not only does Cordelia insist she heard shots coming from the house of Major Dabney the night in question, but saw Rutledge leave the house around that time. She also offers the damning testimony of having seen Lucy Dabney go off with Rutledge from the general store of Chandler Hubble, whose son, Chris, has taken a fancy to the major's daughter. At the time, Cordelia had warned Lucy about spending time with Rutledge, but did she listen? And now look what had happened to a good girl who did not pay her elders heed.

Sergeant Rutledge may not be the greatest of John Ford's westerns (only a few critics have shared the opinion that it is, and then mostly on grounds of its cinematography), and it does not handle its complex and freighted topic with the most sensitive touch. But *Rutledge* is definitely one of those movies that *had* to be made, almost forced up from the quaking soil of 1960s society like a fractured mountain range: the injustices of white toward black placed squarely in the hot spotlight of legal hypocrisy and double-standard: a military courtroom on the outer verges of the U.S. west, recently grabbed from the native peoples whose ancestral homeland it was. And the film is beautifully shot, using a small range of primary colors, muted yet enhanced by the dusty desert canvas on which they are painted. The result gives the movie the somber dignity of a church fresco — that, and the superbly poised performance of Woody Strode, as Braxton Rutledge. The analogy to art is not out of place, since the film itself was said to have been inspired by a painting, Frederick Remington's "Buffalo Soldiers," which depicts black members of the 9th and 10th U.S. Cavalry, so named by the Plains Indians after their first glimpse of these men in winter, muffled up in their buffalo coats.

The history of blacks in the west, many of them former slaves, has not been widely studied, but we know that while many of these men distinguished themselves, as Rutledge does in the film (though not with quite the theatrical derring-do), others were clearly treated to racism covert or overt. Hence Ford's shrewd choice to focus entirely on the trial of Sergeant Rutledge, with flashbacks to the various events leading up to the courtroom showdown. This layering of flashbacks eases the viewer back and forth, never releasing the tension built up block by block from the first to final scenes, in which the release is not quite the relief one is hoping for.[17]

By comparison to Strode's compelling performance, in which he appears all at the same time a man of danger, unpredictability, principle and honor, animal magnetism and selfless fortitude, Billie's bonneted and bustling role, as Cordelia Fosgate, has fooled many critics because on the surface she appears to be up to her usual typecast part, that of ditzy flibbertigibbet, twittering about in laces and feathers and interrupting the film's serious narrative with her obtusities. But in fact, Mrs. Fosgate is one of those preposterously important people who can destroy the lives of others with an ill-chosen remark — an example of what Johann Wolfgang von Goethe meant when he said, "There is nothing more frightening than ignorance in action." Cordelia is that protected, and thus ignorant, bigot, almost without rancor against races other than the safely white, but just sure that they are in some measure inferior to her own, who allows her bigotry to spill like tipped paint on the life of another person, and then joins in the chorus of denouncing the victim stained by nothing more than her own careless hatred.

It is Mrs. Fosgate, so little aware of the savagery inflicted on the south by her Union officer husband and General Sherman that she can brag about the "pretty things" her spouse brought her as spoils of war, who lays the trap of suspicion of Sergeant Rutledge by casting a gimlet eye on his friendship with Lucy, the garrison commander's daughter, whom she warns not to fraternize with him. Nor is she alone in this, among the other ladies and the men of the town. "Brax" Rutledge's black skin becomes a sort of public wall on which Cordelia and her like minded compatriots may scribble the graffiti of their darkest fears. Rutledge becomes, rich in the irony attending all intolerance, the scapegoat for Mrs. Fosgate's own criminal heart. At the movie's end, when the storekeeper confesses not only to having killed the commander and raped and killed Lucy but to having tried to frame his own son for the act, Mrs. Fosgate says chidingly, "Oh, Mr. Hubble!," as if the rapist and murderer were a 12-year-old caught stealing a pie from her window sill.

This is the brilliant essence of Mrs. Fosgate's own criminality — her total lack of all comprehension of what grave circumstances her thoughtless accusations, wild suppositions and flabby memory have foisted onto an innocent man; and worse, her utter inability to realize this. In Mrs. Fosgate we have the self-perpetuating blindess of racism and bigotry, and as Ford gives Mrs. Fosgate the last word in the film, we have to believe he was saving her up to push the point home with the strongest possible force.

"While Ford ostensibly uses Cordelia and the actress who plays her, Billy [sic] Burke, for comic relief," writes William Darby, "[her] shenanigans finally backfire within the more serious framework of the film, and she emerges as a symbol of society's hypocrisy...." Anyone who sees cute Billie Burke in period dress doing her usual pert and perky thing in this film, or sees her role in it as a diversion from serious matters at hand, is obviously not paying attention.[18]

For all the seriousness of filming, and the fact that Billie, as she expressed later on in a letter to Ford, could not have been happier to be working with him, she introduced some of her own style to the dusty location set. Billie's granddaughter Cecilia remembers visiting Billie there, where a tamed John Ford served tea specially for her.

"You should have seen it," she remembers, "all the actors dressed as cowboys and cowhands, sitting down to tea with Oma, each holding his little cup."[19]

Billie was still exhilarated by the film, even though she had been unable to make the premiere, as she wrote to Ford shortly after from Sydney, Australia, in 1961. In a letter on stationery of The Australia Hotel, using two different inks, Billie pens a missive as exuberant as anything she expressed to Nancy Hamilton. She wanted to thank Ford "for the glory of being under your direction." There is a certain forced chattiness to the letter which may indicate Billie felt remiss for not having communicated with Ford sooner, let alone being absent for the premiere. She was in Australia for a *Follies* production, management of which had invited her and granddaughter Florenz to Sydney for the opening night. She loved the energy and open spaces of Australia — "quite a revelation to me" — and what a wonderful place it must be for children (including herself in that tribe, as ever).

It is obvious from various details in the letter that Billie had made a few overtures since *Sergeant Rutledge* had wrapped but had never found Ford where she expected him. "[D]on't forget me entirely," she scribbles, signing the letter "lovingly." Perhaps this is but one of many such letters, like those she sent to Nancy Hamilton and George Cukor, so overly responsive to the slightest attention that the object of her intense affections had to either leave the country or just stop writing back to her. Did Billie press Ford, as she did Cukor, for more work, feeling that he, like Cukor years before, was her savior-director, the man who knew how best to present her and had all the right connections to help her find the perfect vehicle in which to do that? There is no evidence for this, but given Billie's over-the-top approach in these matters, she may well have quickly burnt whatever bridge *Sergeant Rutledge* may have built for her.

In any event, she never did get back in touch with Ford, and the fissure between them pained her terribly — a sad ending to what had been one of her greatest film performances.

> To Mr Ford —
> To have lost your friendship — in these latter years of my career has broken my heart —
> Billie[20]

"Acting wasn't fun anymore," Billie is alleged to have remarked on her retirement in the early 1960s. It is gratifying to see, however, that she did have one last fling at going out with a smile. *Sergeant Rutledge* is often listed as Billie's final film, but it was not — her last appearance was in *Pepe*, the Cantinflas showcase that fell flat on its face not long after being released to a puzzled public. No matter. In a mere cameo, Billie, in an old lady's flowered hat and white gloves, wrests a slingshot away from Pepe (who, of course, cannot figure out how to use it) and lands a shot right on Charles Coburn, whose final film appearance this also was. As Coburn shakes his familiar wattles in astonishment and rage, Billie giggles and scampers away, out of film history.

Her remaining years were spent slowing down from that scamper. She could enjoy life now, which her need to perform, and her fear of poverty, had prevented her from doing. She enjoyed her various animal friends, surrounded as in a private shrine by the bust of Flo, props from Ziegfeld shows, photos and paintings of her glamorous young self, and her desk crowded with photographs and letters, opened and unanswered or tucked away and forgotten as the notes of her memoirs. Biographer Richard Lamparski recalls visiting Billie around this time, and as well as remembering her perfume —*Joy*— and how she rang a small crystal bell when the tea table required clearing. While it amuses him to recall what she said of her little bell—"It's Waterford," she informed him—it was her appearance that most moved him. "I remember thinking," he says, "that I had never seen a more beautiful old lady in my life."[21]

Billie did venture out of the Woodburn Avenue house, mostly to attend services at the Christian Science Church in Beverly Hills (where future playwright William Luce met her; she gave him one of the little red 45 rpm records of her nursery rhymes and a "bright, shining smile"), or to visit friends from her Church circle. One of these was actress Charlotte Greenwood, who had retired, along with her songwriter-turned-manager husband, Martin Broones, to devote all their time to Christian Science.[22]

The story persists, undoubtedly fueled by the characters she is best known for playing, and also by those Hollywood rumor mills she so deplored, that Billie suffered from Alzheimer's Disease at the end of her life—indeed, that she had had to quit acting not so much because it was no longer fun as because she could no longer remember her lines. Cecilia Duncan, who was with her in her last years, dismisses these tales. "She was suffering," she says, "from a case of undiagnosed forgetfulness," and when she died, on May 14, 1970, aged 85 years and nine months, she did so with faculties intact.[23]

In its obituary of May 16, 1970, the *New York Times*, with the benefit of hindsight, published one of the best summing ups of Billie's unique talent ever committed to newsprint: "Addlepated, scatterbrained, twittery, jittery or skittish, Billie Burke appeared in scores of comedies on the stage and screen in a style that was a combination of naiveté and wit."[24]

This sentiment was echoed and amplified at the memorial service in Los Angeles. George Cukor, who had been asked by Patricia Stephenson to speak at the ceremony, rose and told those assembled: "She was an actress in the most romantic tradition, with the magic of the theatre."[25]

That magic, which had sustained Billie's own dreams of a come back far beyond the term of its natural life, never left her. It was the magic of pleasing hundreds of people, as she had done in the gilded theatres of the Broadway of pre–World War I New York, and later in the smart comedies of Tarkington and Maugham, Coward and Novello. That was her first career. Her second started the New Year's Eve of 1914, when she met Florenz Ziegfeld Jr. Billie never became the great actress

Billie Burke's star at 6617 Hollywood Boulevard. Photograph by Les Hayter.

she had believed she had in it her to be, but she was not counting the performance her life with Flo demanded of her, which no amount of lessons in music, dance, elocution or, indeed, man-pleasing, could have prepared her for. Even as it was comedy that, ultimately, tugged all her many scattered talents toward it like iron filings to a magnet and made the best of her as a comedienne, Flo's appearance on the stage of her life drew from her all that was best of her as a person, even when he made her smash crockery or pack her bags to walk out of his life.

She knew, despite Flo's flaws, she that had married the one man who, unlike her theatrical managers, could truly make something of the raw material of self-doubt and pride, sophistication and childishness that was Billie Burke. When he died, she lost anchor and rudder. She sailed on as best she could, chalking up a few outstanding performances along the way, and giving their daughter the solid foundation she needed to start the family tree growing again, always keeping busy, and never giving up on her dreams. In the end, Billie was grateful for it all, even for the things she had not held in much esteem, as she makes clear at the end of her first memoir.

> On clear moonlight nights I walk down the hillside that looks across the sea to Avalon over a spangled array of sparkling lights, like gold nuggets dropped on a dark shawl, and I see the magic of Los Angeles.... And in the town off to the left, the town with the country-village name of Hollywood, there are youngsters coming along who will travel much the same path I have traveled. They will know wealth, happiness, heartaches, and they will lose dreams and recapture dreams. Good luck to them! Let me say this to them: "It's worth it, boys and girls."[26]

Bathed in the footlights of theatrical fame, Billie had once marveled at the crisply sparkling stars over the roof of the Empire Theatre, in 1907 New York. Now she could stand in the evening of her long life and finally find comfort in the lights of Hollywood. She knew, at the end, that it was these that had saved her from darkness.

Appendix: Billie Burke's Performance History

London Performances, 1903–1907

The School Girl, musical play by Henry Hamilton and Paul Potter. Music by Leslie Stuart. Produced at the Prince of Wales Theatre, London, May 9, 1903. CAST: Edna May, Marie Studholm, Violet Cameron, Reginald Somerville, G.P. Huntley, Billie Burke, George Graves, Pauline Chase, Clarita Deval, Norma Whalley, Arthur Roberts.

The Duchess of Dantzic, romantic light opera in three acts by Henry Hamilton, after Sardou. Music by Ivan Caryll. Produced by Robert Courtneidge at the Lyric Theatre, London, October 17, 1903. CAST: Evie Greene, Clare Greet, Irene Edwards, Mea Winfred, Monica Sayer, Marjory Gray, A. Marchand, E. Labare, Pearl Hope, Lawrence Rea, Philip H. Bracy, Holbrook Blinn, Denis O'Sullivan, A.J. Evelyn, Frank Greene, Henry J. Ford, Barry Neame, Claude Dampier, Ford Hamilton, Cecil Cameron, Nellie Souray, Kitty Gordon, Violet Elliot, Adrienne Augarde, Rose Rosslyn, Billie Burke.

The Blue Moon, musical play by Harold Ellis and Percy Greenbank. Music by Howard Talbot and Paul Rubens. Produced by Robert Courtneidge at the Lyric Theatre, London, August 28, 1905. CAST: Florence Smithson, Courtice Pounds, Billie Burke, Walter Passmore, Willie Edouin, Carrie Moore, Fred Allandale, Harold Thorley, Clarence Blakiston, Eleanor Souray, Ruth Saville.

The Belle of Mayfair, musical comedy by C.H. Brookfield and Cosmo Hamilton. Lyrics by Leslie Stiles and George Arthurs. Music by Leslie Stuart. Produced at the Vaudeville Theatre, London, April 11, 1906. CAST: Louie Pounds, Courtice Pounds, Farren Soutar, Edna May, Billie Burke, Camille Clifford.

Mr George, comedy in three acts by Louis N. Parker. Produced at the Vaudeville Theatre, London, April 25, 1907. CAST: Billie Burke, [Sir] Charles Hawtrey, O.B. Clarence, Alice Russon.

Mrs Ponderbury's Past, farcical comedy in three acts by F.C. Burnand (from the French). Produced by A. and S. Gatti at the Vaudeville Theatre, London, June 18, 1907. CAST: [Sir] Charles Hawtrey, Marie Illington, Billie Burke, Mona Harrison, Ernest Graham, Edward Fitzgerald, Charles Troode, Wilfred Draycott, Henri Laurent, L. Williams, Percy R. Goodyer, Gwynne Herbert, Mirabel Hillier.

New York Performances, 1907–1944

My Wife, comedy in four acts by Michael Morton, from the French of Mssrs. Gavault and Charnay. Produced by Charles Frohman at the Empire Theatre, New York, August 31, 1907. (129 performances) CAST: John Drew, Ferdinand Gottschalk, Walter Soderling, Morton Selten, Albert Roccardi, Mario Majeroni, Axel

Bruun, Herbert Budd, Rex McDougall, E. Soldene Powell, Frank Goldsmith, L.C. Howard, Billie Burke, Dorothy Tennant, Ida Greeley Smith, Hope Latham, Kate Pattison Selten, May Galyer.

Love Watches, comedy in four acts by Robert de Flers and Gaston de Caillavet, adapted by Gladys Unger. Produced by Charles Frohman at the Lyceum Theatre, New York, August 27, 1908. (172 performances) CAST: Cyril Heightley, Ernest Lawford, W.H. Crompton, Stanley Dark, Horace Porter, William Claire, William Edgar, Billie Burke, Maude Odell, Kate Meek, Louise Drew, Isabell West, Ida Greeley Smith, Anne Bradley, Laura Clement, Maude Love, Charlotte Shelby.

Mrs. Dot, comedy in three acts by W. Somerset Maugham. Produced by Charles Frohman at the Lyceum Theatre, New York, January 24, 1910. (72 performances) CAST: Julian L'Estrange, Kate Meek, Fred Kerr, Anne Meredith. A. Lionel Hogarth, Edgar MacGregor, Basil Hallam, Billie Burke, Annie Esmond, Ernest Cossart, P.E. McCoy, Mildred Barrett.

Suzanne, comedy in three acts by Frantz Fonson and Fernand Wicheler. Adapted by C. Haddon Chambers. Produced by Charles Frohman at the Lyceum Theatre, New York, December 26, 1910. (64 performances) CAST: Julian L'Estrange, George W. Anson, Conway Tearle, Billie Burke, Harry Harwood, David Glassford, C. Harrison Carter, C.J. Wedgewood, P.E. McCoy, G.H. Beverman, E.R. Sheehy, M.B. Hendel, N.K. Leavitt, Rosa Rand, Alison Skipworth, Jane Galbraith.

The Philosopher in the Apple Orchard, play by E. Harcourt Williams from Anthony Hope's short story. Produced by Charles Frohman at the Lyceum Theatre as curtain raiser to *Suzanne*, from January 20, 1911. CAST: Billie Burke, Lumsden Hare.

The Runaway, comedy in four acts by Pierre Veber and Henri de Gorsse. Adapted by Michael Morton. Produced by Charles Frohman at the Lyceum Theatre, New York, October 9, 1911. (64 performances) CAST: C. Aubrey Smith, George Howell, Henry Miller, Jr., Morton Selten, H.A. Cripps, Edwin Nicander, Harry Barfoot, Emily Wakeman, Josephine

Morse, Isabel West, Jane Evans, Alice Gale, Aline McDermott, Roma Devonne, Adelaide Cumming, Lettie Ford, Billie Burke.

The Mind the Paint Girl, comedy in four acts by Sir Arthur Wing Pinero. Produced by Charles Frohman and directed by Dion G. Boucicault at the Lyceum Theatre, New York, September 9, 1912. (136 performances) CAST: William Raymond, H.E. Herbert, Edward Douglas, John Morley, Arthur Fitzgerald, Barnett Parker, Bernard Merefield, Arthur Luzzi, Neanette Lowrie, Carroll McComas, Edith Campbell, Hazel Leslie, Jeanne Shelby, Anna Rose, Marie Fitzgerald, Morton Selten, Leo Cooper, David Hawthorne, Louis Massen, Kenneth Lee, Cecil Newton, Erskholm E. Clive, Louis H. Geist, Billie Burke, Mabel Frenyear, Ruth Boyce, Vera Mellish, Jeanne Eagels, Lydia Rachel, Louise Reed, J. Palmer Collins, Ernest W. Laceby.

The Amazons, comedy in three acts by Sir Arthur Wing Pinero. Revived by Charles Frohman at the Empire Theatre, New York, April 29, 1913. (48 performances) CAST: Shelley Hull, Morton Selten, Ferdinand GottschalkFritz Williams, Thomas Reynolds, Arthur Fitzgerald, Dorothy Lane, Barnett Parker, Annie Esmond, Miriam Clements, Billie Burke, Lorena Atwood.

The Land of Promise, play in four acts by W. Somerset Maugham. Produced by Charles Frohman at the Lyceum Theatre, New York, December 25, 1913. (76 performances) CAST: Billie Burke, Lumsden Hare, Lillian Kingsbury, Shelley Hull, Norman Tharp, Thomas Reynolds, Barnett Parker, Marion Abbott, Henry Warwick, Gwladys Morris, Mildred Orme, Leopold Lane, Selma Hall.

Jerry, play in three acts by Catherine Chisholm Cushing. Produced by Charles Frohman at the Lyceum Theatre, New York, March 28, 1914. (41 performances) CAST: Gladys Hanson, Billie Burke, Allan Pollock, Thomas Reynolds, Alice John, Shelley Hull, Lumsden Hare, Bernard Thornton.

The Rescuing Angel, play in three acts by Clare Kummer. Produced by Florenz Ziegfeld, Jr., and Arthur Hopkins at the Hudson Theatre, New York, October 8, 1917. (32 performances)

CAST: Billie Burke, Claude Gillingwater, Marie Wainwright, Elmer Brown, Walter Schellin, Dana Desboro, Robert McWade, Richard Barbee, Roland Young, Frederick Perry, Rhoda Beresford.

A Marriage of Convenience, comedy in four acts by Alexandre Dumas. Adapted by Sydney Grundy. Revived at the Henry Miller Theatre, New York, May 1, 1918. (53 performances) CAST: Henry Miller, Billie Burke, Lowell Sherman, Lucille Watson, Frank Kemble Cooper, Frederick Lloyd, Lewis Sealy, Lynn Hammon.

Caesar's Wife, drama in three acts by W. Somerset Maugham. Produced by Florenz Ziegfeld, Jr. at the Liberty Theatre, New York, November 24, 1919. (81 performances) CAST: Norman Trevor, Ernest Glendinning, Harry Green, T. Wigney Percyval, Frederic DeBelleville, Margaret Dale, Hilda Spong, Mrs. Tom A. Wise, Billie Burke.

The Intimate Strangers, a comedy in three acts by Booth Tarkington. Produced by Florenz Ziegfeld, Jr., A.L. Erlanger and Charles Dillingham at the Henry Miller Theatre, New York, November 7, 1921. (91 performances) CAST: Charles Abbe, Alfred Lunt, Billie Burke, Frances Howard, Glenn Hunter, Frank J. Kirk, Elizabeth Patterson, Clare Weldon.

Rose Briar, a comedy in three acts by Booth Tarkington. Produced by Florenz Ziegfeld, Jr. at the Empire Theatre, New York, December 25, 1922. (88 performances) CAST: Billie Burke, Allan Dinehart, Frank Conroy, Julia Hoyt, Richie Ling, Paul Doucet, Florence O'Denishawn, Ethel Remey, Louis Darclee, Mark Haight, Frank McCoy.

Annie Dear, musical comedy in three acts. Book, music and lyrics by Clare Kummer. Produced by Florenz Ziegfeld, Jr., at the Times Square Theatre, New York, November 4, 1924. (103 performances) CAST: John Byam, May Vokes, Florentine Gosnova, Edward Allan, Ernest Truex, Bobby Watson, Billie Burke, Spencer Bentley, Phyllis Cleveland, Mary Lawler, Jack Whiting, Alexander Gray, Spencer Charters, Gaving Gordon, Frank Kingdon, Marion Green, Marjorie Peterson.

The Marquise, play in three acts by Noël Coward. Produced by Kenneth McGowan and Sidney Ross at the Biltmore Theatre, New York, November 14, 1927. (80 performances) CAST: Arthur Byron, Madge Evans, Theodore St. John, Reginald Owen, Rex O'Malley, Harry Lillford, Billie Burke, Dorothy Tree, William Kershaw.

The Happy Husband, comedy in three acts by Harrison Owen. Produced by Gilbert Miller at the Empire Theatre, New York, May 7, 1928. (46 performances) CAST: Billie Burke, A.E. Matthews, Lawrence Grossmith, Irene Browne, Walter Connolly, George Thorpe, John Williams, Ilka Chase, Mackenzie ward, Nancy Ryan, Alice Moffat.

Family Affairs, comedy in three acts by Earle Crooker and Lowell Brentano. Produced by Arthur Hopkins and L. Lawrence Weber at the Maxine Elliott Theatre, New York, December 10, 1929. (7 performances) CAST: Joshope McCallion, Elaine Temple, Cecil Clovelly, Frank Elliot, Billie Burke, Edmund George, Leona Boutelle, Audrey Ridgwell, Bruce Evans.

The Truth Game, comedy in three acts by Ivor Novello. Produced by Lee Shubert at the Ethel Barrymore Theatre, New York, December 27, 1930. (107 performances) CAST: Phoebe Foster, Ivor Novello, Gerald McCarthy, Gwen Day Burroughs, Billie Burke, Burton McEvilly, Jean Fullerton, Dorothie Bigelow, Viola Tree, Albert Garcia Andrews, Forbes Dawson.

This Rock, comedy in three acts by Walter Livingston Faust. Produced by Eddie Dowling at the Longacre Theatre, New York, February 18, 1943. (37 performances) CAST: Harlan Stone, Joyce Van Patten, Joan Sheppard, Zachary Scott, Alastair Kyle, Roland Hogue, Jane Sterling, Billie Burke, Nicholas Joy, Everett Ripley, Lucia Victor, Ethel Morrison, Malcolm Dunn, Gene Lyons, John Farrel, Mabel Taylor, Victor Beecroft, Lorna Lynn, Gerald Matthews, Suzanne Johnston, Louis Volkman, Patsy Flicker, Buddy Millard, Dickie Millard, Richard Leone.

Mrs. January and Mr. X, comedy in three acts by Zoë Akins. Produced by Richard Myers at the Belasco Theatre, New York, March 31, 1944. (43 performances) CAST: Helen Carew, Edward Nannary, Phil Sheridan, Billie Burke, Frank Craven, Roderick Winchell, Robert F. Simon, Mlle Therese Quadri, Barbara Bel Geddes, Bobby Perez, Henry Barnard, Henry Vincent, Dorothy Lambert, Nicholas Joy, Susanna Garnett.

California Performances, 1931–1951

The Vinegar Tree, play in three acts by Paul Osborne. Produced by David Belasco and Homer Curran at the Belasco Theatre, Los Angeles, June 1931, toured in 1941. CAST: Billie Burke, Warren William, William Morris, William Janney, Fulie Dillon, Dorothy Blackburn.

The Mad Hopes, a comedy by Romney Brent. Produced in Los Angeles, 1931.

His Master's Voice, play in three acts by Ivy Low. Produced at the El Capitan Theatre, Hollywood, 1934.

The Marquise, toured California in 1932. CAST: Alan Mowbray, William Stack, Billie Burke, Anita Louise, Morgan Farley, Reginald Sheffield, Herbert Bunston, Cyril Delevanti, Virginia Howard.

The Swallow's Nest, by Zoë Akins, Pasadena Playhouse, June 1951, directed by John Milton. CAST: Billie Burke, Marjorie Steele (Mrs. Huntington Hartford, in her acting debut), Onslow Stevens, George Phelps, Lumsden Hare, Hans Josef Schumm, Roy Gordon.

The Man, Huntington Hartford Theatre in fall 1955, directed by Demetrios Vilan. CAST: Billie Burke, Douglas Dick.

Films, 1916–1960

Peggy (1916), directed by Thomas Ince and Charles Giblyn. CAST: Billie Burke, William H. Thompson, William Desmond, Charles Ray, Nona Thomas, Gertrude Claire, Truly Shattuck.

Gloria's Romance (1916), directed by Colin Campbell and Walter Edwin. CAST: Billie Burke, David Powell, William Roselle, Frank Belcher, William T. Carleton, Jule Power, Henry Weaver, Frank McGlynn, Sr., Helen

Hart, Henry Kolker, Maxfield Moree, Maurice Stewart, Rapley Holmes, Adeliade Hastings, Ralph Bunker, Henry Hallam, Lillian Beck.

The Mysterious Miss Terry (1917), directed by J. Searle Drawley. CAST: Billie Burke, Thomas Meighan, Walter Hiers, Gerald Oliver Smith, George A. Wright, Bessie Hearn.

Arms and the Girl (1917), directed by Joseph Kaufman. CAST: Billie Burke, Thomas Meighan, Louise Bates, J. Malcolm Dunn, Arthur Bauer, William David, George S. Trimble, Harry Lee, May De Lacy.

The Land of Promise (1917), directed by Joseph Kaufman, based on the play by W. Somerset Maugham. CAST: Billie Burke, Thomas Meighan, Helen Tracy, Jack W. Johnston, Mary Alden, Margaret Seddon, Walter McEwen, Grace Studdiford, John Raymond.

Eve's Daughter (1918), directed by James Kirkwood. CAST: Billie Burke, Thomas Meighan, Lionel Atwill, Riley Hatch, Florence Finn, Harriet Ross, Lucille Carney, Mary Navarro, Harry Lee, Clarence Doyle, Jimmy Gormon, Ivy Shannon.

Let's Get a Divorce (1918), directed by Charles Giblyn. CAST: Billie Burke, John Miltern, Pinna Nesbit, Armand Kaliz, Rod La Rocque, Helen Tracy, John Merkyl, Cesare Gravina.

In Pursuit of Polly (1918), directed by Chester "Chet" Withey. CAST: Billie Burke, Thomas Meighan, Frank Losee, A.J. Herbert, William B. Davidson, Alfred Hickman, Ben Deeley.

The Make-Believe Wife (1918), directed by John S. Robertson. CAST: Billie Burke, Alfred Hickman, Ida Darling, David Powell, Wray Page, Isabel O'Madigan, Frances Kaye, Bigelow Cooper, Howard Johnson, F. Gatenbury Bell.

Good Gracious, Annabelle (1919), directed by George Melford, based on the play by Clare Kummer. CAST: Billie Burke, Herbert Rawlinson, Gilbert Douglas, Crauford Kent, Frank Losee, Leslie Casey, Gordon Dana, Delle Duncan, Olga Downs, Thomas Braidon, Billie Wilson.

The Misleading Widow (1919), directed by John S. Robertson, based on the play by H. M.

Harwood and F. Tennyson Jesse. CAST: Billie Burke, James Crane, Frank Mills, Madelyn Clare, Fred Hearn, Mrs. Priestly Morrison, Fred Esmelton, Dorothy Waters.

Sadie Love (1919), directed by John S. Robertson. CAST: Billie Burke, James Crane, Helen Montrose, Hedda Hopper, Jed Prouty, Shaw Lovett, Mrs. Margaret A. Wiggin, May Rogers, Charles Craig, Ida Waterman.

Wanted: A Husband (1919), directed by Lawrence C. Windom, based on a story by Samuel Hopkins Adams. CAST: Billie Burke, James Crane, Margaret Linden, Charles Lane, Edward Lester, Bradley Barker, Helen Greene, Gypsy O'Brien, Kid Broad, Mrs. Priestly Morrison, Frank Goldsmith.

Away Goes Prudence (1920), directed by John S. Robertson. CAST: Billie Burke, Percy Marmont, Maude Turner Gordon, Charles Lane, Dorothy Walters, Bradley Barker, M.W. Rale, Albert Hackett.

The Frisky Mrs. Johnson (1920), directed by Edward Dillon. CAST: Billie Burke, Ward Crane, Jane Warrington, Lumsden Hare, Huntley Gordon, Jean de Briac, Robert Agnew, Leonora von Ottinger, Emily Fitzroy.

The Education of Elizabeth (1921), directed by Edward Dillon, based on the play by Roy Horniman. CAST: Billie Burke, Lumsden Hare, Edith Sharpe, Donald Cameron, Frederick Burton, Frederic March.

The Bill of Divorcement (1932), directed by George Cukor, based on the play by Clemence Dane. CAST: John Barrymore, Billie Burke, David Manners, Katharine Hepburn, Paul Cavanagh, Henry Stephenson, Gayle Evers, Elizabeth Patterson.

Christopher Strong (1933), directed by Dorothy Arzner. CAST: Katharine Hepburn, Colin Clive, Billie Burke, Helen Chandler, Ralph Forbes, Irene Browne, Jack La Rue, Desmond Roberts.

Dinner At Eight (1933), directed by George Cukor, based on the play by Edna Ferber and George S. Kaufman. CAST: Marie Dressler, John Barrymore, Wallace Beery, Jean Harlow, Lionel Barrymore, Lee Tracy, Edmund Lowe,

Billie Burke, Madge Evans, Hilda Vaughn, Harry Beresford.

Only Yesterday (1933), directed by John M. Stahl. CAST: Margaret Sullavan, John Boles, Edna May Oliver, Billie Burke, Benita Hume, Reginald Denny, George Meeker, Jimmy Butler, Noel Francis, Bramwell Fletcher, June Clyde, Jane Darwell.

Where Sinners Meet (1934), directed by J. Walter Ruben. CAST: Diana Wynyard, Clive Brook, Billie Burke, Reginald Owen, Alan Mowbray, Gilbert Emery, Phyllis Barry, Walter Armitage, Katherine Williams, Robert Adair, Vernon Steele.

Finishing School (1934), directed by George Nichols, Jr., and Wanda Tuchock. CAST: Frances Dee, Billie Burke, Ginger Rogers, Bruce Cabot, John Halliday, Beulah Bondi, Sara Haden, Helen Freeman.

We're Rich Again (1934), directed by William A. Seiter. CAST: Edna May Oliver, Billie Burke, Marian Nixon, Reginald Denny, Joan Marsh, Buster Crabbe, Grant Mitchell, Gloria Shea, Edgar Kennedy, Otto Yamaoka.

Forsaking All Others (1934), directed by W.S. Van Dyke. CAST: Robert Montgomery, Joan Crawford, Clark Gable, Charles Butterworth, Billie Burke, Frances Drake, Rosalind Russell.

Society Doctor (1934), directed by George B. Seitz. CAST: Chester Morris, Robert Taylor, Virginia Bruce, Billie Burke, Raymond Walburn, Henry Kolker, Dorothy Peterson, William Henry, Donald Meek.

After Office Hours (1935), directed by Robert Z. Leonard. CAST: Constance Bennett, Clark Gable, Stuart Erwin, Billie Burke, Harvey Stephens, Katharine Alexander, Hale Hamilton, Henry Travers.

Becky Sharp (1935), directed by Rouben Mamoulian, based on the novel by William Makepoeace Thackeray. CAST: Miriam Hopkins, Frances Dee, Cedric Hardwicke, Billie Burke, Alison Skipworth, Nigel Bruce, Alan Mowbray, G.P. Huntley.

Doubting Thomas (1935), directed by David Butler. CAST: Will Rogers, Billie Burke, Alison

Skipworth, Sterling Holloway, Andrew Tombes, Gail Patrick.

She Couldn't Take It (1935), directed by Tay Garnett. CAST: George Raft, Joan Bennett, Walter Connolly, Billie Burke, Lloyd Nolan, Wallace Ford, James Blakeley, Alan Mowbray.

A Feather in Her Hat (1935), directed by Alfred Santell, based on the novel by I.A.R. Wylie. CAST: Pauline Lord, Basil Rathbone, Louis Hayward, Billie Burke, Wendy Barrie, Nydia Westman, Victor Varconi, Thurston Hall.

Splendor (1935), directed by Elliott Nugent, based on the play by Rachel Crothers. CAST: Miriam Hopkins, Joel McCrea, Paul Cavanagh, Helen Westley, Billie Burke, David Niven, Katharine Alexander.

My American Wife (1936), directed by Harold Young. CAST: Francis Lederer, Ann Sothern, Fred Stone, Billie Burke, Ernest Cossart, Grant Mitchell, Hal K. Dawson, Helene Millard, Adrian Morris, Dora Clement.

Piccadilly Jim (1936), directed by Robert Z. Leonard, based on the novel by P.G. Wodehouse. CAST: Robert Montgomery, Frank Morgan, Madge Evans, Eric Blore, Billie Burke, Robert Benchley, Ralph Forbes, Cora Witherspoon.

Craig's Wife (1936), directed by Dorothy Arzner, based on the play by George Kelly. CAST: Rosalind Russell, John Boles, Billie Burke, Jane Darwell, Dorothy Wilson, Alma Kruger, Thomas Mitchell.

Parnell (1937), directed by John M. Stahl, based on the play by Elsie T. Schauffler. CAST: Clark Gable, Myrna Loy, Edna May Oliver, Edmund Gwenn, Alan Marshal, Donald Crisp, Billie Burke.

Topper (1937), directed by Norman Z. MacLeod, based on the novel by Thorne Smith. CAST: Constance Bennett, Cary Grant, Roland Young, Billie Burke, Alan Mowbray, Eugene Pallette, Arthur Lake, Hedda Hopper.

The Bride Wore Red (1937), directed by Dorothy Arzner, based on the play by Ferenc Molnár. CAST: Joan Crawford, Franchot Tone,

Robert Young, Billie Burke, Reginald Owen, Lynne Carver, George Zucco.

Navy Blue and Gold (1937), directed by Sam Wood, based on the book by George Wood. CAST: Robert Young, James Stewart, Florence Rice, Billie Burke, Lionel Barrymore, Tom Brown, Samuel S. Hinds, Paul Kelly.

Everybody Sing (1938), directed by Edwin L. Marin. CAST: Allan Jones, Judy Garland, Fanny Brice, Reginald Owen, Billie Burke, Reginald Gardner, Lynne Carver, Helen Troy.

Merrily We Live (1938), directed by Norman Z. MacLeod. CAST: Constance Bennett, Brian Aherne, Alan Mowbray, Billie Burke (nominated for Oscar, Best Supporting Actress), Patsy Kelly.

The Young in Heart (1938), directed by Richard Wallace, based on the serial by I.A.R. Wylie. CAST: Janet Gaynor, Douglas Fairbanks, Jr., Paulette Goddard, Roland Young, Billie Burke, Minnie Dupree, Henry Stephenson.

Topper Takes a Trip (1939), directed by Norman Z. MacLeod, based on the novel by Thorne Smith. CAST: Constance Bennett, Roland Young, Billie Burke, Alan Mowbray, Verree Teasdale, Franklin Pangborn, Alexander D'Arcy.

Zenobia (1939), directed by Gordon Douglas. CAST: Oliver Hardy, Harry Langdon, Billie Burke, Alice Brady, James Ellison, Jean Parker, June Lang, Olin Howland, J. Farrell MacDonald, Stepin Fetchit, Hattie McDaniel.

Bridal Suite (1939), directed by Wilhelm Thiele. CAST: Annabella, Robert Young, Walter Connolly, Reginald Owen, Gene Lockhart, Arthur Treacher, Billie Burke, Virginia Field, Felix Bressart.

The Wizard of Oz, directed by Victor Fleming, based on the novel by L. Frank Baum. CAST: Judy Garland, Frank Morgan, Ray Bolger, Bert Lahr, Jack Haley, Billie Burke, Margaret Hamilton, Charley Grapewine, Pat Walshe, Clara Blandick, Terry (Toto).

Eternally Yours (1939), directed by Tay Garnett. CAST: Loretta Young, David Niven, Hugh Herbert, Billie Burke, C. Aubrey Smith, Raymond Walburn, Zasu Pitts.

Remember? (1939), directed by Norman Z. MacLeod. CAST: Robert Taylor, Greer Garson, Lew Ayres, Billie Burke, Reginald Owen, George Barbier, Henry Travers.

The Ghost Comes Home (1940), directed by Wilhelm Thiele, based on Georg Kaiser's play. CAST: Frank Morgan, Billie Burke, Ann Rutherford, John Shelton, Reginald Owen, Donald Meek, Nat Pendleton.

And One Was Beautiful (1940), directed by Robert B. Sinclair. CAST: Robert Cummings, Laraine Day, Jean Muir, Billie Burke, Ann Morriss, Esther Dale, Charles Waldron.

Irene (1940), directed by Herbert Wilcox, based on the play by James Montgomery. CAST: Anna Neagle, Ray Milland, Roland Young, Alan Marshal, May Robson, Billie Burke, Arthur Treacher.

The Captain Is a Lady (1940), directed by Robert B. Sinclair, based on the play by Rachael Crothers. CAST: Charles Coburn, Beulah Bondi, Virginia Grey, Helen Broderick, Billie Burke, Dan Dailey, Margery Main, Clem Bevans.

Dulcy (1940), directed by S. Sylvan Simon, based on the play by George S. Kaufman and Marc Connelly. CAST: Ann Sothern, Ian Hunter, Roland Young, Reginald Gardner, Billie Burke, Lynne Carver, Dan Dailey.

Hullaballoo (1940), directed by Edwin L. Marin. CAST: Frank Morgan, Virginia Grey, Dan Dailey, Billie Burke, Nydia Westman, Ann Morriss, Donald Meek.

The Wild Man of Borneo (1941), directed by Robert B. Sinclair, based on the play by Marc Connelly and Herman J. Mankiewicz. CAST: Frank Morgan, Mary Howard, Billie Burke, Donald Meek, Marjorie Main, Connie Gilchrist, Bonita Granville, Dan Dailey.

Topper Returns (1941), directed by Roy Del Ruth. CAST: Joan Blondell, Roland Young, Carole Landis, Billie Burke, Dennis O'Keefe, Patsy Kelly, H.B. Warner.

One Night in Lisbon (1941), directed by Edward H. Griffith, based on the play by John Van Druten. CAST: Fred MacMurray, Madeleine Carroll, Patricia Morison, Billie Burke, John Loder, Dame May Whitty, Edmund Gwenn.

The Man Who Came to Dinner (1942), directed by William Keighley. CAST: Bette Davis, Ann Sheridan, Monty Woolley, Richard Travis, Jimmy Durante, Billie Burke, Reginald Gardner, Mary Wickes.

What's Cookin'? (1942), directed by Edward F. Cline. CAST: The Andrews Sisters, Jane Frazee, Robert Paige, Gloria Jean, Billie Burke, Charles Butterworth, the Jivin' Jacks and Jills.

In This Our Life (1942), directed by John Huston, based on the novel by Ellen Glasgow. CAST: Bette Davis, Olivia de Havilland, George Brent, Dennis Morgan, Charles Coburn, Frank Craven, Billie Burke, Hattie McDaniel.

They All Kissed the Bride (1942), directed by Alexander Hall. CAST: Joan Crawford, Melvyn Douglas, Roland Young, Billie Burke, Allen Jenkins, Andrew Tombes, Helen Parrish.

Girl Trouble (1942), directed by Harold D. Schuster. CAST: Don Ameche, Joan Bennett, Billie Burke, Frank Craven, Alan Dinehart, Helene Reynolds, Fortunio Bonanova.

Hi Diddle Diddle (1943), directed by Andrew L. Stone. CAST: Adolphe Menjou, Martha Scott, Pola Negri, Dennis O'Keeffe, Billie Burke.

So's Your Uncle (1943), directed by Jean Yarbrough. CAST: Billie Burke, Donald Woods, Elyse Knox, Frank Jenks, Robert Lowery, Irving Bacon.

You're a Lucky Fellow, Mr. Smith (1943), directed by Felix E. Feist. CAST: Allan Jones, Evelyn Ankers, Billie Burke, David Bruce, Patsy O'Connor, Stanley Clements.

Gildersleeve on Broadway (1943), directed by Gordon Douglas. CAST: Harold Peary, Billie Burke, Claire Carleton, Richard LeGrand, Freddie Mercer, Leonid Kinskey.

Swing Out, Sister (1945), directed by Edward C. Lilley. CAST: Rod Cameron, Billie Burke, Arthur Treacher, Frances Raeburn, Jacqueline DeWit.

The Cheaters (1945), directed by Joseph Kane. CAST: Joseph Schildkraut, Billie Burke, Eugene Pallette, Ona Munson, Raymond Walburn.

Breakfast in Hollywood (1946), directed by Harold D. Schuster. CAST: Tom Brenneman, Bonita Granville, Beulah Bondi, Edward Ryan, Raymond Walburn, Billie Burke, Zasu Pitts, Hedda Hopper, Nat King Cole.

The Bachelor's Daughters (1946), directed by Andrew L. Stone. CAST: Gail Russell, Claire Trevor, Ann Dvorak, Adolphe Menjou, Billie Burke, Jane Wyatt.

Silly Billie (1948), directed by Jules White. CAST: Billie Burke, Virginia Hunter, Myron Healey, Tim Ryan, Emil Sitka.

Billie Gets Her Man (1948), directed by Edward Bernds. CAST: Billie Burke, Symona Boniface, Tiny Brauer, Heinie Conklin, Virginia S. Ellsworth.

The Barkleys of Broadway (1949), directed by Charles Waters, story by Betty Comden and Adolph Green. CAST: Fred Astaire, Ginger Rogers, Oscar Levant, Billie Burke, Gale Robbins, Jacques François.

And Baby Makes Three (1949), directed by Henry Levin. CAST: Robert Young, Barbara Hale, Robert Carter, Janis Hutton, Billie Burke.

The Boy from Indiana (1950), directed by John Rawlins. CAST: Lon McAllister, Lois Butler, Billie Burke, George Cleveland, Texas Dandy.

Father of the Bride (1950), directed by Vincente Minelli. CAST: Spencer Tracy, Joan Bennett, Elizabeth Taylor, Don Taylor, Billie Burke, Leo G. Carroll.

Three Husbands (1951), directed by Irving Reis. CAST: Eve Arden, Ruth Warrick, Vanessa Brown, Howard Da Silva, Shepperd Strudwick, Robert Carnes, Emlyn Williams, Billie Burke.

Father's Little Dividend (1951), directed by Vincente Minelli. CAST: Spencer Tracy, Joan Bennett, Elizabeth Taylor, Don Taylor, Billie Burke, Moroni Olson.

Small Town Girl (1953), directed by László Kardos. CAST: Jane Powell, Farley Granger, Ann Miller, S.K. Sakall, Robert Keith, Bobby Van, Billie Burke.

The Young Philadelphians (1959), directed by Vincent Sherman, based on the novel by Richard Powell. CAST: Paul Newman, Barbara Rush, Alexis Smith, Brian Keith, Diane Brewster, Billie Burke.

Sergeant Rutledge (1960), directed by John Ford. CAST: Jeffrey Hunter, Constance Towers, Billy Burke, Woody Strode, Juano Hernandez, Willis Bouchey.

Pepe (1961), directed by George Sidney. CAST: Cantinflas, Dan Dailey, Shirley Jones, Carlos Montalban, with cameos by Sammy Davis, Jr., Bing Crosby, Debbie Reynolds, Zsa Zsa Gabor, Billie Burke, Hedda Hopper, Greer Garson.

Radio

The Ziegfeld Follies of the Air 1932

Good News of 1939 1938

The Rudy Vallee Hour 1939

The Gulf Screen Guild Theater 1939

The Rudy Vallee Sealtest Show 1940–41

The Pepsodent Show 1941

The Billie Burke Show 1943–1946

Duffy's Tavern 1944

The Sealtest Village Store 1944

Mail Call 1944

The Charlie McCarthy Show 1944–47

Tribute to Ethel Barrymore 1945

The Rudy Vallee Show 1945

Show Stoppers 1946

The Danny Kaye Show 1946

WOR 25th Anniversary 1947

Your Movietown Radio Theatre 1948

The Eddie Cantor Pabst Blue Ribbon Show 1948

Family Theater 1948–52

This Is Show Business 1949

The Martin and Lewis Show 1949

The Bill Stern Colgate Sports Newsreel 1949

Stagestruck 1954

Biography in Sound 1955–56

Television

Author Meets [The] Critics, Joe Laurie, Jr. and Harry Hershfield, NBC (1949).

Texaco Star Theatre, NBC (1949).

The Bigelow Show, CBS (1949).

The Ed Wynn Show, CBS (1950).

Dr. Heidegger's Experiment (1950—1 episode), with Billie Burke, Halliwell Hobbes, Gene Lockhart and Tom Poston.

Stop the Music, ABC (1950).

Don McNeill TV Club, ABC (1951).

Bigelow Theatre: "Dear Amanda," CBS (1951).

All Star Revue, NBC (1951).

Doc Corkle (1952 — 3 episodes), with Eddie Mayehoff, Billie Burke, Chester Conklin, Hope Emerson and Connie Marshall.

I've Got a Secret, CBS (1953).

The Best of Broadway: "Arsenic and Old Lace," CBS (1955 — Season 1, Episode 5), directed by Herbert B. Swope, with John Alexander, Orson Bean, Richard Bishop, Patricia Breslin, Billie Burke, Bruce Gordon, Helen Hayes.

The Eddie Cantor Comedy Theatre: "The Big Bargain," SYN (1955 —1 episode), with Eddie Cantor, Billie Burke, James Gleason.

Who Said That?, ABC (1955).

Matinee Theatre: "Mother Was a Bachelor," NBC (1956).

Playhouse 90: "The Star Wagon" (1957 — Season 1, Episode 17), directed by Vincent J. Donehue, with Richard Joy, Eddie Bracken, Diana Lynn, Jackie Coogan, Margaret Hayes, William Bishop, Billie Burke; "Rumors of Evening" (1958 — Season 2, Episode 32), directed by John Frankenheimer, with Barbara Bel Geddes, Billie Burke, Dave Guard, Patricia Hitchcock, John Kerr, Robert Loggia.

Art Linkletter's House Party, CBS (1958).

77 Sunset Strip: "Publicity Brat" (1960–1 episode), directed by Leslie H. Martinson, with Efrem Zimbalist, Jr., Roger Smith, Louis Quinn, Pamela Britton, Billie Burke.

Chapter Notes

Preface

1. Donald Spoto, "Billie Burke: The Wizard of Oz's Good Witch in Beverly Hills," *Architectural Digest*, April 1996.

Chapter 1

1. Billie Burke, *With a Feather on My Nose*, p. 16.
2. *Ibid.*, pp. 10–11 and p. 92. Cousin Lucy told Billie (according to Billie) she remembered Blanche's silk petticoats rustling as if saying, "Dollar a yard, dollar a yard." It could well be Lucy was a former servant of Cecilia Beatty's from Zanesville, but nothing I have found indicates she could have been a slave of Cecilia Beatty's family from New Orleans. In any event, Billie would later refer to her grandmother's abolitionist writings, which does not jibe with the focus on Cousin Lucy's ex-slave status. Another peculiar claim, this made by Billie as late as 1945, was that her grandmother Beatty was "along with Harriet Beecher Stowe, [a writer of] articles against the South's treatment of the Negro slaves." Again, there is no obvious record of any of this. See *The Milwaukee Journal*, August 19, 1945.
3. Ada Patterson, *Theatre Magazine*, pp. 300–302 (no date but clearly published in 1908); author interview with Mr. and Mrs. William Stephenson, August 10, 2007; 1850 Census, Muskingum Co., District 116, Union Township, October 15, 1850, p. 450. When Blanche and Billie sailed from Liverpool on the *Mauretania* in August 1913, Blanche correctly gave her birth place as Zanesville, though she took nearly ten years off her age; Billie's entry gives her birth year as 1887 instead of 1884. The Asfordby information is given in Douglas Richardson, *Magna Carta Ancestry: A Study in Colonial and Medieval Families* (Baltimore: Ge-

nealogical, July 30, 2005), pp. 17–18. Billie's royal ancestor was King Henry II "Curtmantle," through his illegitimate son William de Longespee. Through his mother, Nancy Sarchet, John Beatty was descended from numerous French families long settled on Guernsey in the Channel Islands.
4. Burke, *Feather*, p. 8.
5. 1880 Census, taken at 819 Fourteenth Street, Washington, D.C., June 11, 1880.
6. Fred D. Pfening, "Circus Songsters," *Bandwagon* 7.6 (November-December 1963), pp. 10–12; Burke, *Feather*, p. 4. See "Biographical Sketch of William Ethelbert Burke, America's Greatest Clown."
7. Burke, *Feather*, pp. 3–8; "Biographical Sketch of William Ethelbert Burke, America's Greatest Clown."
8. Burke-Beatty marriage certificate, Stephenson family archives; *www.littlechurch.org/history.html*.
9. Burke, *Feather*, p. 9. Billie's granddaughter, Cecilia Duncan, does remember contact with the Hodkinson children; one of the old family recipes still enjoyed by Blanche's descendants was invented by "Uncle George," Blanche's son (Stephenson interview, August 10, 2007).
10. Burke, *Feather*, pp. 9–10; Patterson, pp. 300–303.
11. Burke, *Feather*, p. 11; *New York Times*, December 1894 and June 1895; Patterson, pp. 300–303.
12. *Telegraph*, November 22, 1908; Burke, *Feather*, pp. 11–13.

Chapter 2

1. Burke, *Feather*, pp. 15–18.
2. *Ibid.*, p. 8; *Olympians of the Sawdust Circle*, *www.circushistory.org*.

3. Burke, *Feather*, p. 19; Patricia Ziegfeld, *The Ziegfelds' Girl* [hereafter *TZG*], pp.3–4.

4. Burke, *Feather*, p. 20.

5. *Ibid.*, pp. 20–21.

6. *Ibid.*, p. 22.

7. See the Wisconsin *Superior Telegram*, April 10, 1909, which claims Billie debuted in Vienna in 1902, toured Hungary, Russia, Germany and France, and made her UK debut in Glasgow.

8. Burke, *Feather*, pp. 24–25; Patterson.

9. Ellwood Anaheim, Florodora Musical Research Project, *http://www.geocities.com/musictheater/floro/floro.html*.

10. Billie was to repay Stuart thirteen years later when, as the toast of Broadway and wife of Flo Ziegfeld, she welcomed Stuart out to Burkeley Crest, telling him that had it not been for him there would have been no such grandeur for her to live in. In December 1917, Stuart was listed as co-writer, with Gene Buck, for Flo's new *Midnight Frolic*. Stuart contributed at least one song ("Cutey"), but the production was fraught with trouble, the height of which came in the form of a fire that decimated the wardrobe, then a spate of frigid weather that delayed the arrival of the sets from Boston, and assorted other headaches. See Andrew Lamb, *Leslie Stuart: Composer of Florodora*, pp. 250–251.

11. Burke, *Feather*, pp. 26–29.

12. *Ibid.*, p. 29.

13. *Ibid.*, pp. 29–30.

14. *Ibid.*, p. 31 and pp. 33–35; Nancy Hamilton-Billie Burke letters [hereafter NH-BB letters], Howard Gotlieb Archival Research Center at Boston University. For Cary ancestry, see Alan Freer, A.C.I.B., Society of Genealogists, London, "The Descendants of William the Conqueror," *http://www.william1.co.uk/t28.htm*. Frank Cary's wife, Mary Farrell, was a descendant on her mother's side of the Viscounts Gormanston; and according to one of their descendants, Mary was very much in the mould, physically speaking, of Billie Burke.

15. Burke, *Feather*, pp. 35–36.

16. *Ibid.*, pp. 39–40; "The Best Stage Liar of His Time," *The Times*, Arts section, December 18, 1958.

17. Burke, *Feather*, pp. 39–40.

18. *Ibid.*, pp. 40–42.

19. *Ibid.*, pp. 42–44.

20. *Ibid.*, pp. 43–45.

21. Isaac F. Marcosson and Daniel Frohman, *Charles Frohman, Manager and Man*, James M. Barrie's foreword.

22. Burke, *Feather*, pp. 45–47 and p. 61.

Chapter 3

1. Burke, *Feather*, p. 68.

2. John Drew, *My Years on the Stage*, pp. 1–4 and pp. 163–167; Marcosson and Frohman, *Frohman*, p. 135.

3. Burke, *Feather*, p. 48 and pp. 57–61.

4. Stephenson interview, August 10, 2007.

5. Burke, *Feather*, pp. 49–53; Drew, pp. 208–209.

6. *New York Times*, June 9, 1907.

7. *New York Times*, September 1, 1907.

8. Burke, *Feather*, pp. 55–56; Internet Broadway Database [hereafter IBDB].

9. Burke, *Feather*, p. 68 and p. 70.

10. *Ibid.*, pp. 70–71.

Chapter 4

1. Burke, *Feather*, pp. 71–72. Billie was not always so approving of New York's discerning circles. In the August 1, 1909, edition of the *New York World* she criticized New York society for worshiping titles and money more than European society did: "The exclusiveness of New York is sheer cowardice," she is reported to have said. "New York society is so tiresomely limited and narrow." Billie Burke papers, USC-Doheny Library.

2. Burke, *Feather*, p. 92; *New York Times*, August 18, 1909; Patterson, pp. 300–302; *Yonkers Herald*, October 1908.

3. Burke, *With Powder on My Nose*, p. 119; Richard Lamparski interview, July 4, 2007. The half-hour show was a pilot. According to Lamparski, NBC chose not to finance the series after taping five or six segments. In 1934, when Billie was performing *Her Master's Voice* in Los Angeles, her success at obtaining enough swank clothes and then some for the play — six changes' worth — was thought sufficient to warrant an article on the subject in the *Los Angeles Times* on December 23, 1934.

4. Burke, *Feather*, pp. 75–79 and p. 89; and Ziegfeld, *TZG*, p. 19.

5. *New York Times*, July 18, 1908, and July 19, 1908.

6. Burke, *Feather*, p. 89; *New York Times*, August 28, 1908.

7. Billie Burke papers, 1908–1909 scrapbook, USC-Doheny Library.

8. *New York Commercial*, November 19, 1908.

9. Burke, *Feather*, pp. 87–89; *New York Times*, September 20, 1908.

10. Billie Burke papers, 1908–1909 scrapbook,

USC-Doheny Library, undated clipping and Otto R. Rietschlin note from February 25, 1909.

11. *New York Times*, November 8, 1908.

Chapter 5

1. *New York Times*, November 15, 1008.
2. *New York Times*, January 15, 1909.
3. Billie Burke papers, 1908–1909 scrapbook, USC-Doheny Library, *Springfield Republican*, January 29, 1909.
4. *New York Times*, January 29, 1909, and February 2, 1909; Frohman telegram in Billie Burke papers, USC-Doheny Library; Burke, *Feather*, pp. 89–93.
5. *New York Times*, June 29, 1916; *New York World*, July 8, 1909.
6. Burke, *Feather*, pp. 93–94; *Washington Post*, September 18, 1910.
7. *Washington Post*, September 18, 1910; *New York Times*, June 29, 1916.
8. *New York Times*, July 11, 1909; *Saginaw News*, June 8, 1909, in Billie Burke papers, 1908–1909 scrapbook, USC-Doheny Library.
9. *New York Times*, May 16, 1909.
10. Burke, *Feather*, p. 94; *New York Times*, May 16, 1909.
11. Billie Burke papers, 1908–1909 scrapbook, USC-Doheny Library.
12. Burke, *Feather*, pp. 95–96.

Chapter 6

1. Patterson, pp. 300–302.
2. *Ibid.*
3. *St. Louis Times*, February 21, 1909; Billie Burke papers, 1908–1909 scrapbook, USC-Doheny Library.
4. Billie Burke papers, 1908–1909 scrapbook, USC-Doheny Library.
5. Burke, *Feather*, pp. 103–105; Stanley Jackson, *Caruso*, pp. 181–182.
6. Ted Morgan, *Maugham: A Biography*, pp. 169–170.
7. Burke, *Feather*, p. 107.
8. Unsigned review, *Illustrated London News*, May 2, 1908; J.T. Grein, *Sunday Times*, May 3, 1908.
9. Burke, *Feather*, p. 108; *Fort Wayne Journal Gazette*, January 8, 1911.
10. *New York Times*, January 25, 1910, and January 30, 1910.
11. Burke, *Feather*, pp. 109–110.

12. IBDB, Adele Cheridah; *New York Times*, September 10, 1910, and September 28, 1910.
13. *New York Times*, December 6, 1910; Anthony Hope, "The Philosopher in the Apple Orchard."
14. *New York Times*, October 10, 1911.

Chapter 7

1. *New York Times*, November 26, 1911; Dr. Richard Ziegfeld, *The Ziegfeld Touch* [hereafter *TZT*], pp. 105–106; and Ziegfeld, *TZG*, pp. 46–48.
2. Billie Burke papers, 1908–1909 scrapbook, USC-Doheny Library, note from Maxine from January 1909, asking Billie to come to tea; this may have been the occasion when Maxine advised Billie on her finances.
3. The Shuberts may have been unwelcome to both Frohman and Ziegfeld, but they were to bail out both Billie and the Follies after Flo's death in 1932.
4. Burke, *Feather*, pp. 97–100.
5. *Ibid.*, p. 112.
6. Don Gillan, "Actresses and the Peerage," *www.stagebeauty.net*; Duchess of Leinster, *So Brief a Dream*, p. 109; and Sir Arthur Wing Pinero, *The Mind the Paint Girl*.
7. Pinero, *The Mind the Paint Girl*, Act I.
8. F. Scott Fitzgerald, *The Beautiful and the Damned*, Chapter 1, p. 11.
9. Michael R. Booth and Joel H. Kaplan, *The Edwardian Theatre: Essays on Performance and the Stage*, pp. 50–52; and *Los Angeles Examiner*, January 11, 1953.
10. *New York Times*, September 10, 1912.
11. Burke, *Feather*, pp. 112–113.
12. *New York Times*, April 29, 1913; and Burke, *Feather*, pp. 114–115.

Chapter 8

1. *New York Times*, October 31, 1910, and January 5, 1914.
2. Morgan, *Maugham: A Biography*, p. 165 and p. 177.
3. *New York Times*, January 5, 1914.
4. Calder, *Willie*, p. 172.
5. Robert G. Lawrence, "The Land of Promise: Canada, as Somerset Maugham Saw It in 1914," *Theatre Research in Canada* 4.1 (Spring 1983); Trevor W. Sissing, "How They Kept Canada Almost Lily White," *Saturday Night* 85. 9 (1970).

6. Burke, *Feather*, pp. 116–118; *New York World*, August 1, 1909, Billie Burke papers, USC-Doheny Library.

7. Ziegfeld, *TZT*, pp. 12–13.

8. E. Douglas Bomberger, *Brainard's Biographies of American Musicians*, pp. 302–305.

9. Burke, *Feather*, p. 135.

10. Ziegfeld, *TZT*, pp. 16–19; *Los Angeles Times*, July 23, 1932; Burke, *Feather*, p. 137.

11. Ziegfeld, *TZT*, pp. 20–29; Burke, *Feather*, pp. 137–139.

12. John Kenrick, "Ziegfeld 101," *http://www.musicals101.com/ziegheld.htm*; Burke, *Feather*, pp. 139–145.

13. Burke, *Feather*, p. 144.

14. *Ibid.*, pp. 119–120.

15. *Ibid.*, p. 121.

16. *Ibid.*, p. 123.

17. *Ibid.*, 126–129.

18. *Ibid.*, pp. 121–130.

Chapter 9

1. *New York Times*, March 10, 1914, March 16, 1914, and March 30, 1914.

2. Burke-Ziegfeld marriage certificate, Stephenson family archives.

3. Burke, *Feather*, pp. 130–133.

4. *Ibid.*, pp. 130–133.

5. Ziegfeld, *TZT*, p. 56 and pp. 147–148.

6. *New York Times*, April 26, 1914; Burke, *Powder*, pp. 54–55.

7. Burke, *Feather*, pp. 156 and p. 165.

8. Bernard Sobel, *Broadway Heartbeat*, pp. 118–119.

9. *New York Times*, October 22, 1914.

10. Marcosson and Frohman, *Frohman*, pp. 381–387.

11. Ziegfeld, *TZT*, p. 72.

12. *New York Times*, May 26, 1915.

Chapter 10

1. Lewis Jacobs, *Rise of the American Film*, pp. 3–6 and pp. 81–85; Burke, *Feather*, pp. 166–167.

2. Burke, *Feather*, pp. 167–168.

3. *Ibid.*, pp. 168–169. Rumors circulated later that there was more between Billie and Thomas Ince than a strictly professional relationship. If true, it is easy to ascribe such an affair to her frustrations over Flo's philandering. She was not yet a mother (motherhood toned down her rebelliousness considerably), and if photos can be relied on

as proof of any kind — we shall consider later in this book whether they can be relied on for anything at all — the extant stills of Billie and Ince on the set of *Peggy* are full of captures of close moments between star and director. On the other hand, Billie depended on her directors to an almost obsessive degree, and the intimacy may display just that and nothing more. Anthony Slide interview, September 5, 2007.

4. Billie Burke papers, USC-Doheny Library.

5. Billie Burke papers, script of *Peggy*, USC-Doheny Library; *New York Times*, January 17, 1916.

6. Burke, *Feather*, p. 168 and pp. 170–173.

7. Stuart McIver, *Dreamers, Schemers and Scalawags, Vol. 1*, pp. 28–30.

8. Burke telegram to Ziegfeld, Ziegfeld-Burke papers, New York Public Library.

9. Ziegfeld, *TZT*, p. 74; Ziegfeld, *TZG*, pp. 26–28; Sobel, p. 111; Burke, *Feather*, p. 177. According to Patricia Ziegfeld Stephenson, she was named for a friend of Billie's who lived in England.

Chapter 11

1. Burke, *Feather*, p. 203.

2. Sobel, p. 111.

3. George Bernard Shaw, Epistle Dedicatory to Arthur Bingham Wakely, *Man and Superman*.

4. Sobel, p. 114.

5. Ziegfeld-Burke papers, New York Public Library.

6. Burke, *Powder*, p. 42.

7. Sobel, p. 111; Hedda Hopper, *From Under My Hat*, p. 234.

8. Ziegfeld, *TZG*, p. 46 and pp. 64–65.

9. Ziegfeld, *TZT*, pp. 107–108; Ziegfeld, *TZG*, pp. 47–50.

10. Burke, *Feather*, p. 156.

Chapter 12

1. Burke, *Feather*, pp. 191–192.

2. *New York Times*, May 5, 1918.

3. *New York Times*, October 9, 1917.

4. Burke, *Feather*, p. 194.

5. *Ibid.*, pp. 193–195.

6. *Ibid.*, p. 195.

7. Ziegfeld, *TZT*, pp. 83–84.

8. Burke, *Feather*, p. 208.

9. *Ibid.*, pp. 175–176.

10. *Ibid.*, 208; and Ziegfeld, *TZG*, pp. 183–186.

11. Ziegfeld, *TZT*, pp. 84–85.

12. *New York Times*, November 25, 1919.

13. Alexander Klein, ed., *Empire City: A Treasury of New York*, p. 256; Marion Meade, *Bobbed Hair and Bathtub Gin*, pp. 7–8.

Chapter 13

1. Burke, *Feather*, p. 197.

2. Booth Tarkington, *Intimate Strangers*, Act I, p. 25.

3. *New York Times*, November 7, 1921.

4. *Pittsburgh Dispatch*, March 12, 1922; *Pittsburgh Sunday Post*, March 12, 1922, in Billie Burke papers, USC-Doheny Library.

5. Undated clipping, undated with no byline or newspaper title, in Billie Burke papers, USC-Doheny Library.

6. Louise Landis, undated with no newspaper title, Billie Burke papers, USC-Doheny Library.

7. *New York Times*, February 8, 1922.

8. Burke, *Feather*, p. 203.

9. Ziegfeld, *TZT*, p. 95.

10. *Ibid.*, pp. 103–104.

11. *New York Times*, July 24, 1922.

12. Burke, *Feather*, p. 209; *New York Times* July 24, 1922, and July 25, 1922.

13. Burke, *Feather*, p. 210 and p. 213.

14. *Ibid.*, p. 201.

15. Gerald Bordman, *American Theatre: A Chronicle of Comedy and Drama*, p. 197.

16. *New York Times*, December 26, 1922.

17. Burke, *Feather*, p. 205.

18. Burke, *Powder*, p. 96.

19. Burke, *Feather*, p. 206.

20. Stephenson interview, August 10, 2007.

21. Ziegfeld, *TZT*, p. 112; Burke, *Feather*, pp. 212–214.

22. Burke, *Feather*, p. 215.

23. Ziegfeld, *TZG*, pp. 117–119; Burke, *Feather*, pp. 215–216.

24. Ziegfeld, *TZT*, p. 111.

25. Bordman, *American Musical Theatre*, pp. 394–395.

26. *New York Times*, November 5, 1924.

27. Sobel, p. 122.

28. Burke, *Feather*, p. 207.

Chapter 14

1. *New York Times*, February 28, 1925, and February 24, 1926.

2. *New York Times*, June 26, 1926; Ziegfeld, *TZT*, pp. 38–39; *New York Times*, November 7, 1926.

3. *New York Times*, December 10, 1926. The cornerstone box was removed from the rubble of the Ziegfeld Theatre after its razing in 1966 and is now in the Billy Rose Theatre Collection at the New York Public Library.

4. *New York Times*, November 13, 1927.

5. Noël Coward, *The Collected Plays of Noël Coward. Play Parade, Vol. III*; *New York Times*, November 15, 1927; Sobel, p. 114.

6. *New York Times*, May 8, 1928; and Brooks Atkinson, "The Case for Beauty and Ugliness," *New York Times*, December 22, 1929. As late as 1932, Billie would lend her name and photograph to Lux Soap advertisements in which she claimed to be 39 years old — taking almost a decade off her real age. And when a rumor was spread in 1933 that Billie was a patient of Paris plastic surgeon Dr. Bove, she went "hysterical" and ordered United Artists, her publicity handlers, to ensure that her name was stricken from Bove's list and that the *Los Angeles Times* strike all mention of the alleged relationship from its pages. This was, as in the days of Flo, duly done. Billie's "hysterical" reaction, as reported, would seem a bit overdone if the story were untrue; on the other hand, she could probably see lucrative endorsement opportunities go out the window if she did not refute or, in this case, quash the story. Note from June 27, 1933, Billie Burke papers, USC-Doheny Library. In her memoir, *Life Is a Banquet*, Rosalind Russell describes discovering during the filming of *Craig's Wife* that Billie used tape to lift her face (p. 241).

7. Burke, *Feather*, p. 219.

Chapter 15

1. Burke, *Feather*, p. 220.

2. Harold J. Bierman, Jr., "The 1929 Stock Market Crash," *http://eh.net/encyclopedia/article/Bierman.Crash*.

3. Ziegfeld, *TZT*, p. 154.

4. Burke, *Feather*, p. 221.

5. Eddie Cantor, with Jane Kesner Ardmore, *Take My Life*, pp. 31–32, p. 146 and p. 253; Laurence Bergreen, *As Thousands Cheer: The Life of Irving Berlin*, pp. 291–292; and Sobel, pp. 193–194.

6. Burke, *Feather*, pp. 221–222.

7. *Ibid.*, p. 219.

8. *New York Times*, December 29, 1930.

9. Ziegfelt, *TZT*, p. 155; Burke, *Feather*, pp. 222–223.

10. Sobel, p. 112.

11. Ziegfeld, *TZG*, pp. 197–200.

12. *New York Times*, September 15, 1930, and November 20, 1930.

13. Burke, *Feather*, p. 252; Paul Osborn, *The Vinegar Tree*, Act I.

14. *Los Angeles Times*, July 1, 1931.

15. Burke, *Feather*, p. 225.

16. Ziegfeld, *TZT*, pp. 161–162.

17. Charles Higham, *Ziegfeld*, pp. 212–215, p. 217.

18. Burke, *Feather*, pp. 225–226.

19. Ziegfeld, *TZT*, pp. 164–165; Burke, *Feather*, pp. 233–234.

20. Burke, *Feather*, pp. 234–235; Ziegfeld, *TZT*, p. 166; Patrick McGilligan, *A Double Life: George Cukor*, p. 2, p. 8, p. 81.

21. Burke, *Feather*, pp. 235–236.

22. *Ibid.*, p. 236; Katharine Hepburn, *Me*, p. 132.

23. *New York Times*, July 15, 1932. The *Los Angeles Times* reported on July 16, 1932, and July 17, 1932, that Flo was merely resting at "a New Mexico ranch," but this does not jibe with Billie's account and sounds manufactured to throw the press off the scent.

24. *New York Times*, July 19, 1932; Burke, *Feather*, pp. 236–237, p. 238.

Chapter 16

1. Burke, *Feather*, pp. 236–237, p. 239.

2. *Ibid.*, pp. 238–239.

3. *Ibid.*, p. 239; Ziegfeld, *TZT*, p. 167.

4. Burke, *Feather*, pp. 239–240; Ziegfeld, *TZT*, pp. 167–168; and Ziegfeld, *TZG*, p. 204.

5. George Cukor's typed and hand-corrected eulogy given at Burke's memorial service [hereafter abbreviated as Cukor MS]; Burke, *Feather*, p. 240 and p. 248.

6. Cukor MS; Burke, *Feather*, p. 242; *Los Angeles Times* July 25, 1932; *New York Times*, July 23, 1932, July 24, 1932, and July 25, 1932.

7. Ziegfeld, *TZG*, p. 204; Cukor MS.

8. Burke, *Powder*, pp. 67–68.

9. Burke, *Feather*, p. 241.

Chapter 17

1. Burke, *Feather*, p. 248.

2. *The Washington Post*, August 8, 1937.

3. Ziegfeld, *TZT*, pp. 170–171; Burke, *Feather*, p. 247, p. 251.

4. Burke, *Feather*, p. 251.

5. George Jean Nathan and Charles Angoff, *Theatre Book of the Year, 1943–1944*, pp. 271–274.

6. Cukor MS.

7. *New York Times*, August 24, 1033.

8. McGilligan, pp. 95–96.

9. *New York Times*, August 24, 1933.

10. *New York Times*, October 8, 1933.

Chapter 18

1. *New York Times*, April 22, 1933.

2. *New York Times* June 6, 1934; Ziegfeld, *TZT*, p. 172.

3. *Los Angeles Evening Herald & Express*, May 10, 1935.

4. *New York Times*, June 2, 1935.

5. Thackeray, *Vanity Fair*, XI, pp. 614–15.

6. *Morning Telegraph*, May 23, 1935. Though not depicted as such in the film's extremely abbreviated version of Thackeray's novel, Lady Bareacres is a very grand but impoverished Englishwoman who, though disgusted with upstart and tarty Becky Sharp's brilliant rise in society, cannot bestir herself or her feckless husband to emulate Becky's resourcefulness.

7. *Morning Telegraph*, May 23, 1935; *New York Times*, June 2, 1935; Barbara Rush interview, August 23, 2007.

8. It is a measure of Billie's forgiving nature (a quality often found in people with otherwise explosive tempers like hers) that the year following her return to New York, she co-founded The Ziegfeld Club with her former publicist, Bernard Sobel. Though the organization began its life as an advertisement of Ziegfeldian proportions for *The Great Ziegfeld*, Billie and Sobel set it up as a charitable organization to help out ex–*Follies* girls living with illness or in poverty — perhaps inspired by the most pathetic case of them all, Lillian Lorraine. Her several marriages, temperamental character, fondness for big spending and, worst of all, her alcoholism, drove Lorraine off the stage and into a life of cheap apartments and poverty, in which state she died in 1955. The Ziegfeld Club still exists today in the precincts of the Central Presbyterian Church at 593 Park Avenue; given that one known *Follies* Girl, Doris Eaton Travis, is known to survive, the Club directs most of its assistance to Broadway Cares/Equity Fights AIDS, the Episcopal Actors' Guild, and the Actors' Fund of America Retirement Home in Englewood, NJ. See *www.thenationalziegfeldclubinc.com.*

9. *New York Times*, April 30, 1940.

10. Burke, *Feather*, p. 255.

11. *New York Times*, February 19, 1943.

12. *New York Times*, April 1, 1944; *Time*, April 10, 1944; Burke, *Feather*, p. 257.

Chapter 19

1. L. Frank Baum, *The Wizard of Oz*.

2. Aljean Harmetz, *The Making of The Wizard of Oz*, p. 193.

3. John Fricke, Jay Scarfone, and William Stillman, *The Wizard of Oz: The Official 50th Anniversary Pictorial History*, p. 8.

4. Harmetz, pp. 272–274.

5. *Ibid.*, p. 127, p. 129, p. 179; John Fricke interview, August 20, 2007. During the making of *Craig's Wife* in 1936, Rosalind Russell observed that "when Billie Burke ... came on the lot, great trumpets sounded." Russell lost count of the dogs, servants, makeup man "and then some guys carrying a big tray with a potty on it," which was covered in monogrammed satin, with Billie following up at the end of the parade (Rosalind Russell, with Charis Chase, *Life Is a Banquet*, p. 58).

6. Meinhardt Raabe, *Memories of a Munchkin: An Illustrated Walk Down the Yellow Brick Road*, pp. 122–123.

7. Fricke, p. 50; Burke, *Feather*, p. 258.

8. Salman Rushdie, *The Wizard of Oz*, p. 42.

9. *Ibid.* For purposes of contrast, consider Lena Horne's Glinda in *The Wiz* (1978): she is truly a sorceress in the traditional mode, a vivid and intense Queen of the Night, but she is bent not on vengeance but justice for the lost Dorothy. The sequined babies suspended about her in the night sky underscore her warm maternal nature.

10. Fricke interview, August 20, 2007; Cecilia Duncan interview, August 10, 2007. I would add that Billie recorded, several years after the making of *Oz*, a small 45 rmp record of nursery rhymes on which she sings "Twinkle, Twinkle Little Star." Listening to this recording, made in her late 50s, of Billie's real singing voice, as well as the singing she did at the end of each "Billie Burke Show," and comparing it to the singing she does in *Oz*, I can only conclude that the voice in the film score and the voice on the record are the same. The record, given by Billie Burke to playwright William Luce in the early 1950s in Los Angeles, is in the author's collection.

11. Harmetz, p. 20.

12. Fricke interview, August 20, 2007.

13. *Ibid.*

14. *Los Angeles Times*, August 10, 1939; *Los Angeles Examiner*, August 10, 1939; *Chicago Sunday Tribune*, August 27, 1939; *Dallas Morning Star*, August 27, 1939.

Chapter 20

1. McGilligan, p. 341.

2. *Los Angeles Times*, May 16, 1958.

3. *The Milwaukee Journal*, August 19, 1945.

4. Spoto; Stephenson interview and tour of house, August 10, 2007.

5. Stephenson interview, August 10, 2007; Ziegfeld, *TZG*, p. 205.

6. Stephenson interview, August 10, 2007; Ziegfeld, *TZG*, pp. 206–207.

7. Burke, *Powder*, p. 191, p. 193.

8. Richard Lamparski interview, July 4, 2007. It is ironic that the children came to call Billie Oma or that they even had a German nurse: in an interview with the *Los Angeles Times* in June 1918, Billie spoke about her part in a war-themed film and said she did not want to see any Germans in any movie in which she acted. "Miss Burke has nursed a secret dislike of Germans which, she says, she has never felt free to disclose" until the Kaiser set loose mayhem by helping to start World War I. Billie claimed that before being placed in a French convent she had been put in a German school by Billy Burke and Blanche, where German officers had amused themselves by pushing her into the gutter. All of this supposedly happened at age six, which does not square with the fact that Billie was still living with her parents in the New York area at that time. *Los Angeles Times* June 30, 1918.

9. Burke, *Powder*, p. 69; Stephenson interview, August 10, 2007.

10. Billie's cattle ranch hint is interesting, in that it was at a dude ranch, location unnamed, where she met and was impressed by character actor Hank Worden, so much so she gave him introductions in Hollywood that helped establish his film career. Worden was a good friend and colleague of country singer Tex Ritter, who by the 1930s was a star of film and radio. Ritter didn't marry till the early 1940s. Was he the unnamed "cattleman"?

11. Stephenson interview, August 10, 2007.

12. *Los Angeles Times*, June 26, 1951.

13. Stephenson interview, August 10, 2007.

14. "The Billie Burke Show," April 27, 1946; John Dunning, *On the Air: The Encyclopedia of Old-Time Radio*.

15. NH-BB letters, Howard Gotlieb Archival Research Center at Boston University.

16. "Barretts of Wimpole Street," autographed program, 1944; Missouri Digital Heritage, Bernard Becker Medical Library, Washington University School of Medicine.

17. NH-BB letter undated but clearly written in 1946; my dating is based on a combination of the Russia reference and the fact that Billie had just seen Bernstein's *On the Town*, which she did not like though she loved Jerome Robbins' choreography. The play she refers to may have been Zoë Akins' *The Swallow's Nest*, which she did perform in Los Angeles.

18. NH-BB letter, which I date to 1947, as the radio show is over and Billie mentions Patricia's young son Robert, born in 1946, as if he is no longer a newborn.

19. NH-BB letter, circa 1947. I date this letter based on Billie's reference to Ray Bolger being the star of Hamilton's 1946 show, *Three to Make Ready*, and the fact that Billie refers to "having worked" with Bolger on *The Wizard of Oz*, which is to say, post-1939.

20. *Time*, December 5, 1949.

21. NH-BB letter, circa 1952.

22. NH-BB letter, dated per Billie's mention of working on the "horse opera," Kit's opening night, Berlin's *Lady Liberty*, and reference to *Mrs. January*.

23. NH-BB letter, February 11, 1952.

24. NH-BB letter, November 20, 1953.

25. Tennessee Williams, *The Glass Menagerie*, Scene Two.

26. *Los Angeles Times*, January 26, 1953.

27. Jim Crabtree interview March 31, 2008, and written recollections.

28. NH-BB, November 20, 1953.

29. *New York Times*, May 22, 1957.

30. *Washington Post*, December 31, 1958.

31. *New York Times*, October 4, 1958; Burke, *Powder*, pp. 241–244.

Chapter 21

1. Sobel, pp. 112–114.

2. Burke, *Powder*, pp. 247–248.

3. *Ibid.*, pp. 16–17.

4. Stephenson interview, August 10, 2007.

5. Burke, *Powder*, pp. 23–28.

6. *Ibid.*, p. 237.

7. *Ibid.*, p. 236.

8. *Ibid.*, p. 238.

9. *Ibid.*, pp. 245–246.

10. *Ibid.*, p. 247.

11. *Ibid.*

12. *Ibid.*, pp. 242–243.

13. *New York Times*, May 22, 1959.

14. *Newsweek*, June 1, 1959.

15. Barbara Rush interview, August 23, 2007.

16. "Losing and finding John Ford's 'Sergeant Rutledge,'" *Historical Journal of Film, Radio and Television*, June 1997.

17. *Ibid.*

18. Darby, *John Ford's Westerns: A Thematic Analysis*, p. 121.

19. Stephenson interview, August 10, 2007.

20. Burke to Ford, John Ford Mss., Lilly Library, Indiana University, Bloomington, IN.

21. Richard Lamparski interview, July 19, 2007.

22. Stephenson interview, August 10, 2007; Cecilia Duncan recalls driving Billie over to Charlotte and Martin's house on Rodeo Drive.

23. Though it is obviously romantic to think so, since so many observers seem to believe it, the verdigrised bronze figure of a mourning young woman at the site of Billie Burke's grave at Kensico Cemetery, Valhalla, in Westchester County, New York, is not a marker for her but for her mother, Blanche. Billie's grave marker, like Flo's, is a simple bronze rectangle flush with the ground.

24. *New York Times*, May 19, 1970.

25. Cukor MS.

26. Burke, *Feather*, pp. 259–260.

Bibliography

Newspapers and Magazines

Fort Wayne Journal Gazette
Illustrated London News
Journal of Commerce
New York Commercial
New York Globe
New York Times
New York World
Newsweek
Pittsburgh Dispatch
Pittsburgh Sunday Post
Saginaw News (Michigan)
St. Louis Times
Springfield Republican
Sunday Times
The Daily Mail
The Daily News
The Daily Telegraph
The London Sphere
The Morning Telegraph
Theatre Magazine
Time Magazine
The Washington Post
Wisconsin Superior Telegram
Yonkers Herald

Articles

Annaheim, Ellwood. Florodora Musical Research Project. http://www.geocities.com/musicthea ter/floro/floro.html.

"The Best Stage Liar of His Time." *The Times*, Arts section, December 18, 1958. www.little church.org/history.html.

Bierman, Harold, Jr. "The 1929 Stock Market Crash." http://eh.net/encyclopedia/article/Bier man.Crash.

Brantley, Ben. "Critic's Notebook: 'Why Oz Is a State of Mind in Gay Life and Drag Shows.'" *New York Times*, June 28, 1994.

"The Descendants of William the Conqueror," created by Alan Freer. http://www.william1.co. uk/t28.htm.

Fliotsos, Anne. "Much More Than a Good Witch." *Studies in Popular Culture* 23.1, 2000.

Gillan, Don. "Actresses and the Peerage." www. stagebeauty.net.

Kenrick, John. "Ziegfeld 101." http://www.musi cals101.com/ziegheld.htm.

Lawrence, Robert G. "The Land of Promise: Canada, as Somerset Maugham Saw It in 1914." *Theatre Research in Canada* 4.1, Spring 1983.

"Losing and finding John Ford's 'Sergeant Rutledge.'" *Historical Journal of Film, Radio and Television*, June 1997.

Olympians of the Sawdust Circle. www.circushis tory.org.

Pfening, Fred D. "Circus Songsters." *Bandwagon* 7.6, Nov.-Dec. 1963.

Spoto, Donald. "Billie Burke: The Wizard of Oz's Good Witch in Beverly Hills." *Architectural Digest*, April 1996.

Interviews

Jim Crabtree interview with the author and written recollections, March 31, 2008.

Richard Lamparski interviews with the author, July 4, 2007, and July 19, 2007.

Barbara Rush interview with author, August 23, 2007.

Anthony Slide interview with author, September 2, 2007.

Patricia and William Stephenson interview with the author, August 10, 2007.

Archives

"Barretts of Wimpole Street" autographed program, 1944, Missouri Digital Heritage.

Bernard Becker Medical Library, Washington University School of Medicine

Billie Burke collection, New York Public Library.

Billie Burke papers, University of Southern California, Doheny Cinematic Arts Library.

Billie Burke-John Ford letters, John Ford Mss., Lilly Library, Bloomington, Indiana.

Burke-Beatty marriage certificate, Stephenson family archives.

Burke-Ziegfeld marriage certificate, Stephenson family archives.

1850 Census, Muskingum Co., District 116, Union Township, October 15, 1850.

1880 Census, Washington, D.C., 819 Fourteenth Street, June 11, 1880.

Internet Broadway Database.

Internet Movie Database.

Nancy Hamilton-Billie Burke letters, Howard Gotlieb Archival Research Center at Boston University.

Ziegfeld-Burke papers, New York Public Library.

Recordings

Burke, Billie. *Billie Burke's Nursery Selections*, 45 rpm disk containing Burke's recitation and singing of "Mary Had a Little Lamb," "Three Little Mice," "Twinkle, Twinkle Little Star," "Simple Simon," and "Rockabye Bay." Undated, recording studio unknown. (Author's collection)

Books

Barnum, Bailey, and Hutchinson. *Biographical Sketch of William Ethelbert Burke, America's Greatest Clown*. 1882.

Basinger, Jeanine. *The Star Machine*. New York: Alfred A. Knopf, 2007.

Baum, L. Frank. *The Wizard of Oz*. George M. Hill, 1900.

Bergreen, Laurence. *As Thousands Cheer: The Life of Irving Berlin*. New York: Da Capo Press, 1996.

Bomberger, E. Douglas, ed. *Brainard's Biographies of American Musicians*. Westport, CT: Greenwood Press, 1999.

Bondeson, Jan, *The Feejee Mermaid and Other Essays in Natural and Unnatural History*. Ithaca: Cornell University Press, 1999.

Booth, Michael R., and Joel H. Kaplan. *The Edwardian Theatre: Essays on Performance and the Stage*. Cambridge: Cambridge University Press, 1996.

Bordman, Gerald. *American Musical Theatre: A Chronicle*. New York: Oxford University Press, 1992.

_____. *American Theatre: A Chronicle of Comedy and Drama, 1914–1930*. New York: Oxford University Press, 1995.

Brown, Catherine Hayes. *Letters to Mary*. New York: Random House, 1940.

Brown, Jared. *The Fabulous Lunts: A Biography of Alfred Lunt and Lynne Fontanne*. Bloomington, IN: AuthorHouse, 2005.

Burke, Billie. *With a Feather on My Nose*. New York: Appleton-Century-Crofts, 1949.

_____. *With Powder on My Nose*. New York: Coward-McCann, 1959.

Calder, Robert. *Willie: The Life of W. Somerset Maugham*. London: Heinemann, 1989.

Cantor, Eddie, with Jane Kesner Ardmore. *Take My Life*. New York: Cooper Square Press, 2000.

Clarke, Gerald. *Get Happy: The Life of Judy Garland*. New York: Delta Trade, 2000.

Coward, Noël. *Autobiography (Present Indicative, Future Indefinite & Past Conditional)*. London: Methuen, 1986.

_____. *The Collected Plays of Noël Coward. Play Parade, Vol. III*. London: William Heinemann, 1950.

Darby, William. *John Ford's Westerns: A Thematic Analysis, with a Filmography*. Jefferson, N.C.: McFarland, 1996.

Drew, John. *My Years on the Stage*. New York: Dutton, 1922.

Dunning, John. *On the Air: The Encyclopedia of Old-Time Radio*. New York: Oxford University Press, 1998.

Eyman, Scott. *Mary Pickford: From Here to Hollywood*. Toronto: HarperCollins, 1990.

Fitzgerald, F. Scott. *The Beautiful and the Damned*. New York: Scribner's, 1922.

Forbes-Robertson, Sir Johnston. *A Player Under Three Reigns*. Boston: Little Brown, 1925.

Fricke, John, Jay Scarfone, and William Stillman. *The Wizard of Oz: The Official 50th Anniversary Pictorial History*. New York: Warner, 1989.

Genthe, Arnold. *As I Remember*. New York: Reynal & Hitchcock, 1936.

glbtq, an encyclopedia of gay, lesbian, bisexual, transgender & queer culture. General editor Claude J. Summers. Chicago: glbtq, 2002.

Guiles, Fred Lawrence. *Marion Davies: A Biography*. New York: McGraw-Hill, 1972.

Harmetz, Aljean. *The Making of the Wizard of Oz*. New York: Hyperion, 1977.

Hepburn, Katharine. *Me*. New York: Alfred A. Knopf, 1991.

Higham, Charles. *Ziegfeld*. London: W.H. Allen, 1973.

Hope, Anthony. *The Philosopher in the Apple Orchard*. 1911.

Hopper, Hedda. *From Under My Hat*. New York: Doubleday, 1952.

Inman, David M. *Performers' Television Credits, 1948–2000. Vol. 1: A–F*. Jefferson, N.C.: McFarland, 2001.

Jackson, Stanley. *Caruso*. London: W.H. Allen, 1972.

Jacobs, Lewis. *The Rise of the American Film: A Critical History*. New York: Harcourt Brace, 1939.

Klein, Alexander, ed. *Empire City: A Treasury of New York*. New York: Ayer, 1990.

Kotsilbas-Davis, James. *The Barrymores: The Royal Family in Hollywood*. New York: Crown, 1981.

Lamb, Andrew. *Leslie Stuart: Composer of Florodora*. New York: Routledge, 2002.

Le Gallienne, Eva. *At 33*. New York: Longmans, Green, 1940.

Leinster, Duchess of. *So Brief a Dream: The Recollections of Rafaelle, Duchess of Leinster*. Arthur Barker. 1971.

Marcosson, Isaac F., and Daniel Frohman. *Charles Frohman, Manager and Man*. New York: Harper & Brothers, 1916.

Marion, Frances. *Off with Their Head!: A Serio-Comic Tale of Hollywood*. New York: MacMillan, 1972.

Maugham, W. Somerset. *Caesar's Wife*. London: Heinemann, 1922.

_____. *The Land of Promise*. New York: Bickers & Sons, 1913.

_____. *Mrs. Dot*. London: Heinemann, 1912.

McGilligan, Patrick. *A Double Life: George Cukor*. New York: St. Martin's Press, 1991.

McIver, Stuart. *Dreamers, Schemers and Scalawags, Vol. 1*. Sarasota: Pineapple Press, 1994.

Meade, Marion. *Bobbed Hair and Bathtub Gin*. New York: Random House, 2004.

Molnár, Ferenc. "The Swan." In *The Plays of Ferenc Molnár*. New York: Vanguard Press, 1929.

Monaco, James, and the editors of *Baseline*. *The Encyclopedia of Film*. New York: Perigee, 1991.

Morgan, Ted. *Maugham: A Biography*. New York: Simon & Schuster, 1980.

Morrison, Michael. *John Barrymore: Shakespearean Actor*. New York: Cambridge University Press, 1997.

Nathan, George Jean, and Charles Angoff, contributor. *Theatre Book of the Year 1943–1944*. Rutherford, N.J.: Farleigh Dickinson University Press, 1972.

Novello, Ivor. *The Truth Game*. London and New York: French, 1928.

Osborn, Paul. *The Vinegar Tree*. New York: Farrar & Rinehart, 1931.

Parish, James Robert, and Vincent Terrace. *The Complete Actors' Television Credits, 1949–1988. Vol. 2: Actresses*. Lanham, MD: Scarecrow, 1990.

Pettit, Rhonda S. *The Critical Waltz: Essays on the Work of Dorothy Parker*. Rutherford, N.J.: Farleigh Dickinson University Press, 2005.

Pickford, Mary. *Sunshine and Shadow*. New York: Doubleday, 1955.

Pinero, Sir Alfred Wing. *The Mind the Paint Girl*. London: Heinemann, 1912.

Porter, Darwin. *Katharine The Great: A Lifetime of Secrets Revealed*. New York: Blood Moon Productions, 2004.

Prouty, Howard H., ed. *Variety Television Reviews. Vols, 4 and 15*. New York: Garland, 1989–1991.

Raabe, Meinhardt. *Memories of a Munchkin: An Illustrated Walk Down the Yellow Brick Road*. Washington, D.C.: Backstage Books, 2005.

Richardson, Douglas. *Magna Carta Ancestry: A Study in Colonial and Medieval Families*. Baltimore: Genealogical, 2005.

Rigdon, Walter, ed. *The Biographical Encyclopedia & Who's Who of the American Theatre*. New York: Heinemann, 1966.

Rushdie, Sir Salman. *The Wizard of Oz*. BFI Film Classics. London: British Film Institute, 1992.

Russell, Rosalind, with Chris Chase. *Life Is a Banquet*. New York: Random House, 1977.

Shaw, George Bernard. *Man and Superman*. Westminster: Archibald Constable, 1903.

Singer, Thomas, ed. *The Vision Thing: Man, Politics and Psyche in the World*. London: Routledge, 2000.

Slide, Anthony. *Silent Topics: Essays on Undocumented Areas of Silent Film*. Lanham, MD: Scarecrow, 2005.

Sobel, Bernard. *Broadway Heartbeat*. New York: Hermitage House, 1953.

Tarkington, Booth. *Intimate Strangers: A Comedy in Three Acts*. New York: Samuel French, 1921.

Thackeray, William Makepeace. *Vanity Fair*. New York: R.F. Fenno, 1905.

Wallace, Irving. *The Fabulous Showman: The Life and Times of P.T. Barnum*. New York: Alfred A. Knopf, 1959.

Williams, Tennessee. *The Glass Menagerie.* New York: Dramatists Play Service, 1948.

Ziegfeld, Patricia. *The Ziegfelds' Girl: Confessions of an Abnormally Happy Childhood.* Boston: Little, Brown, 1964.

Ziegfeld, Dr. Richard. *The Ziegfeld Touch: The Life and Times of Florenz Ziegfeld, Jr.* New York: Harry N. Abrams, 1993.

Index